BIOGRAPHIES

Al Ewing is a comics writer and novelist based in York, UK who has written extensively for *2000AD*. Most recently, he has been scripting high-profile Marvel titles *Captain America and the Mighty Avengers, Loki: Agent of Asgard* and *Iron Man: Fatal Frontier*.

Rob Williams began his comics career with *CLA$$WAR*, and now writes regular runs at *2000AD* (*Judge Dredd: Titan, Low Life, Trifecta, Ichabod Azrael*) Marvel (*Thanos, Spider-Man, Revolutionary War*) as well as licensed titles like *Indiana Jones* and *Star Wars*, and his creator-owned successes *Ordinary* and *The Royals*. He lives in Bristol, UK.

Simon Fraser is a world traveling artist, born in Scotland, now based in New York City. Best known as the co-creator of *Nikolai Dante for 2000AD*, Fraser has drawn for *Judge Dredd, Grindhouse, Family, Hell House* and his own series, *Lilly MacKenzie*.

Boo Cook is known for his stunning covers and interiors on *Elephantmen*, and for thrilling readers on *2000AD*, drawing the adventures of *Judge Dredd, Harry Kipling, Anderson: Psi Division, Damnation Station* and many more. He lives in Eastbourne, UK.

Warren Pleece is a comic artist and graphic novelist of over 20 years experience – working for *2000AD*, DC, Dark Horse and many more – on titles such as *True Faith, Hellblazer, The Invisibles, Deadenders* and *Incognegro*. He lives in Brighton, UK.

Gary Caldwell has been coloring Simon Fraser's work for over twenty years, as Simon's right-hand man. Based in Scotland, he quietly knocks his pages out of the park every time.

Hi-Fi Colour Design was founded in 1998 by Brian and Kristy Miller and provides digital color for comic books, toys, video games, and animation, and tutorials on color through masterdigitalcolor.com.

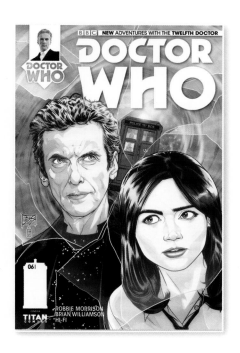

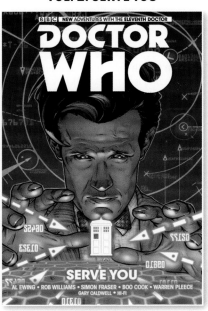

THE TRIUMPHANT FIRST COLLECTIONS! AVAILABLE NOW!

BBC NEW ADVENTURES WITH THE TWELFTH DOCTOR
DOCTOR WHO
TERRORFORMER
ROBBIE MORRISON • DAVE TAYLOR
HI-FI

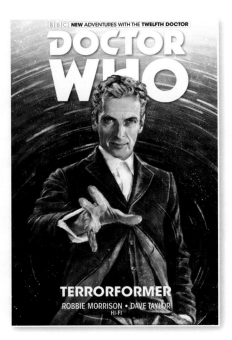

DOCTOR WHO: THE TWELFTH DOCTOR VOL. 1: TERRORFORMER

COLLECTS DOCTOR WHO: THE TWELFTH DOCTOR ISSUES #1-5

ON SALE NOW $19.99 / $22.95 CAN

ISBN: 9781782761778

DOCTOR WHO: THE TENTH DOCTOR VOL. 1: REVOLUTIONS OF TERROR

BBC NEW ADVENTURES WITH THE TENTH DOCTOR
DOCTOR WHO
REVOLUTIONS OF TERROR
NICK ABADZIS • ELENA CASAGRANDE • ARIANNA FLOREAN

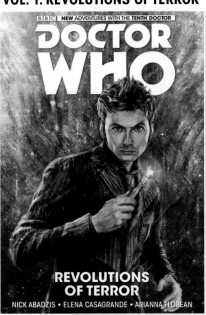

ISBN: 9781782761730

ON SALE NOW - $19.99 / $22.95 CAN

DOCTOR WHO: THE ELEVENTH DOCTOR VOL. 1: AFTER LIFE

BBC NEW ADVENTURES WITH THE ELEVENTH DOCTOR
DOCTOR WHO
AFTER LIFE
AL EWING • ROB WILLIAMS • SIMON FRASER • BOO COOK
GARY CALDWELL • HI-FI

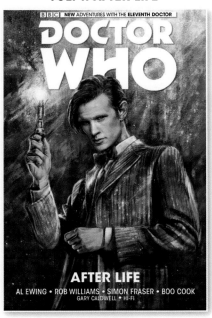

ISBN: 9781782761747

ON SALE NOW - $19.99 / $22.95 CAN

TITAN COMICS

For information on how to subscribe to our great Doctor Who titles, or to purchase them digitally for your favorite device, visit:

WWW.TITAN-COMICS.COM

BBC
DOCTOR WHO
THE ELEVENTH DOCTOR

COVER GALLERY

8A

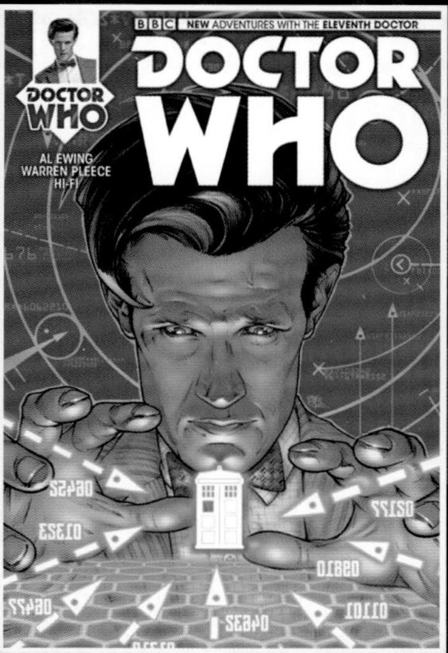
BBC NEW ADVENTURES WITH THE ELEVENTH DOCTOR
DOCTOR WHO
DOCTOR WHO
AL EWING
WARREN PLEECE
HI-FI

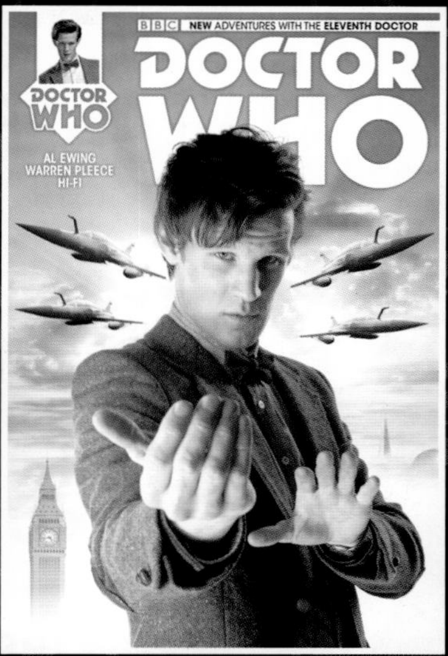
BBC NEW ADVENTURES WITH THE ELEVENTH DOCTOR
DOCTOR WHO
DOCTOR WHO
AL EWING
WARREN PLEECE
HI-FI

8B

9A

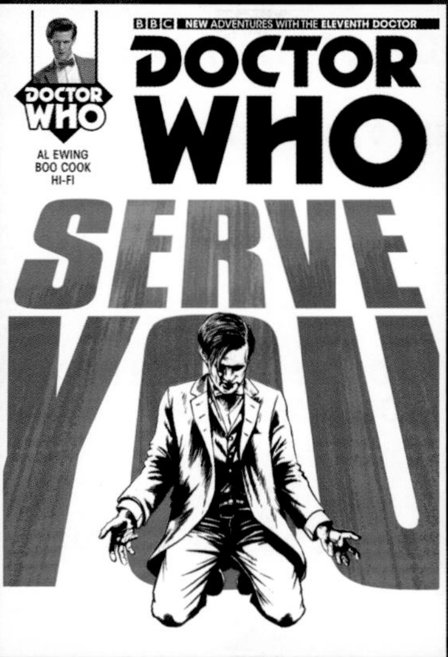
BBC NEW ADVENTURES WITH THE ELEVENTH DOCTOR
DOCTOR WHO
DOCTOR WHO
AL EWING
BOO COOK
HI-FI
SERVE

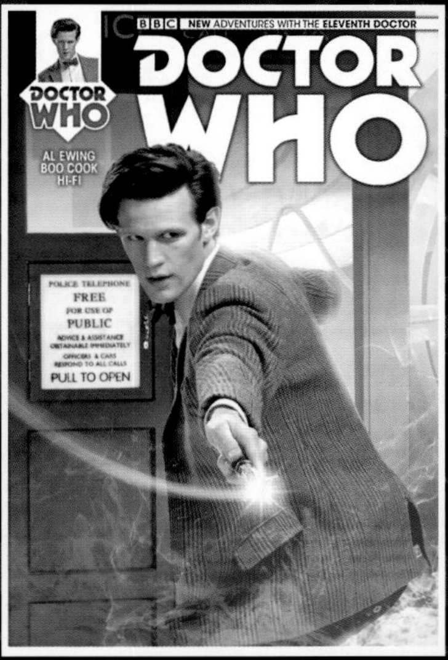
BBC NEW ADVENTURES WITH THE ELEVENTH DOCTOR
DOCTOR WHO
DOCTOR WHO
AL EWING
BOO COOK
HI-FI
POLICE TELEPHONE
FREE
FOR USE OF
PUBLIC
PULL TO OPEN

9B

10A

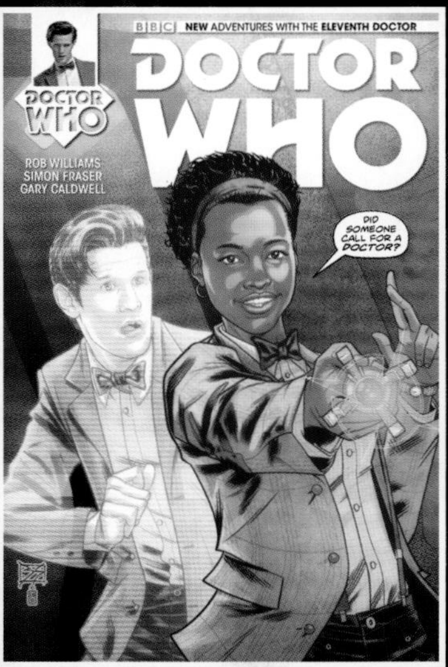
BBC NEW ADVENTURES WITH THE ELEVENTH DOCTOR
DOCTOR WHO
DOCTOR WHO
ROB WILLIAMS
SIMON FRASER
GARY CALDWELL
DID SOMEONE CALL FOR A DOCTOR?

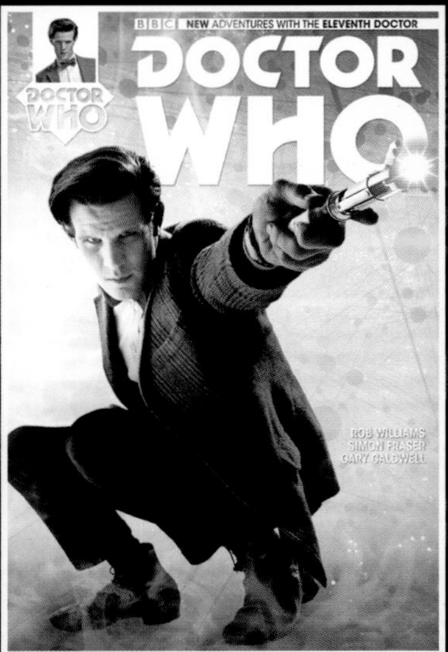
BBC NEW ADVENTURES WITH THE ELEVENTH DOCTOR
DOCTOR WHO
DOCTOR WHO
ROB WILLIAMS
SIMON FRASER
GARY CALDWELL

10B

#8 A: Boo Cook
#8 B: AJ/Rob Farmer

#9 A: Brian Williamson
#9 B: AJ

#10 A: Blair Shedd
#10 B: AJ/Rob Farmer

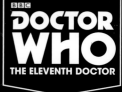

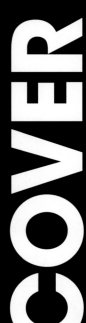

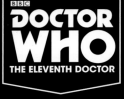

BBC DOCTOR WHO THE ELEVENTH DOCTOR

COVER GALLERY

6A

BBC NEW ADVENTURES WITH THE ELEVENTH DOCTOR
DOCTOR WHO
ROB WILLIAMS
SIMON FRASER
GARY CALDWELL
POLICE PUBLIC CALL BOX

6B

BBC NEW ADVENTURES WITH THE ELEVENTH DOCTOR
DOCTOR WHO
ROB WILLIAMS
SIMON FRASER
GARY CALDWELL

7A

BBC NEW ADVENTURES WITH THE ELEVENTH DOCTOR
DOCTOR WHO
ROB WILLIAMS
WARREN PLEECE
HI-FI
DOCTOR
DOCTOR

7B

BBC NEW ADVENTURES WITH THE ELEVENTH DOCTOR
DOCTOR WHO
ROB WILLIAMS
WARREN PLEECE
HI-FI

7C

BBC NEW ADVENTURES WITH THE ELEVENTH DOCTOR
DOCTOR WHO
ROB WILLIAMS
WARREN PLEECE
HI-FI

#6 A: Verity Glass
#6 B: AJ
#7 A: Mariano Laclaustra
#7 B: AJ/Rob Farmer
#7 C: AJ

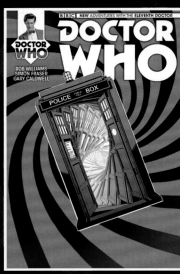

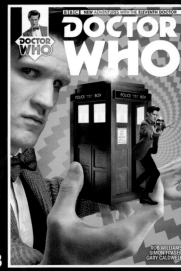

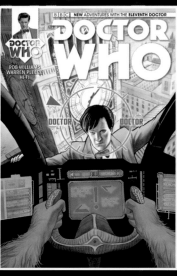

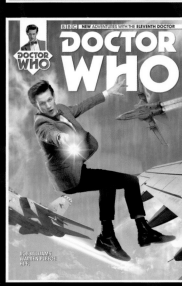

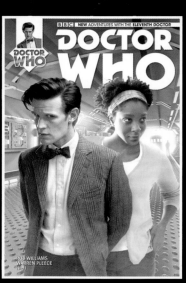

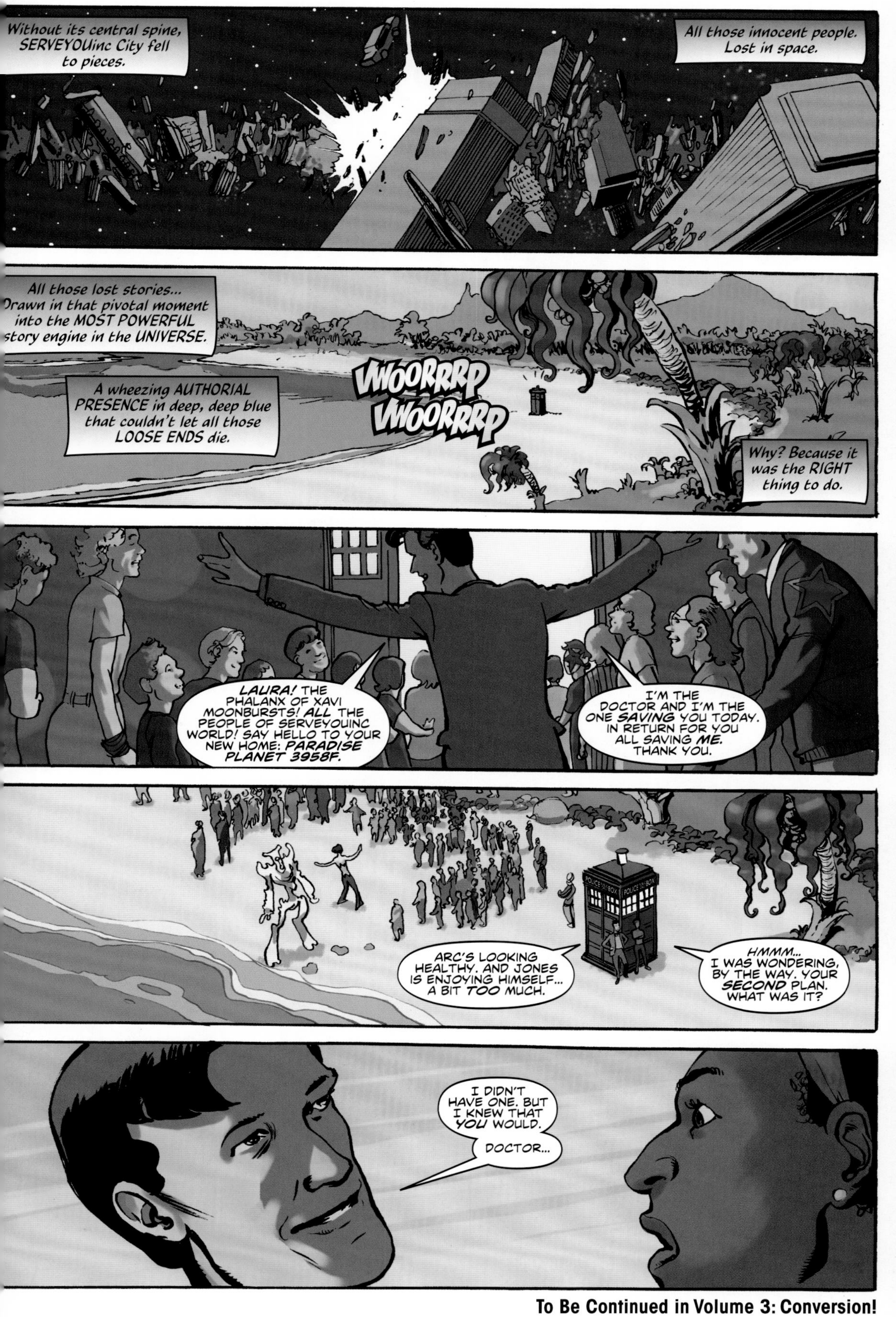
Without its central spine, SERVEYOUinc City fell to pieces.
All those innocent people. Lost in space.
All those lost stories... Drawn in that pivotal moment into the MOST POWERFUL story engine in the UNIVERSE.
A wheezing AUTHORIAL PRESENCE in deep, deep blue that couldn't let all those LOOSE ENDS die.
VWOORRRP VWOORRRP
Why? Because it was the RIGHT thing to do.
LAURA! THE PHALANX OF XAVI MOONBURSTS! ALL THE PEOPLE OF SERVEYOUINC WORLD! SAY HELLO TO YOUR NEW HOME: PARADISE PLANET 3958F.
I'M THE DOCTOR AND I'M THE ONE SAVING YOU TODAY. IN RETURN FOR YOU ALL SAVING ME. THANK YOU.
ARC'S LOOKING HEALTHY. AND JONES IS ENJOYING HIMSELF... A BIT TOO MUCH.
HMMM... I WAS WONDERING, BY THE WAY. YOUR SECOND PLAN. WHAT WAS IT?
I DIDN'T HAVE ONE. BUT I KNEW THAT YOU WOULD.
DOCTOR...

To Be Continued in Volume 3: Conversion!

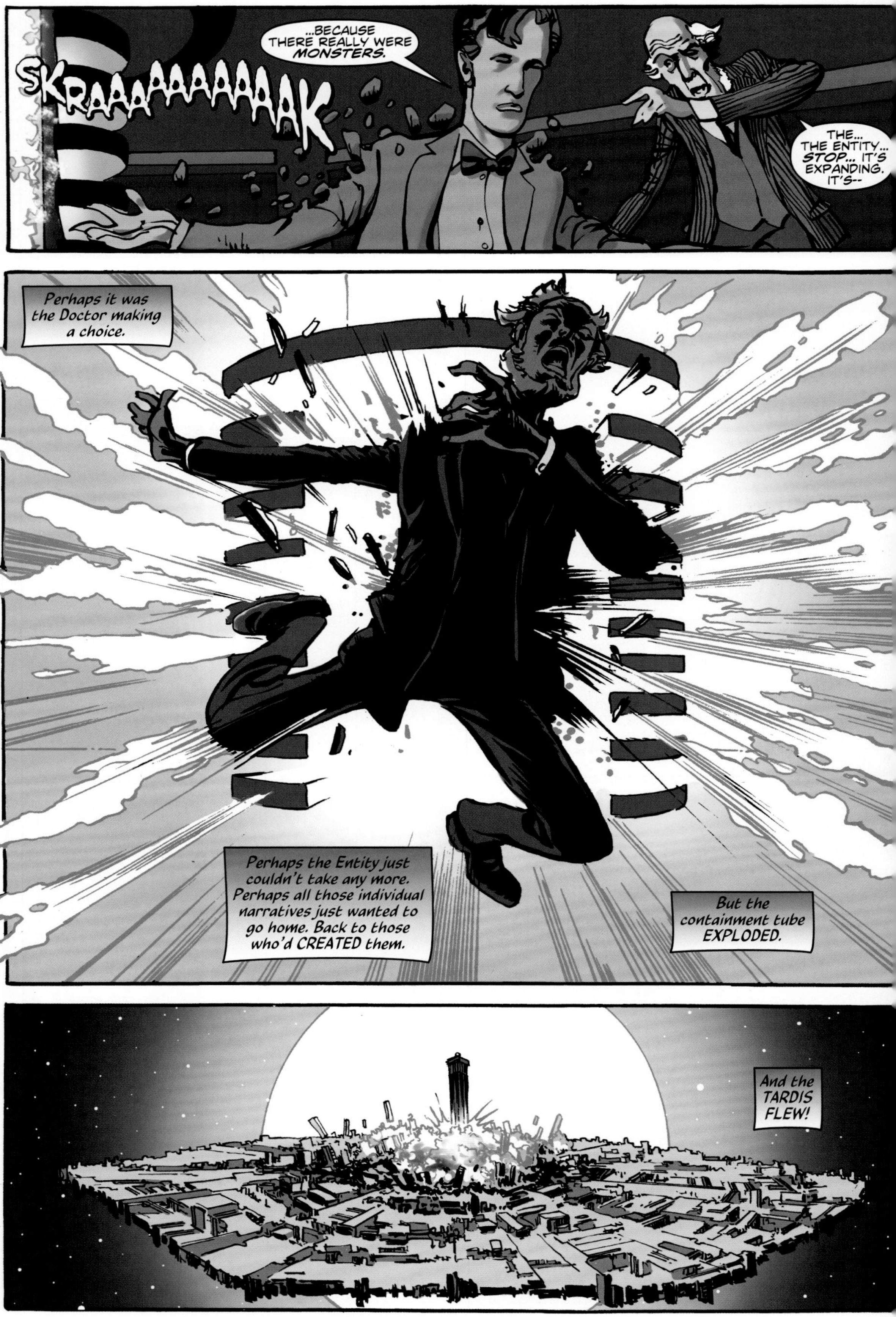
SKRAAAAAAAAAAK
...BECAUSE THERE REALLY WERE MONSTERS.
THE... THE ENTITY... STOP... IT'S EXPANDING. IT'S--
Perhaps it was the Doctor making a choice.
Perhaps the Entity just couldn't take any more. Perhaps all those individual narratives just wanted to go home. Back to those who'd CREATED them.
But the containment tube EXPLODED.
And the TARDIS FLEW!

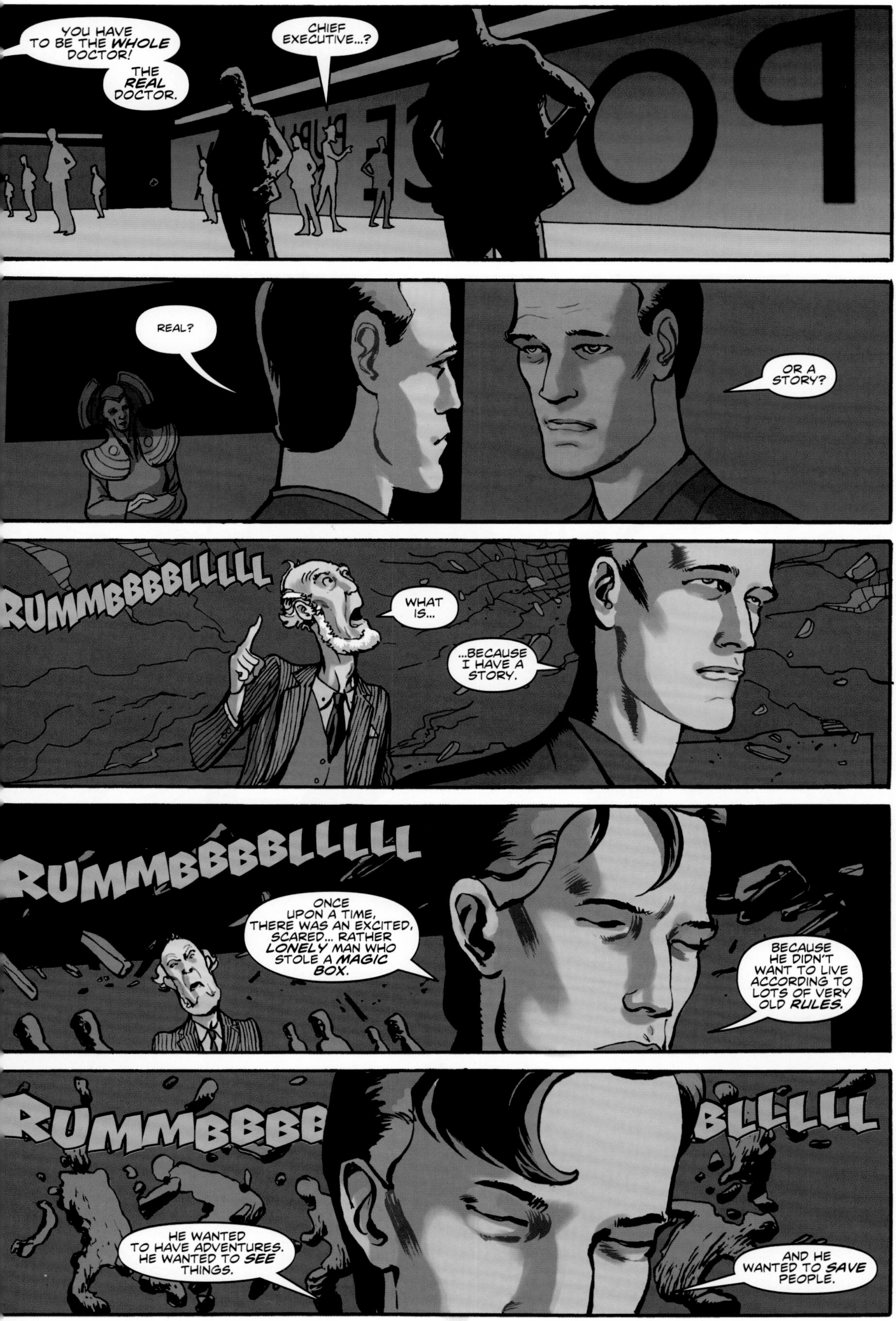

YOU HAVE TO BE THE WHOLE DOCTOR!
THE REAL DOCTOR.
CHIEF EXECUTIVE...?
REAL?
OR A STORY?
RUMMBBBBLLLLL
WHAT IS...
...BECAUSE I HAVE A STORY.
RUMMBBBBLLLLL
ONCE UPON A TIME, THERE WAS AN EXCITED, SCARED... RATHER LONELY MAN WHO STOLE A MAGIC BOX.
BECAUSE HE DIDN'T WANT TO LIVE ACCORDING TO LOTS OF VERY OLD RULES.
RUMMBBBB
BLLLLL
HE WANTED TO HAVE ADVENTURES. HE WANTED TO SEE THINGS.
AND HE WANTED TO SAVE PEOPLE.

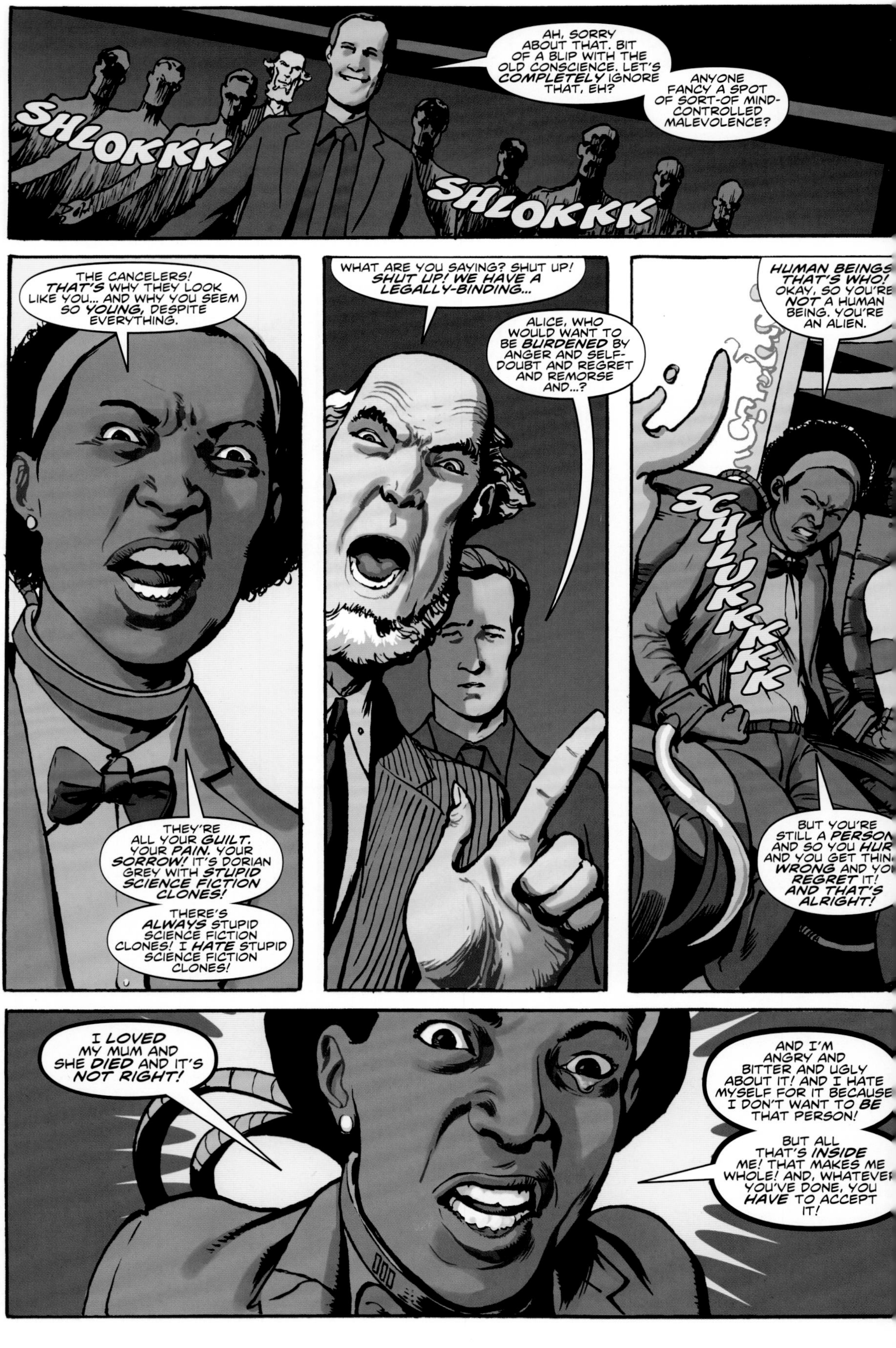

SHLOKKK
AH, SORRY ABOUT THAT. BIT OF A BLIP WITH THE OLD CONSCIENCE. LET'S COMPLETELY IGNORE THAT, EH?
ANYONE FANCY A SPOT OF SORT-OF MIND-CONTROLLED MALEVOLENCE?
SHLOKKK
THE CANCELERS! THAT'S WHY THEY LOOK LIKE YOU... AND WHY YOU SEEM SO YOUNG, DESPITE EVERYTHING.
THEY'RE ALL YOUR GUILT. YOUR PAIN. YOUR SORROW! IT'S DORIAN GREY WITH STUPID SCIENCE FICTION CLONES!
THERE'S ALWAYS STUPID SCIENCE FICTION CLONES! I HATE STUPID SCIENCE FICTION CLONES!
WHAT ARE YOU SAYING? SHUT UP! SHUT UP! WE HAVE A LEGALLY-BINDING...
ALICE, WHO WOULD WANT TO BE BURDENED BY ANGER AND SELF-DOUBT AND REGRET AND REMORSE AND...?
HUMAN BEINGS THAT'S WHO! OKAY, SO YOU'RE NOT A HUMAN BEING. YOU'RE AN ALIEN.
SCHLUKKKK
BUT YOU'RE STILL A PERSON AND SO YOU HUR AND YOU GET THIN WRONG AND YO REGRET IT! AND THAT'S ALRIGHT!
I LOVED MY MUM AND SHE DIED AND IT'S NOT RIGHT!
AND I'M ANGRY AND BITTER AND UGLY ABOUT IT! AND I HATE MYSELF FOR IT BECAUSE I DON'T WANT TO BE THAT PERSON!
BUT ALL THAT'S INSIDE ME! THAT MAKES ME WHOLE! AND, WHATEVEF YOU'VE DONE, YOU HAVE TO ACCEPT IT!

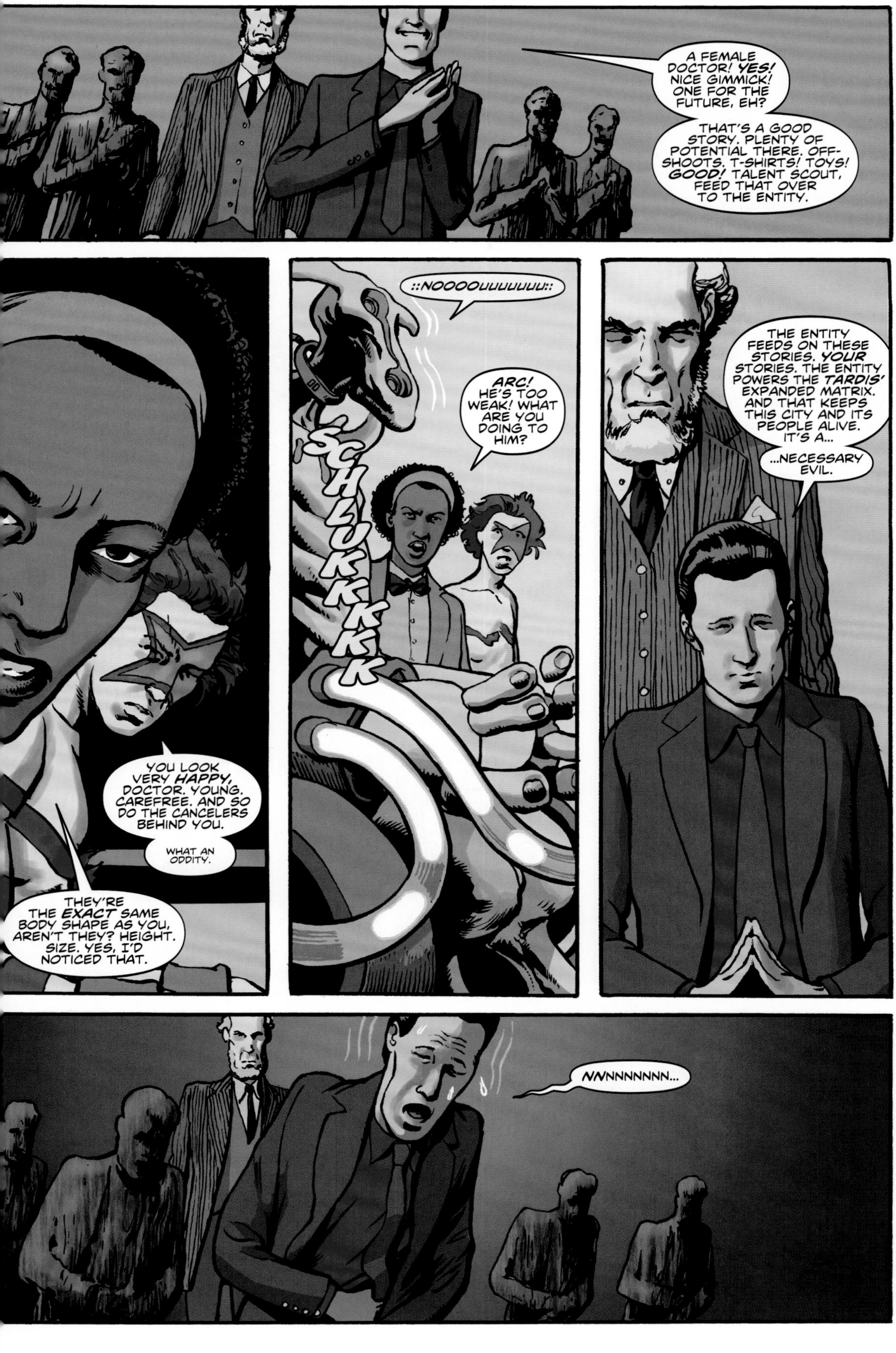
A FEMALE DOCTOR! YES! NICE GIMMICK! ONE FOR THE FUTURE, EH?
THAT'S A GOOD STORY. PLENTY OF POTENTIAL THERE. OFF-SHOOTS. T-SHIRTS! TOYS! GOOD! TALENT SCOUT, FEED THAT OVER TO THE ENTITY.
YOU LOOK VERY HAPPY, DOCTOR. YOUNG. CAREFREE. AND SO DO THE CANCELERS BEHIND YOU.
WHAT AN ODDITY.
THEY'RE THE EXACT SAME BODY SHAPE AS YOU, AREN'T THEY? HEIGHT. SIZE. YES, I'D NOTICED THAT.
::NOOOOuuuuuuu::
ARC! HE'S TOO WEAK! WHAT ARE YOU DOING TO HIM?
SCHLUKKKKK
THE ENTITY FEEDS ON THESE STORIES. YOUR STORIES. THE ENTITY POWERS THE TARDIS' EXPANDED MATRIX. AND THAT KEEPS THIS CITY AND ITS PEOPLE ALIVE. IT'S A...
...NECESSARY EVIL.
NNNNNNNNN...

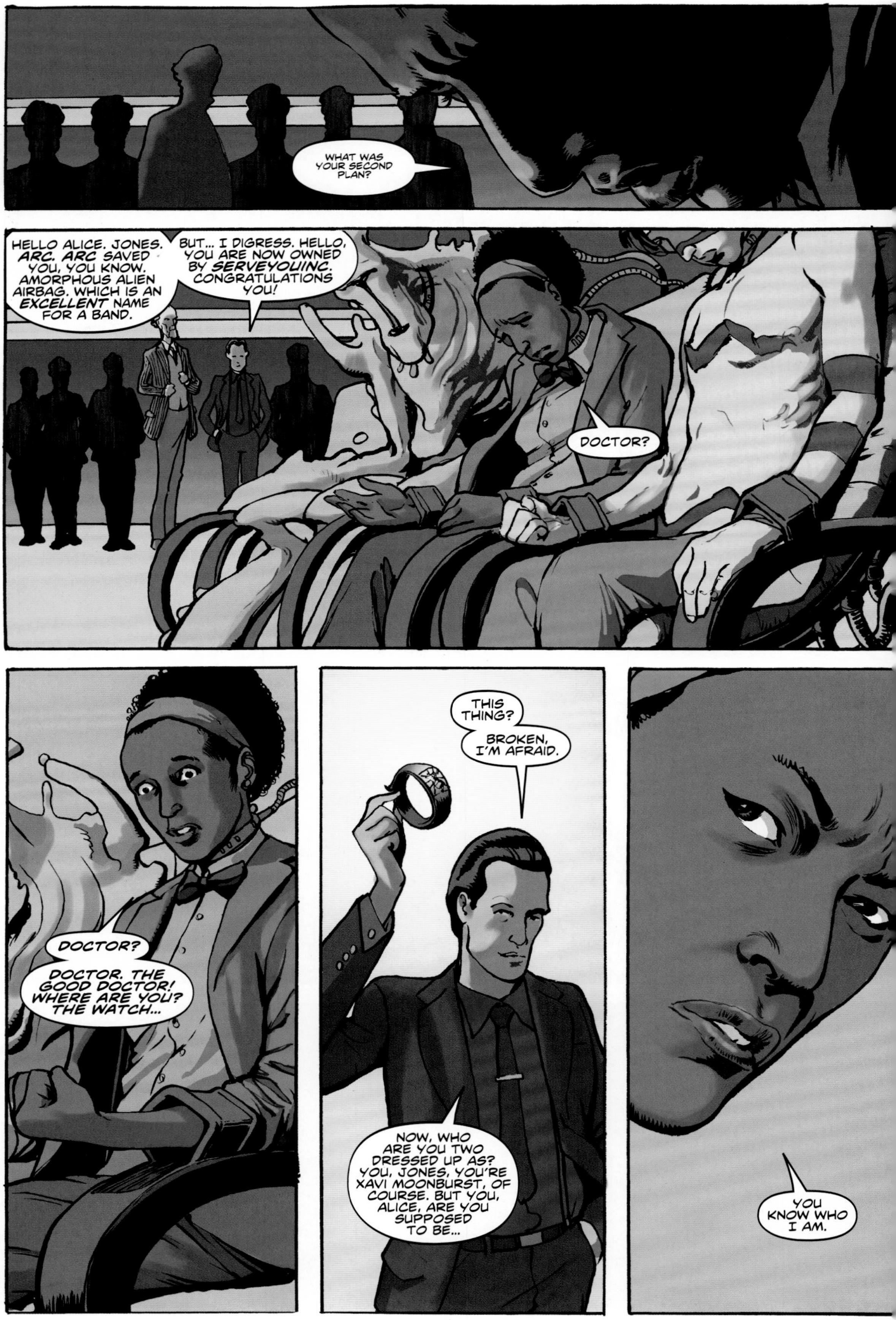
WHAT WAS YOUR SECOND PLAN?
HELLO ALICE. JONES. ARC. ARC SAVED YOU, YOU KNOW. AMORPHOUS ALIEN AIRBAG. WHICH IS AN EXCELLENT NAME FOR A BAND.
BUT... I DIGRESS. HELLO, YOU ARE NOW OWNED BY SERVEYOUINC. CONGRATULATIONS YOU!
DOCTOR?
DOCTOR?
DOCTOR. THE GOOD DOCTOR! WHERE ARE YOU? THE WATCH...
THIS THING?
BROKEN, I'M AFRAID.
NOW, WHO ARE YOU TWO DRESSED UP AS? YOU, JONES, YOU'RE XAVI MOONBURST, OF COURSE. BUT YOU, ALICE, ARE YOU SUPPOSED TO BE...
YOU KNOW WHO I AM.

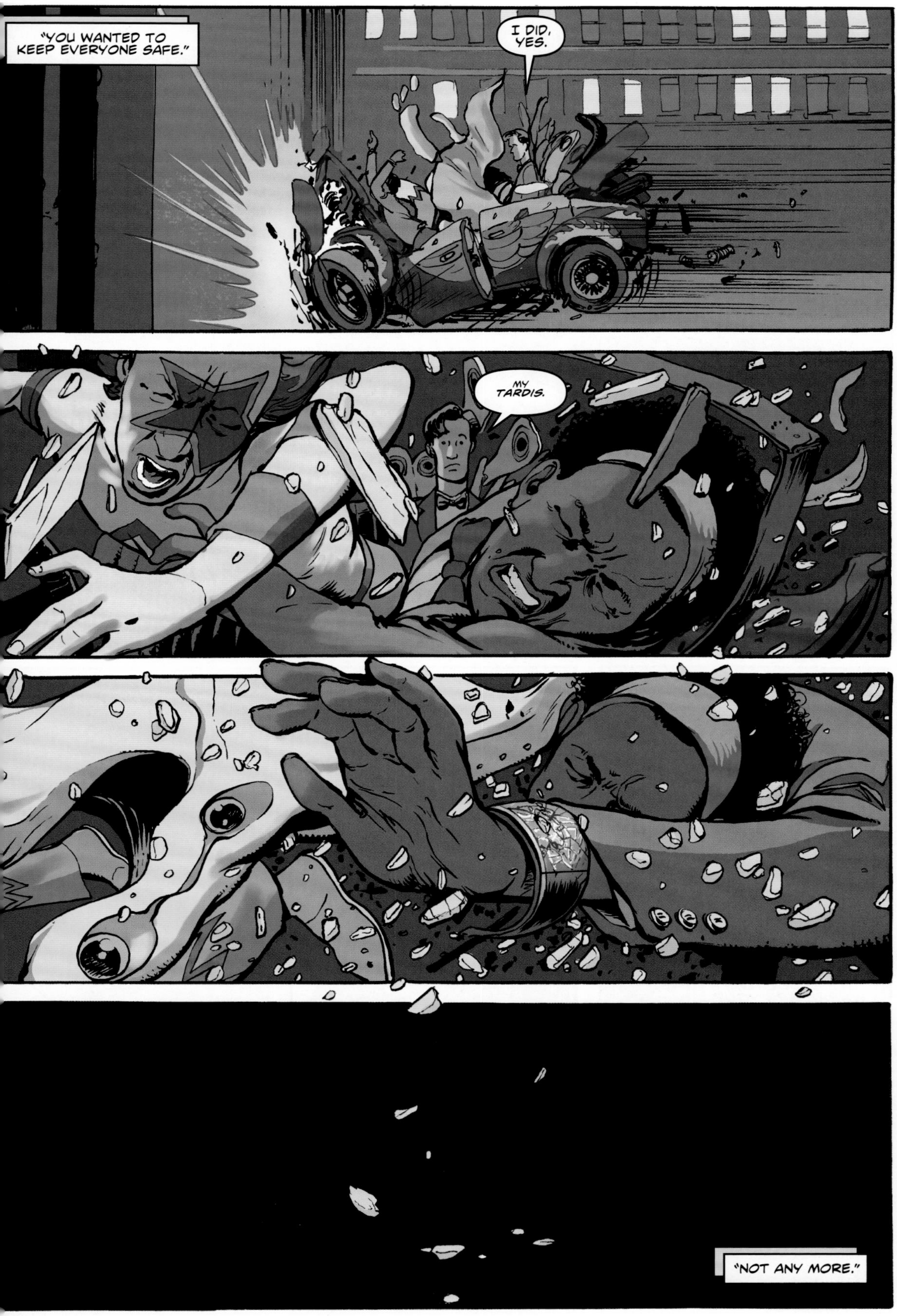
"YOU WANTED TO KEEP EVERYONE SAFE."
I DID, YES.
MY TARDIS.
"NOT ANY MORE."

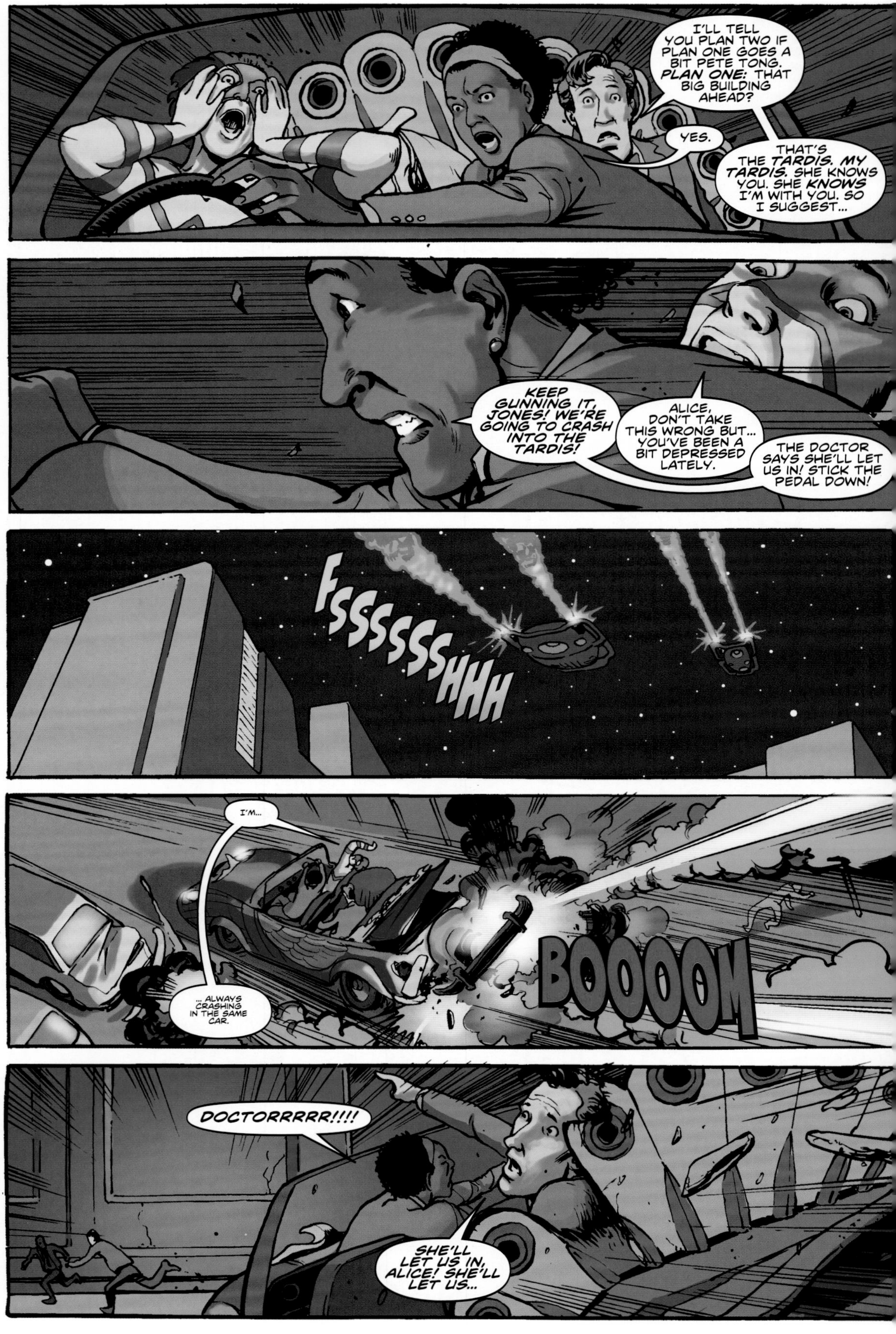
I'LL TELL YOU PLAN TWO IF PLAN ONE GOES A BIT PETE TONG. PLAN ONE: THAT BIG BUILDING AHEAD?
YES.
THAT'S THE TARDIS. MY TARDIS. SHE KNOWS YOU. SHE KNOWS I'M WITH YOU. SO I SUGGEST...
KEEP GUNNING IT, JONES! WE'RE GOING TO CRASH INTO THE TARDIS!
ALICE, DON'T TAKE THIS WRONG BUT... YOU'VE BEEN A BIT DEPRESSED LATELY.
THE DOCTOR SAYS SHE'LL LET US IN! STICK THE PEDAL DOWN!
FSSSSSSHHH
I'M...
... ALWAYS CRASHING IN THE SAME CAR.
BOOOOM
DOCTORRRRR!!!!
SHE'LL LET US IN, ALICE! SHE'LL LET US...

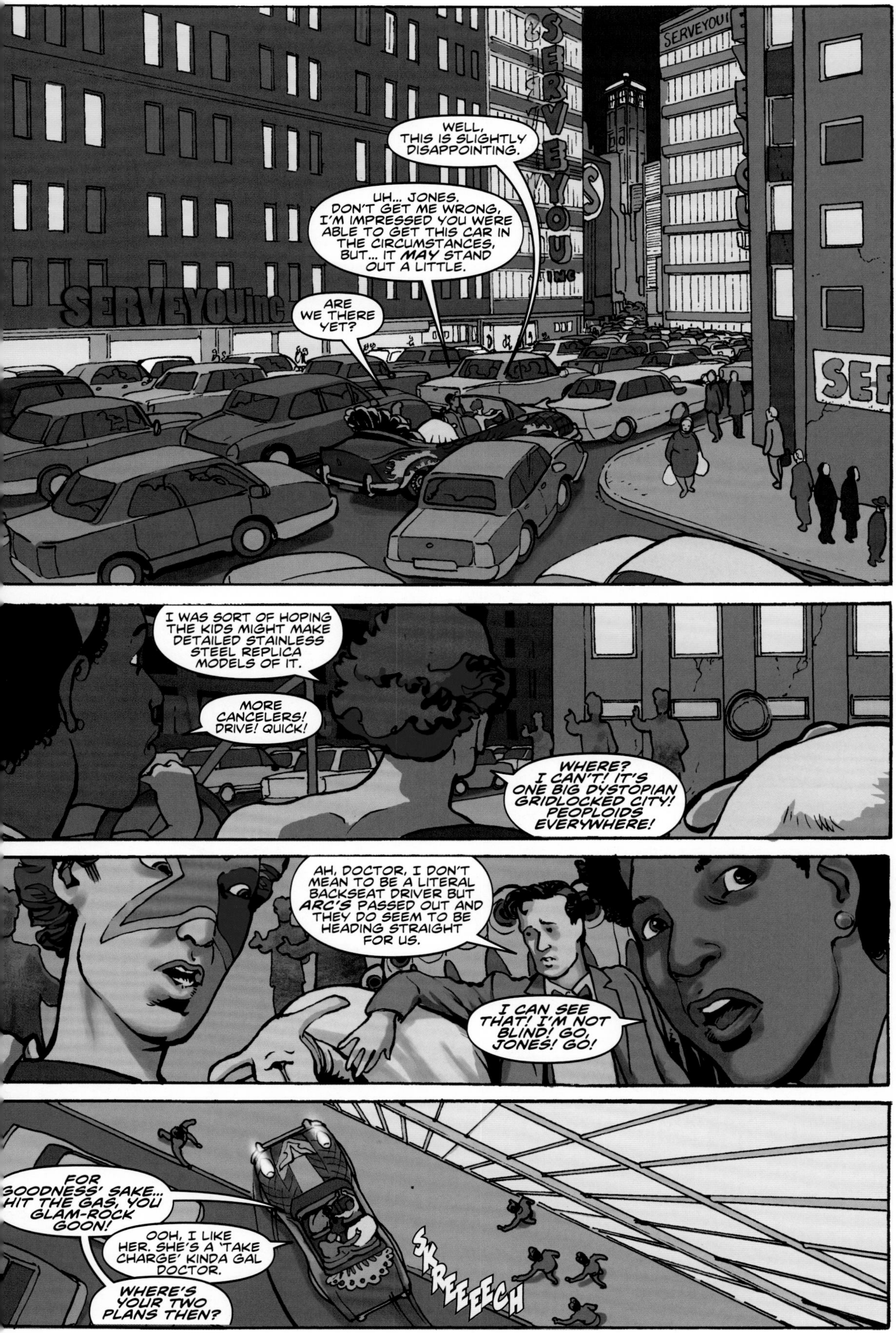
SERVEYOU
SERVEYOU
SERVEYOUinc
WELL, THIS IS SLIGHTLY DISAPPOINTING.
UH... JONES. DON'T GET ME WRONG, I'M IMPRESSED YOU WERE ABLE TO GET THIS CAR IN THE CIRCUMSTANCES, BUT... IT *MAY* STAND OUT A LITTLE.
ARE WE THERE YET?
I WAS SORT OF HOPING THE KIDS MIGHT MAKE DETAILED STAINLESS STEEL REPLICA MODELS OF IT.
MORE CANCELERS! DRIVE! QUICK!
WHERE? I CAN'T! IT'S ONE BIG DYSTOPIAN GRIDLOCKED CITY! PEOPLOIDS EVERYWHERE!
AH, DOCTOR, I DON'T MEAN TO BE A LITERAL BACKSEAT DRIVER BUT *ARC'S* PASSED OUT AND THEY DO SEEM TO BE HEADING STRAIGHT FOR US.
I CAN SEE THAT! I'M NOT BLIND! GO, JONES! GO!
FOR GOODNESS' SAKE... HIT THE GAS, YOU GLAM-ROCK GOON!
OOH, I LIKE HER. SHE'S A 'TAKE CHARGE' KINDA GAL DOCTOR.
WHERE'S YOUR TWO PLANS THEN?
SKREEEEECH

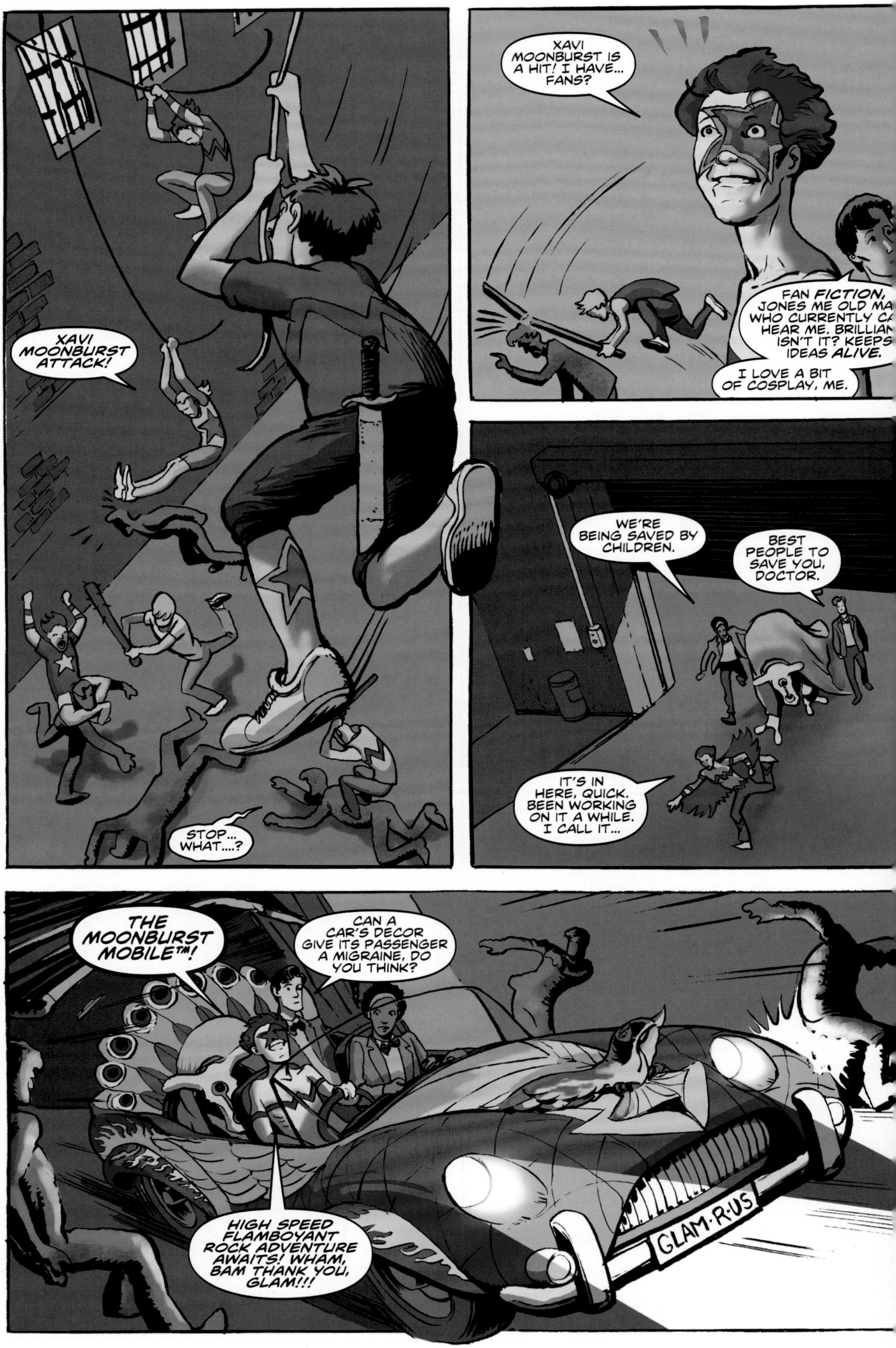
XAVI MOONBURST ATTACK!
STOP... WHAT....?
XAVI MOONBURST IS A HIT! I HAVE... FANS?
FAN FICTION, JONES ME OLD MA
WHO CURRENTLY C
HEAR ME. BRILLIAN
ISN'T IT? KEEPS
IDEAS ALIVE.
I LOVE A BIT OF COSPLAY, ME.
WE'RE BEING SAVED BY CHILDREN.
BEST PEOPLE TO SAVE YOU, DOCTOR.
IT'S IN HERE, QUICK. BEEN WORKING ON IT A WHILE. I CALL IT...
THE MOONBURST MOBILE™!
CAN A CAR'S DECOR GIVE ITS PASSENGER A MIGRAINE, DO YOU THINK?
HIGH SPEED FLAMBOYANT ROCK ADVENTURE AWAITS! WHAM, BAM THANK YOU, GLAM!!!
GLAM·R·US

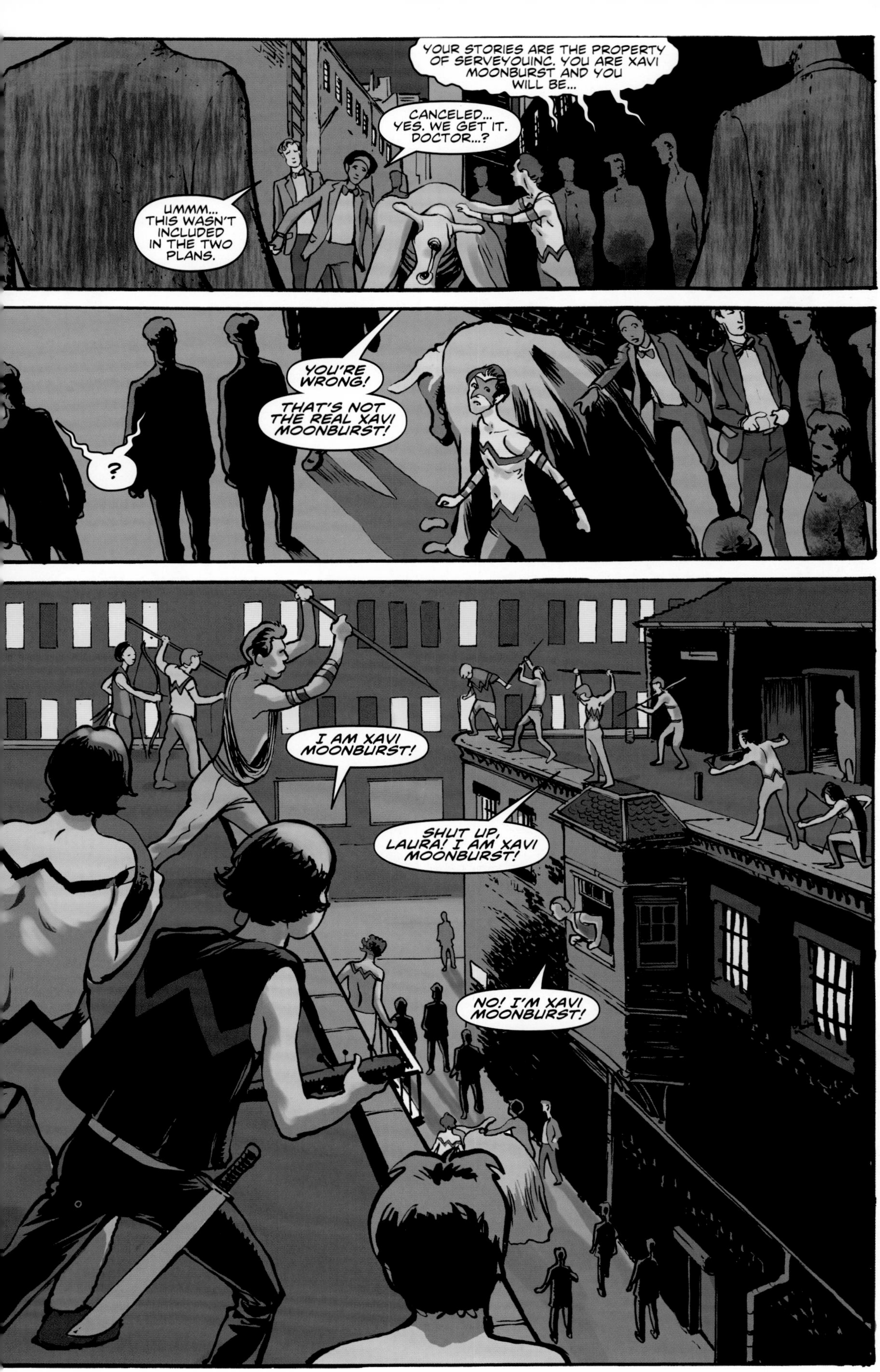
YOUR STORIES ARE THE PROPERTY OF SERVEYOUINC. YOU ARE XAVI MOONBURST AND YOU WILL BE...
CANCELED... YES. WE GET IT. DOCTOR...?
UMMM... THIS WASN'T INCLUDED IN THE TWO PLANS.
YOU'RE WRONG!
THAT'S NOT THE REAL XAVI MOONBURST!
?
I AM XAVI MOONBURST!
SHUT UP, LAURA! I AM XAVI MOONBURST!
NO! I'M XAVI MOONBURST!

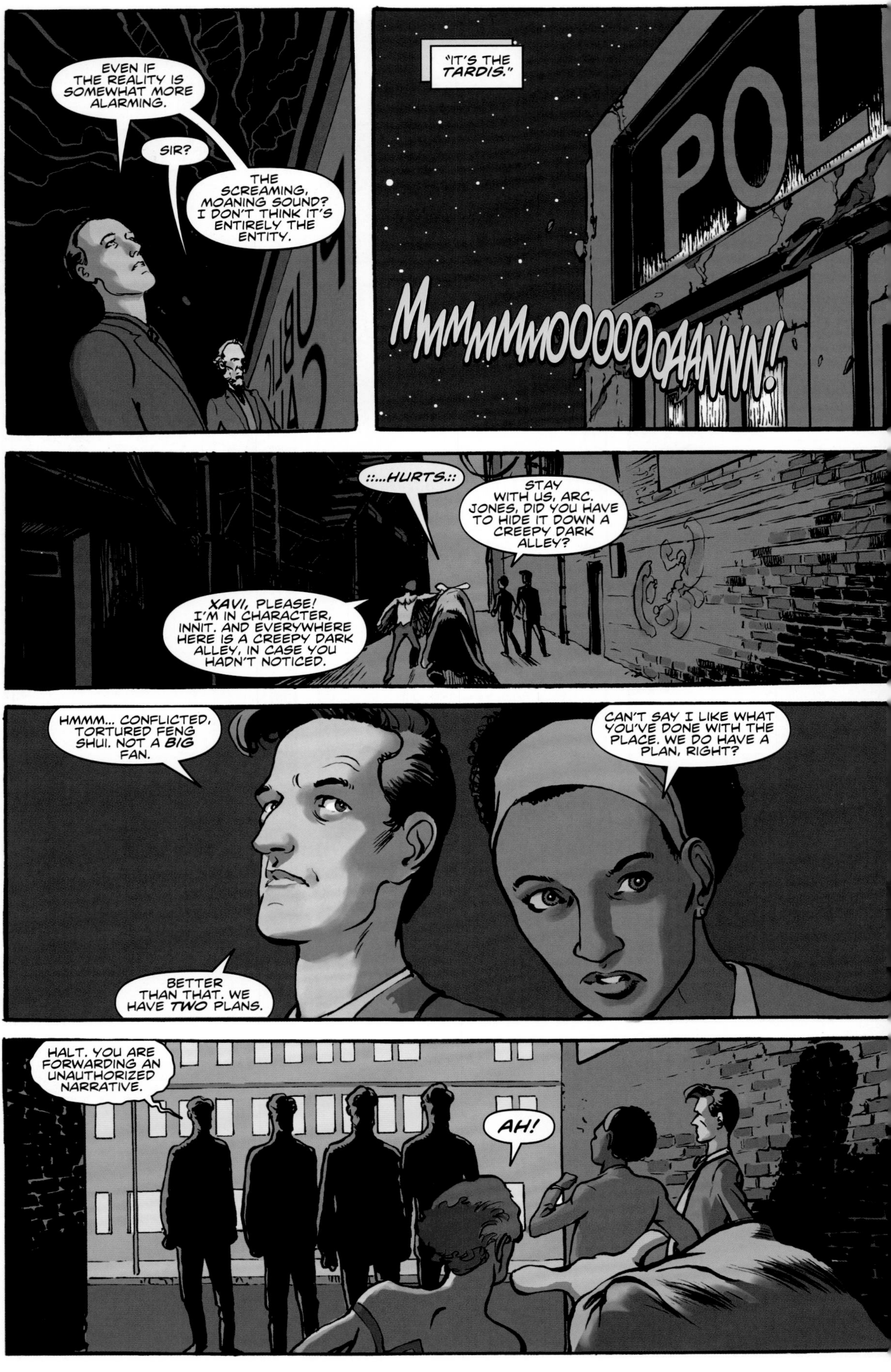
EVEN IF THE REALITY IS SOMEWHAT MORE ALARMING.
SIR?
THE SCREAMING, MOANING SOUND? I DON'T THINK IT'S ENTIRELY THE ENTITY.
"IT'S THE TARDIS."
POL
MMMMMMOOOOOOOAANNN!
::...HURTS.::
STAY WITH US, ARC. JONES, DID YOU HAVE TO HIDE IT DOWN A CREEPY DARK ALLEY?
XAVI, PLEASE! I'M IN CHARACTER, INNIT. AND EVERYWHERE HERE IS A CREEPY DARK ALLEY, IN CASE YOU HADN'T NOTICED.
HMMM... CONFLICTED, TORTURED FENG SHUI. NOT A BIG FAN.
CAN'T SAY I LIKE WHAT YOU'VE DONE WITH THE PLACE. WE DO HAVE A PLAN, RIGHT?
BETTER THAN THAT. WE HAVE TWO PLANS.
HALT. YOU ARE FORWARDING AN UNAUTHORIZED NARRATIVE.
AH!

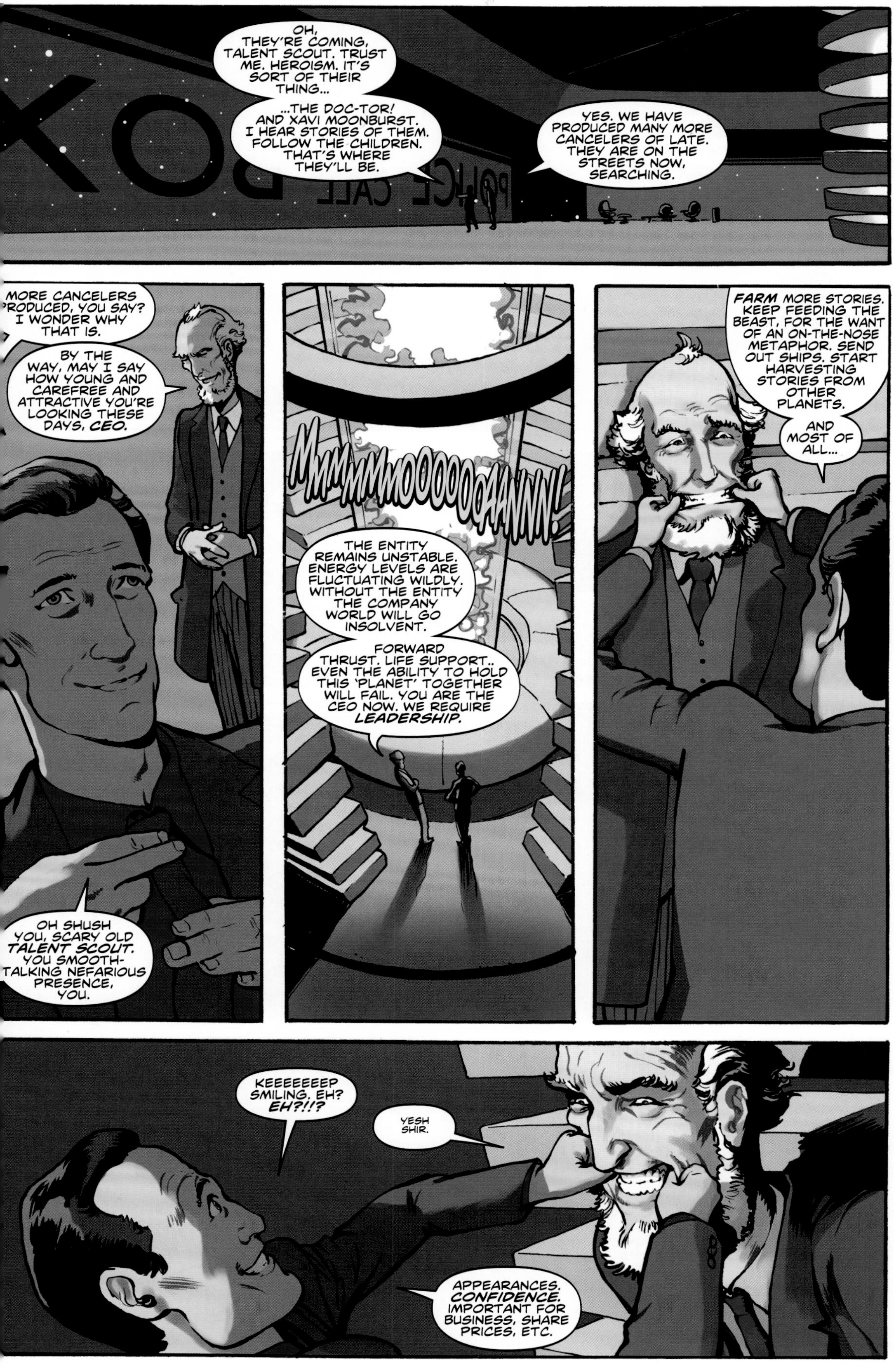

OH, THEY'RE COMING, TALENT SCOUT. TRUST ME. HEROISM. IT'S SORT OF THEIR THING...
...THE DOC-TOR! AND XAVI MOONBURST. I HEAR STORIES OF THEM. FOLLOW THE CHILDREN. THAT'S WHERE THEY'LL BE.
YES. WE HAVE PRODUCED MANY MORE CANCELERS OF LATE. THEY ARE ON THE STREETS NOW, SEARCHING.
POLICE CALL BOX
MORE CANCELERS PRODUCED, YOU SAY? I WONDER WHY THAT IS.
BY THE WAY, MAY I SAY HOW YOUNG AND CAREFREE AND ATTRACTIVE YOU'RE LOOKING THESE DAYS, CEO.
OH SHUSH YOU, SCARY OLD TALENT SCOUT. YOU SMOOTH-TALKING NEFARIOUS PRESENCE, YOU.
MMMMMMOOOOOOAANNN!
THE ENTITY REMAINS UNSTABLE. ENERGY LEVELS ARE FLUCTUATING WILDLY. WITHOUT THE ENTITY THE COMPANY WORLD WILL GO INSOLVENT.
FORWARD THRUST. LIFE SUPPORT.. EVEN THE ABILITY TO HOLD THIS 'PLANET' TOGETHER WILL FAIL. YOU ARE THE CEO NOW. WE REQUIRE LEADERSHIP.
FARM MORE STORIES. KEEP FEEDING THE BEAST, FOR THE WANT OF AN ON-THE-NOSE METAPHOR. SEND OUT SHIPS. START HARVESTING STORIES FROM OTHER PLANETS.
AND MOST OF ALL...
KEEEEEEEP SMILING. EH? EH?!!?
YESH SHIR.
APPEARANCES. CONFIDENCE. IMPORTANT FOR BUSINESS, SHARE PRICES, ETC.

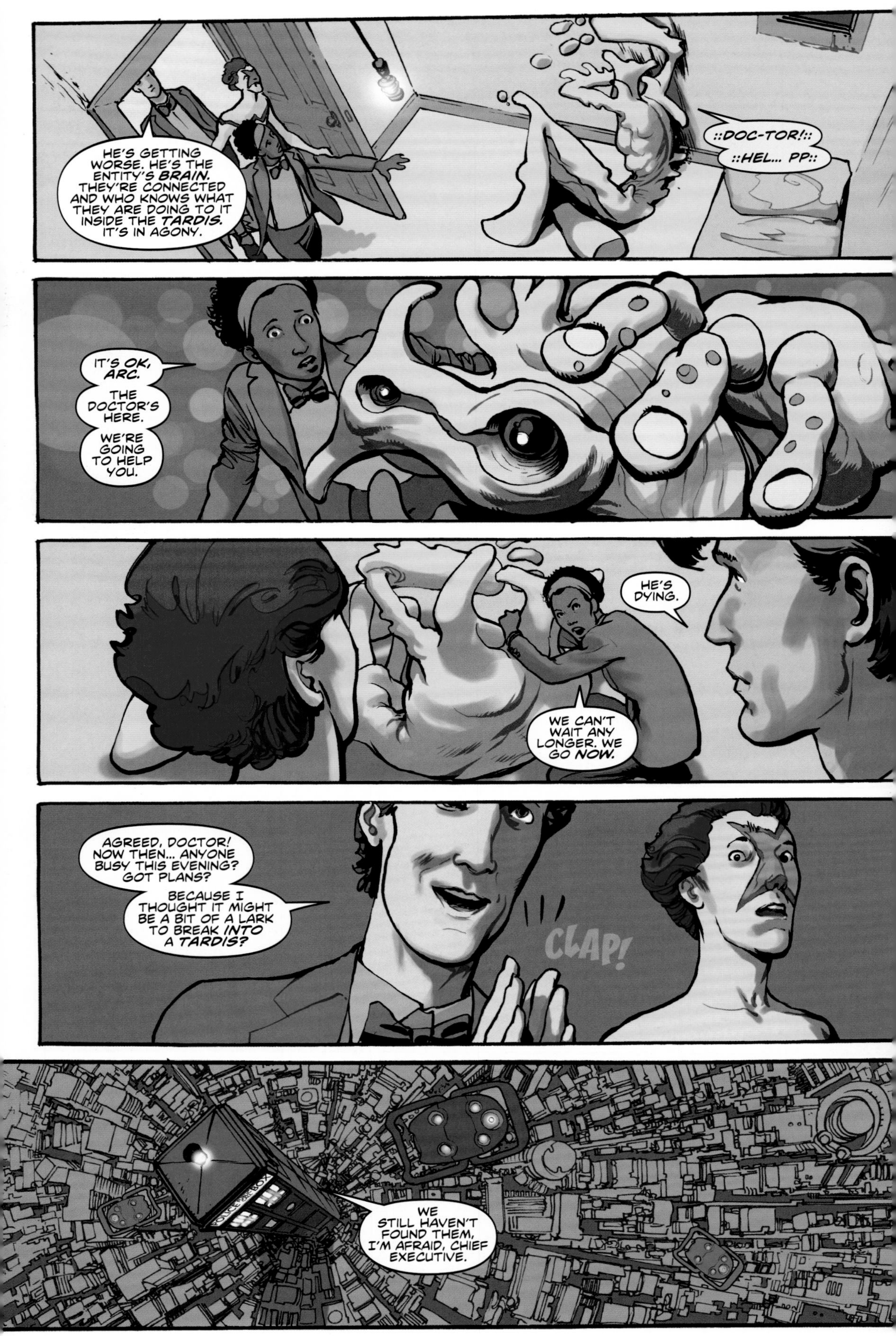
HE'S GETTING WORSE. HE'S THE ENTITY'S BRAIN. THEY'RE CONNECTED AND WHO KNOWS WHAT THEY ARE DOING TO IT INSIDE THE TARDIS. IT'S IN AGONY.
::DOC-TOR!::
::HEL... PP::
IT'S OK, ARC.
THE DOCTOR'S HERE.
WE'RE GOING TO HELP YOU.
HE'S DYING.
WE CAN'T WAIT ANY LONGER. WE GO NOW.
AGREED, DOCTOR! NOW THEN... ANYONE BUSY THIS EVENING? GOT PLANS?
BECAUSE I THOUGHT IT MIGHT BE A BIT OF A LARK TO BREAK INTO A TARDIS?
CLAP!
WE STILL HAVEN'T FOUND THEM, I'M AFRAID, CHIEF EXECUTIVE.

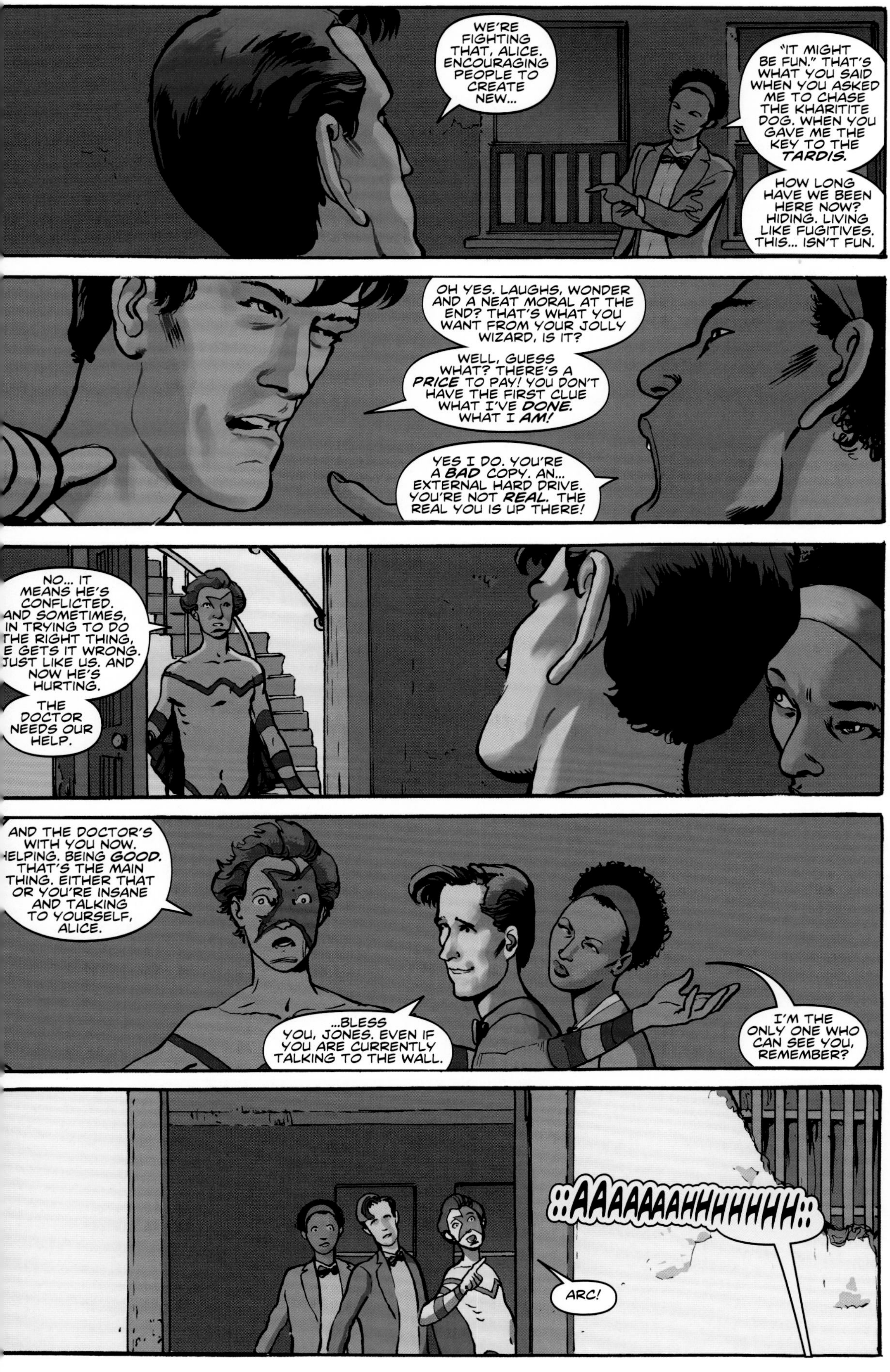

WE'RE FIGHTING THAT, ALICE. ENCOURAGING PEOPLE TO CREATE NEW...
"IT MIGHT BE FUN." THAT'S WHAT YOU SAID WHEN YOU ASKED ME TO CHASE THE KHARITITE DOG. WHEN YOU GAVE ME THE KEY TO THE TARDIS.
HOW LONG HAVE WE BEEN HERE NOW? HIDING. LIVING LIKE FUGITIVES. THIS... ISN'T FUN.
OH YES. LAUGHS, WONDER AND A NEAT MORAL AT THE END? THAT'S WHAT YOU WANT FROM YOUR JOLLY WIZARD, IS IT?
WELL, GUESS WHAT? THERE'S A PRICE TO PAY! YOU DON'T HAVE THE FIRST CLUE WHAT I'VE DONE. WHAT I AM!
YES I DO. YOU'RE A BAD COPY. AN... EXTERNAL HARD DRIVE. YOU'RE NOT REAL. THE REAL YOU IS UP THERE!
NO... IT MEANS HE'S CONFLICTED. AND SOMETIMES, IN TRYING TO DO THE RIGHT THING, E GETS IT WRONG. JUST LIKE US. AND NOW HE'S HURTING.
THE DOCTOR NEEDS OUR HELP.
AND THE DOCTOR'S WITH YOU NOW. HELPING. BEING GOOD. THAT'S THE MAIN THING. EITHER THAT OR YOU'RE INSANE AND TALKING TO YOURSELF, ALICE.
...BLESS YOU, JONES. EVEN IF YOU ARE CURRENTLY TALKING TO THE WALL.
I'M THE ONLY ONE WHO CAN SEE YOU, REMEMBER?
::AAAAAAAHHHHHHH::
ARC!

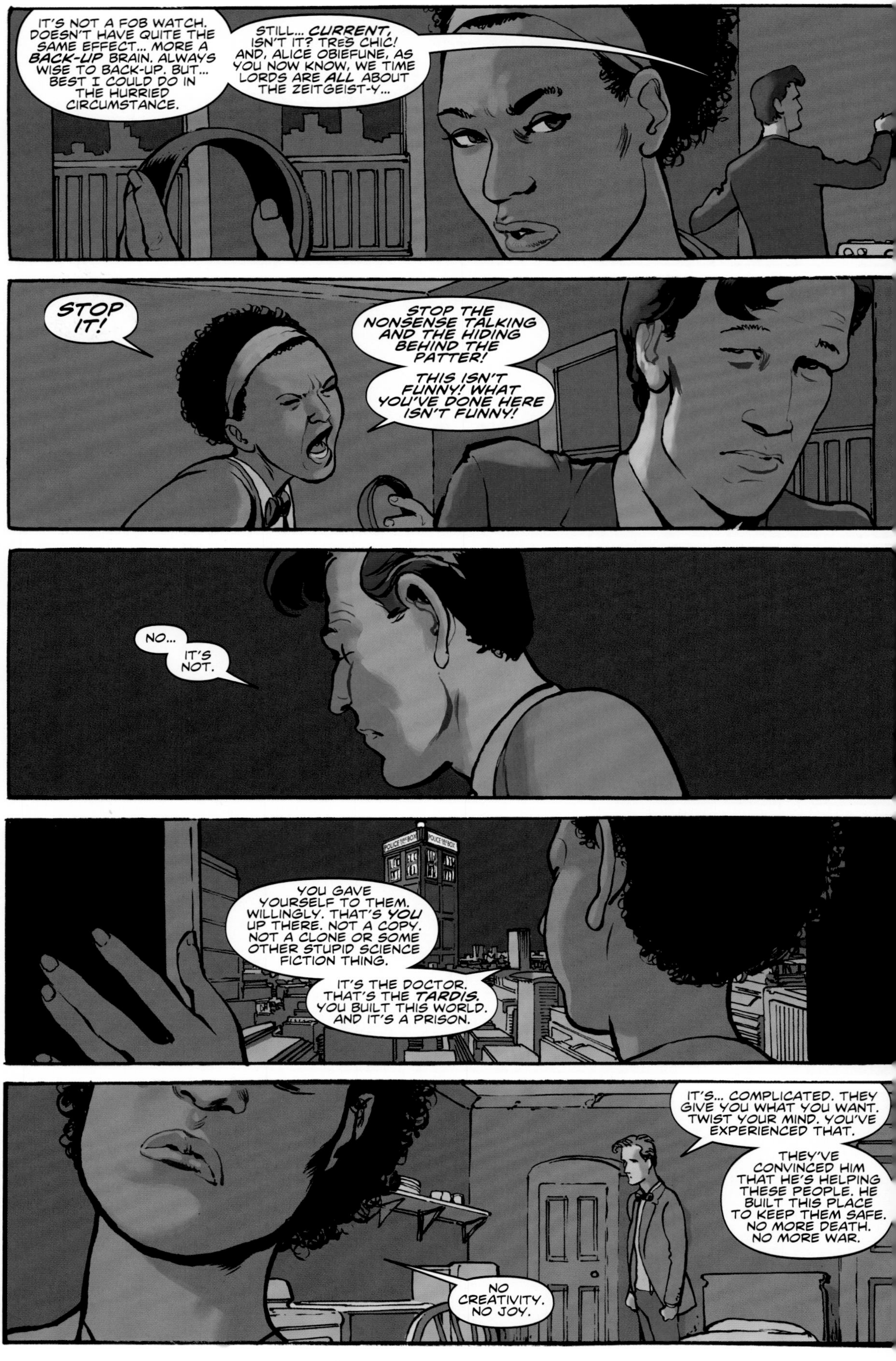
IT'S NOT A FOB WATCH. DOESN'T HAVE QUITE THE SAME EFFECT... MORE A BACK-UP BRAIN. ALWAYS WISE TO BACK-UP. BUT... BEST I COULD DO IN THE HURRIED CIRCUMSTANCE.
STILL... CURRENT, ISN'T IT? TRÈS CHIC! AND, ALICE OBIEFUNE, AS YOU NOW KNOW, WE TIME LORDS ARE ALL ABOUT THE ZEITGEIST-Y...
STOP IT!
STOP THE NONSENSE TALKING AND THE HIDING BEHIND THE PATTER!
THIS ISN'T FUNNY! WHAT YOU'VE DONE HERE ISN'T FUNNY!
NO... IT'S NOT.
YOU GAVE YOURSELF TO THEM. WILLINGLY. THAT'S YOU UP THERE. NOT A COPY. NOT A CLONE OR SOME OTHER STUPID SCIENCE FICTION THING.
IT'S THE DOCTOR. THAT'S THE TARDIS. YOU BUILT THIS WORLD. AND IT'S A PRISON.
POLICE BOX
IT'S... COMPLICATED. THEY GIVE YOU WHAT YOU WANT. TWIST YOUR MIND. YOU'VE EXPERIENCED THAT.
THEY'VE CONVINCED HIM THAT HE'S HELPING THESE PEOPLE. HE BUILT THIS PLACE TO KEEP THEM SAFE. NO MORE DEATH. NO MORE WAR.
NO CREATIVITY. NO JOY.

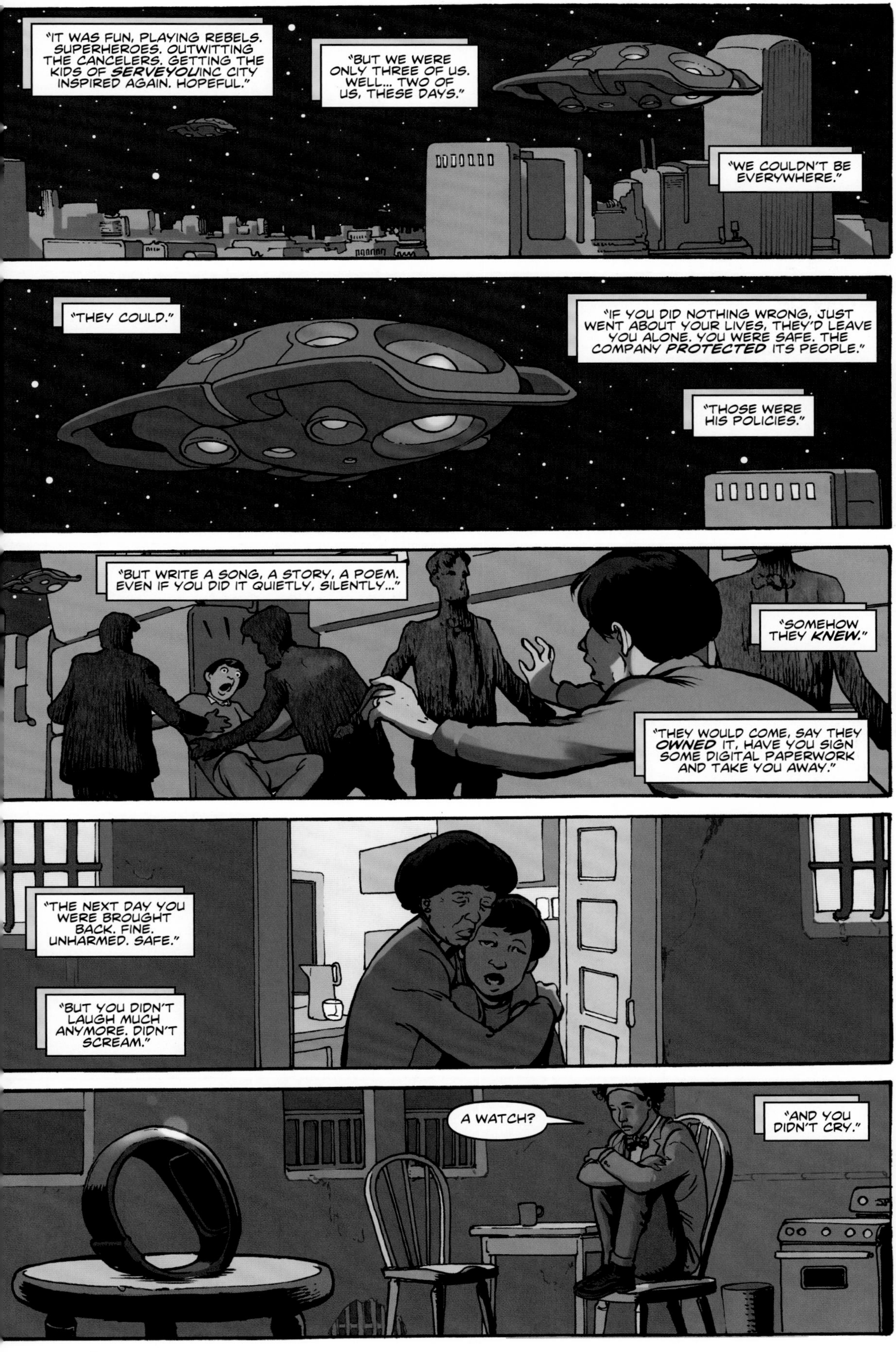
"IT WAS FUN, PLAYING REBELS. SUPERHEROES. OUTWITTING THE CANCELERS. GETTING THE KIDS OF SERVEYOUINC CITY INSPIRED AGAIN. HOPEFUL."
"BUT WE WERE ONLY THREE OF US. WELL... TWO OF US, THESE DAYS."
"WE COULDN'T BE EVERYWHERE."
"THEY COULD."
"IF YOU DID NOTHING WRONG, JUST WENT ABOUT YOUR LIVES, THEY'D LEAVE YOU ALONE. YOU WERE SAFE. THE COMPANY PROTECTED ITS PEOPLE."
"THOSE WERE HIS POLICIES."
"BUT WRITE A SONG, A STORY, A POEM. EVEN IF YOU DID IT QUIETLY, SILENTLY..."
"SOMEHOW THEY KNEW."
"THEY WOULD COME, SAY THEY OWNED IT, HAVE YOU SIGN SOME DIGITAL PAPERWORK AND TAKE YOU AWAY."
"THE NEXT DAY YOU WERE BROUGHT BACK. FINE. UNHARMED. SAFE."
"BUT YOU DIDN'T LAUGH MUCH ANYMORE. DIDN'T SCREAM."
A WATCH?
"AND YOU DIDN'T CRY."

CHAPTER 10

THE OTHER DOCTOR

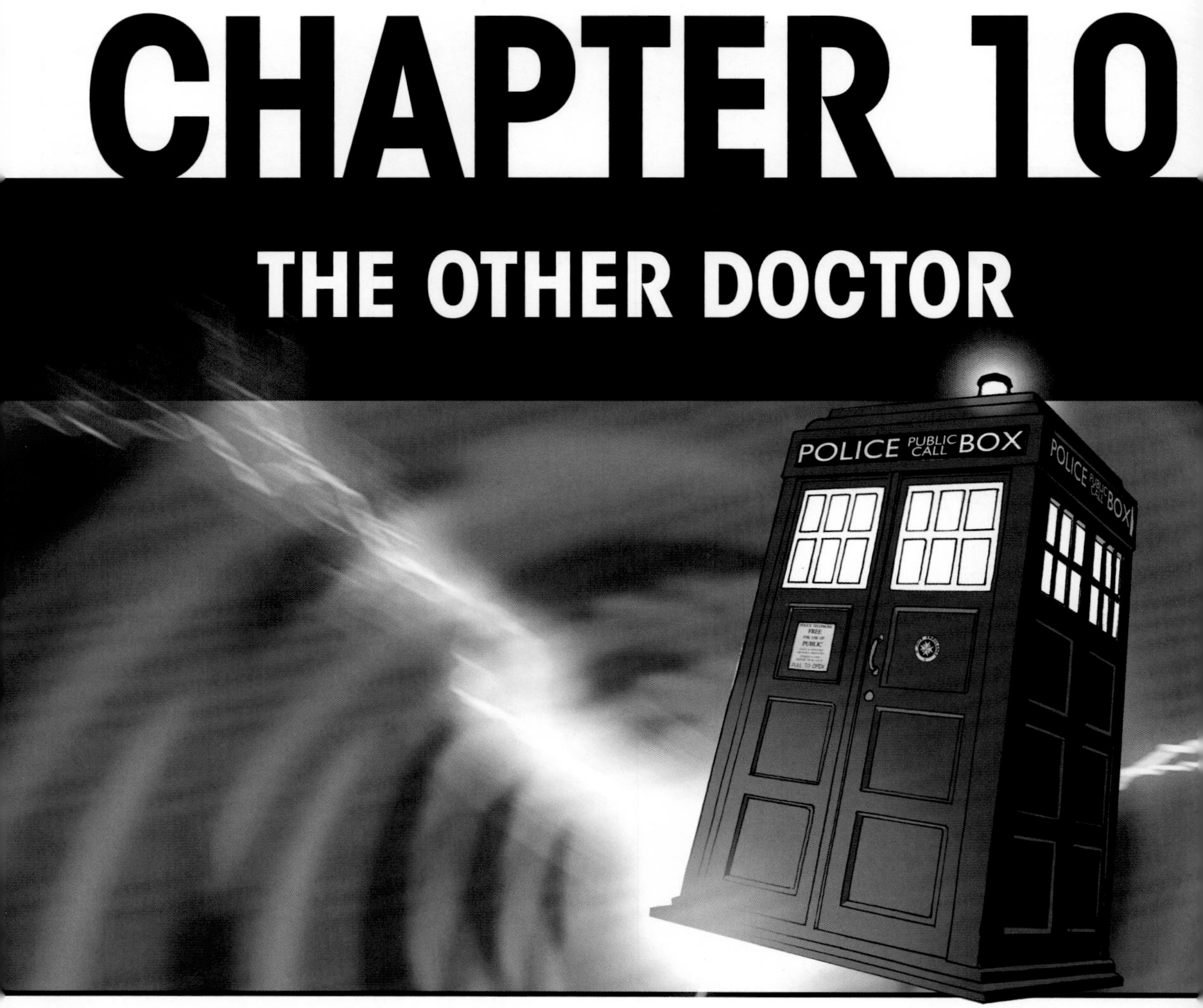
POLICE PUBLIC CALL BOX

WRITER
ROB WILLIAMS

ARTIST
SIMON FRASER

COLORIST
GARY CALDWELL

LETTERER
RICHARD STARKINGS AND COMICRAFT'S JIMMY BETANCOURT

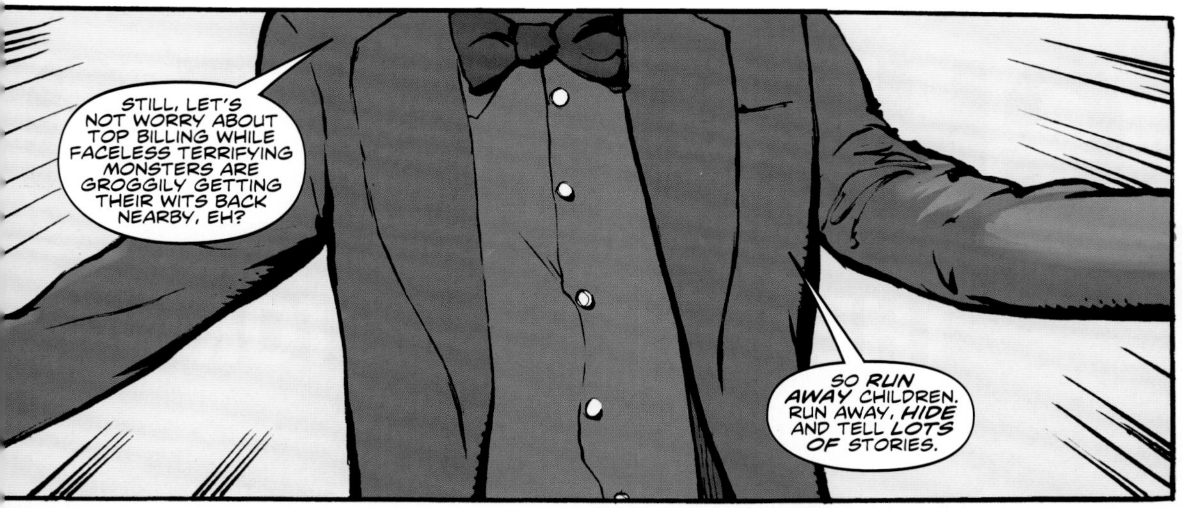
STILL, LET'S NOT WORRY ABOUT TOP BILLING WHILE FACELESS TERRIFYING MONSTERS ARE GROGGILY GETTING THEIR WITS BACK NEARBY, EH?
SO RUN AWAY CHILDREN. RUN AWAY, HIDE AND TELL LOTS OF STORIES.

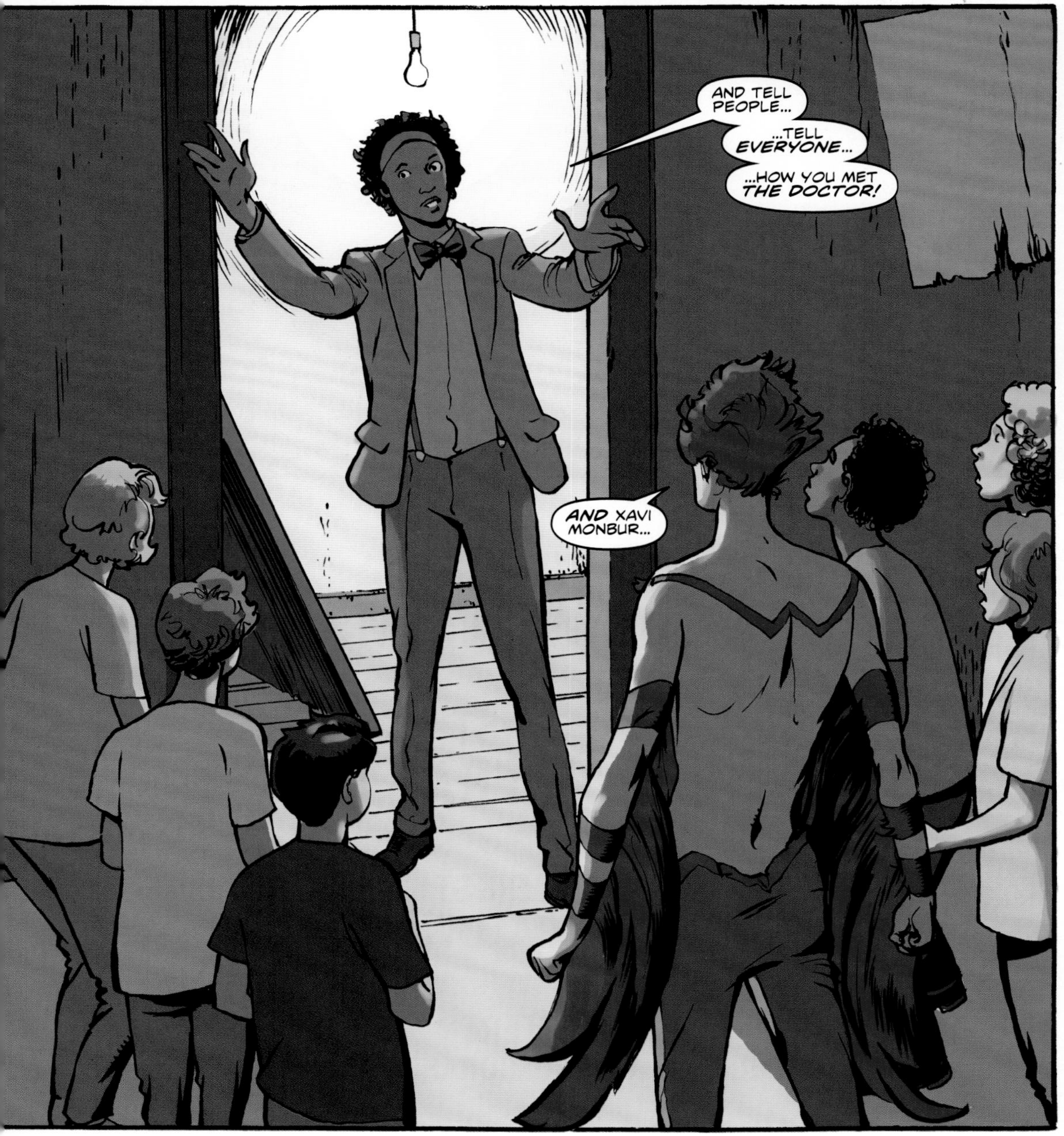
AND TELL PEOPLE...
...TELL EVERYONE...
...HOW YOU MET THE DOCTOR!
AND XAVI MONBUR...

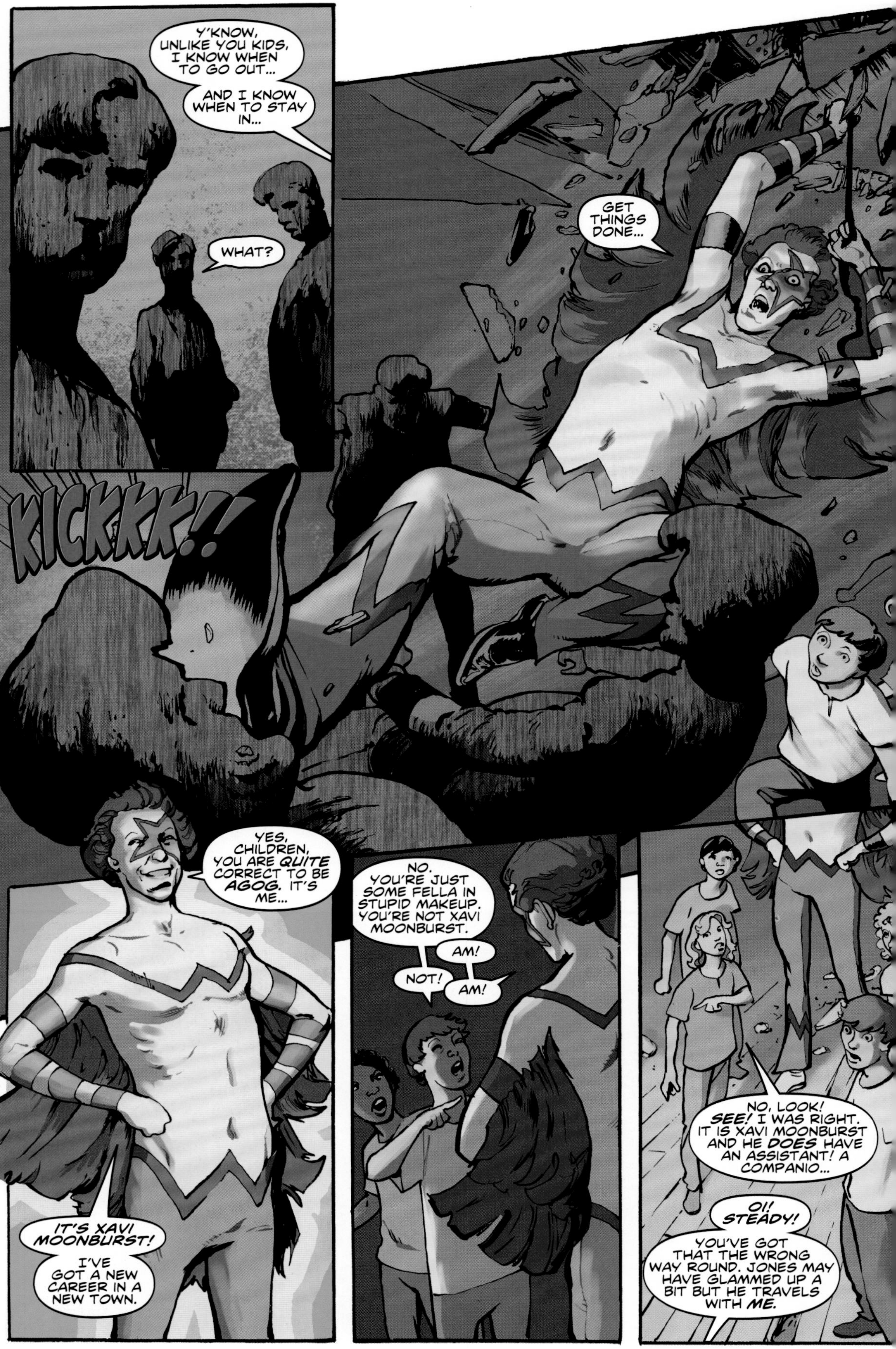

Y'KNOW, UNLIKE YOU KIDS, I KNOW WHEN TO GO OUT...
AND I KNOW WHEN TO STAY IN...
WHAT?
GET THINGS DONE...
KICKKK!!
YES, CHILDREN, YOU ARE QUITE CORRECT TO BE AGOG. IT'S ME...
IT'S XAVI MOONBURST!
I'VE GOT A NEW CAREER IN A NEW TOWN.
NO. YOU'RE JUST SOME FELLA IN STUPID MAKEUP. YOU'RE NOT XAVI MOONBURST.
AM!
NOT!
AM!
NO, LOOK! SEE! I WAS RIGHT. IT IS XAVI MOONBURST AND HE DOES HAVE AN ASSISTANT! A COMPANIO...
OI! STEADY!
YOU'VE GOT THAT THE WRONG WAY ROUND. JONES MAY HAVE GLAMMED UP A BIT BUT HE TRAVELS WITH ME.

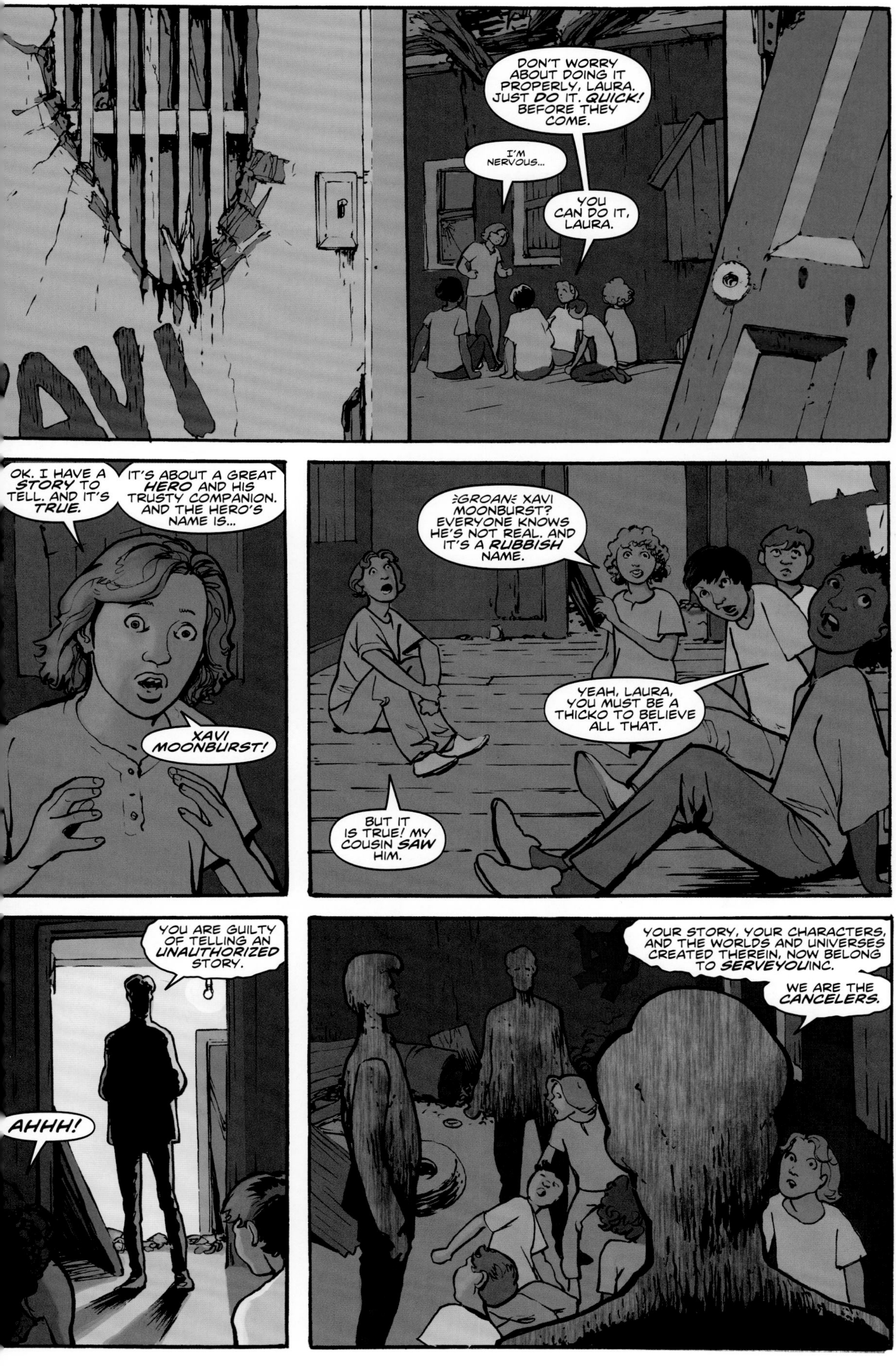
DON'T WORRY ABOUT DOING IT PROPERLY, LAURA. JUST DO IT. QUICK! BEFORE THEY COME.
I'M NERVOUS...
YOU CAN DO IT, LAURA.
OK. I HAVE A STORY TO TELL. AND IT'S TRUE.
IT'S ABOUT A GREAT HERO AND HIS TRUSTY COMPANION. AND THE HERO'S NAME IS...
XAVI MOONBURST!
GROAN XAVI MOONBURST? EVERYONE KNOWS HE'S NOT REAL. AND IT'S A RUBBISH NAME.
YEAH, LAURA, YOU MUST BE A THICKO TO BELIEVE ALL THAT.
BUT IT IS TRUE! MY COUSIN SAW HIM.
YOU ARE GUILTY OF TELLING AN UNAUTHORIZED STORY.
AHHH!
YOUR STORY, YOUR CHARACTERS, AND THE WORLDS AND UNIVERSES CREATED THEREIN, NOW BELONG TO SERVEYOUINC.
WE ARE THE CANCELERS.

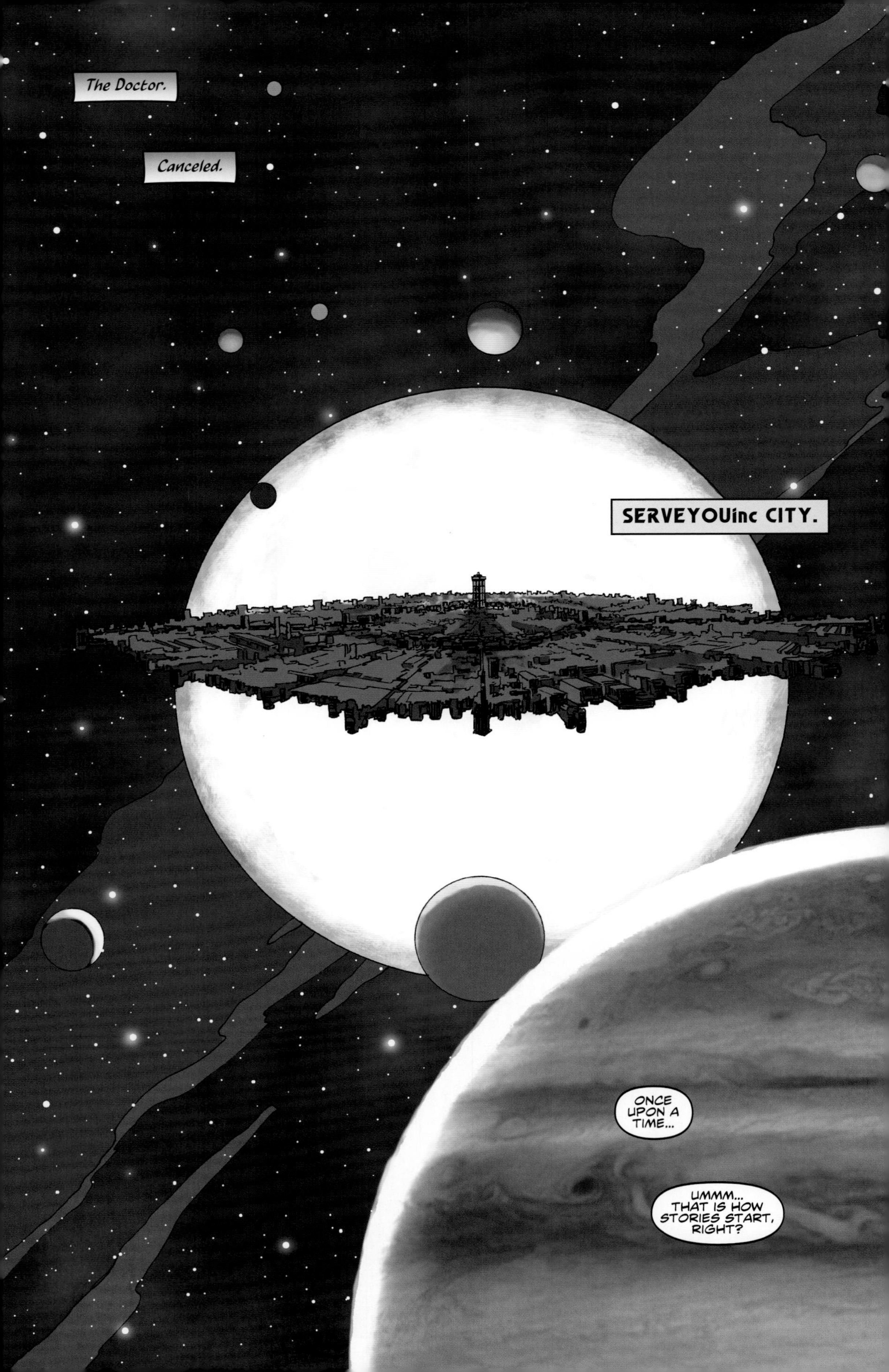
The Doctor.
Canceled.
SERVEYOUinc CITY.
ONCE UPON A TIME...
UMMM... THAT IS HOW STORIES START, RIGHT?

The Doctor felt better than he had in years.

AAAAAAAAAAAA...

It was just a shame the Entity kept screaming like that from within the containment tube.

AAAAAAAAAAAAA...

YOU ARE DOING THE *RIGHT* THING.

YES...

COULD SOMEONE STOP THAT *SCREAMING* PLEASE? IT'S MILDLY GRATING.

POLI

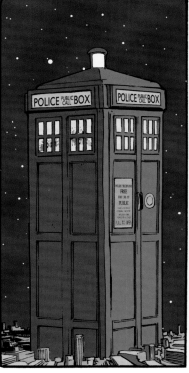

POLICE PUBLIC BOX   POLICE PUBLIC BOX

As Chief Operating Officer of SERVEYOUinc The Doctor had created a SAFE world where he could ensure the people he had collected from their worlds were PROTECTED.

And in doing so had HEALED himself.

No more monsters. No more stories.

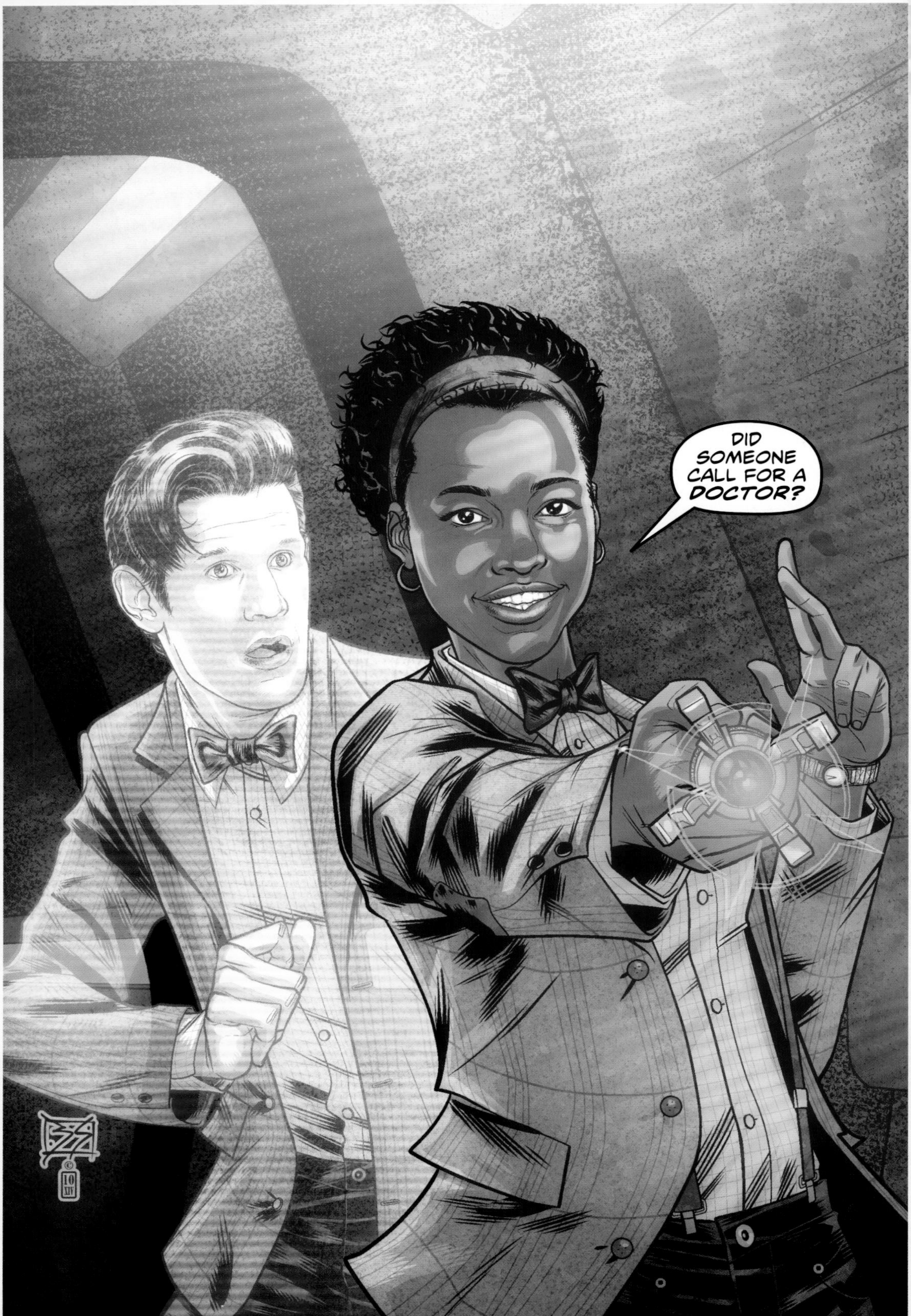
DID SOMEONE CALL FOR A DOCTOR?

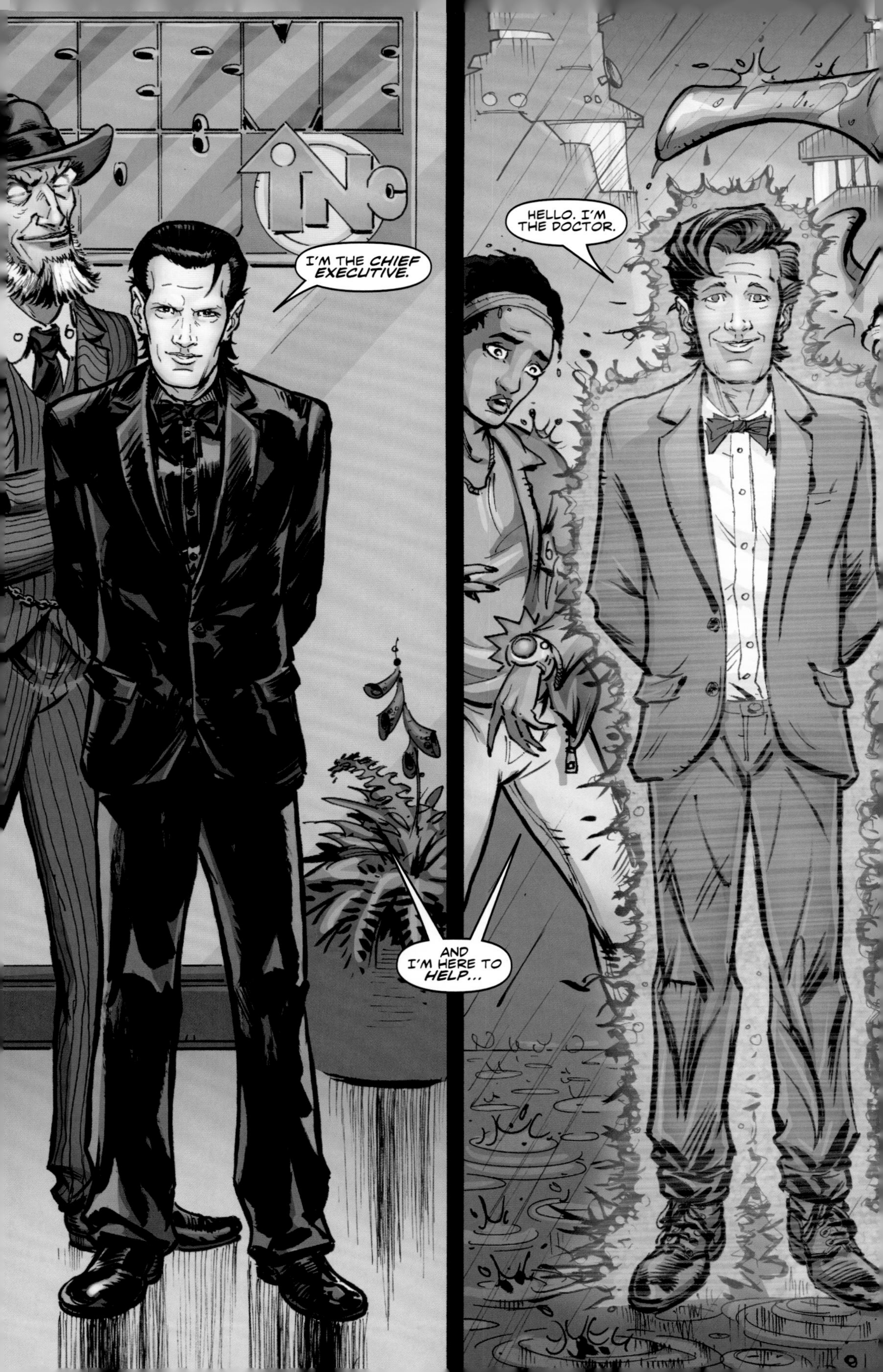
I'M THE CHIEF EXECUTIVE.
HELLO. I'M THE DOCTOR.
AND I'M HERE TO HELP...

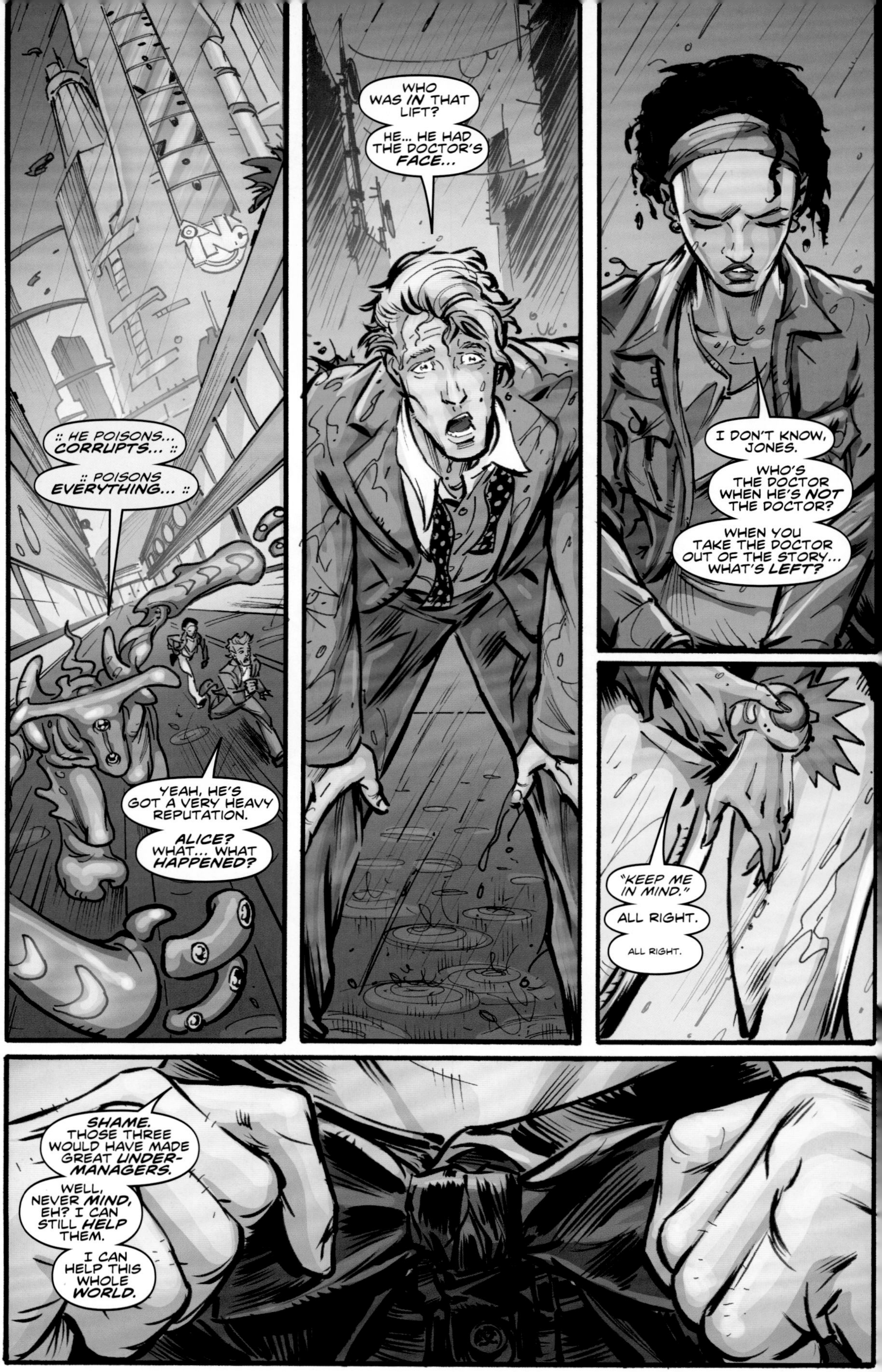
:: HE POISONS... CORRUPTS... ::
:: POISONS EVERYTHING... ::
YEAH, HE'S GOT A VERY HEAVY REPUTATION.
ALICE? WHAT... WHAT HAPPENED?
WHO WAS IN THAT LIFT?
HE... HE HAD THE DOCTOR'S FACE...
I DON'T KNOW, JONES.
WHO'S THE DOCTOR WHEN HE'S NOT THE DOCTOR?
WHEN YOU TAKE THE DOCTOR OUT OF THE STORY... WHAT'S LEFT?
"KEEP ME IN MIND."
ALL RIGHT.
ALL RIGHT.
SHAME. THOSE THREE WOULD HAVE MADE GREAT UNDER-MANAGERS.
WELL, NEVER MIND, EH? I CAN STILL HELP THEM.
I CAN HELP THIS WHOLE WORLD.

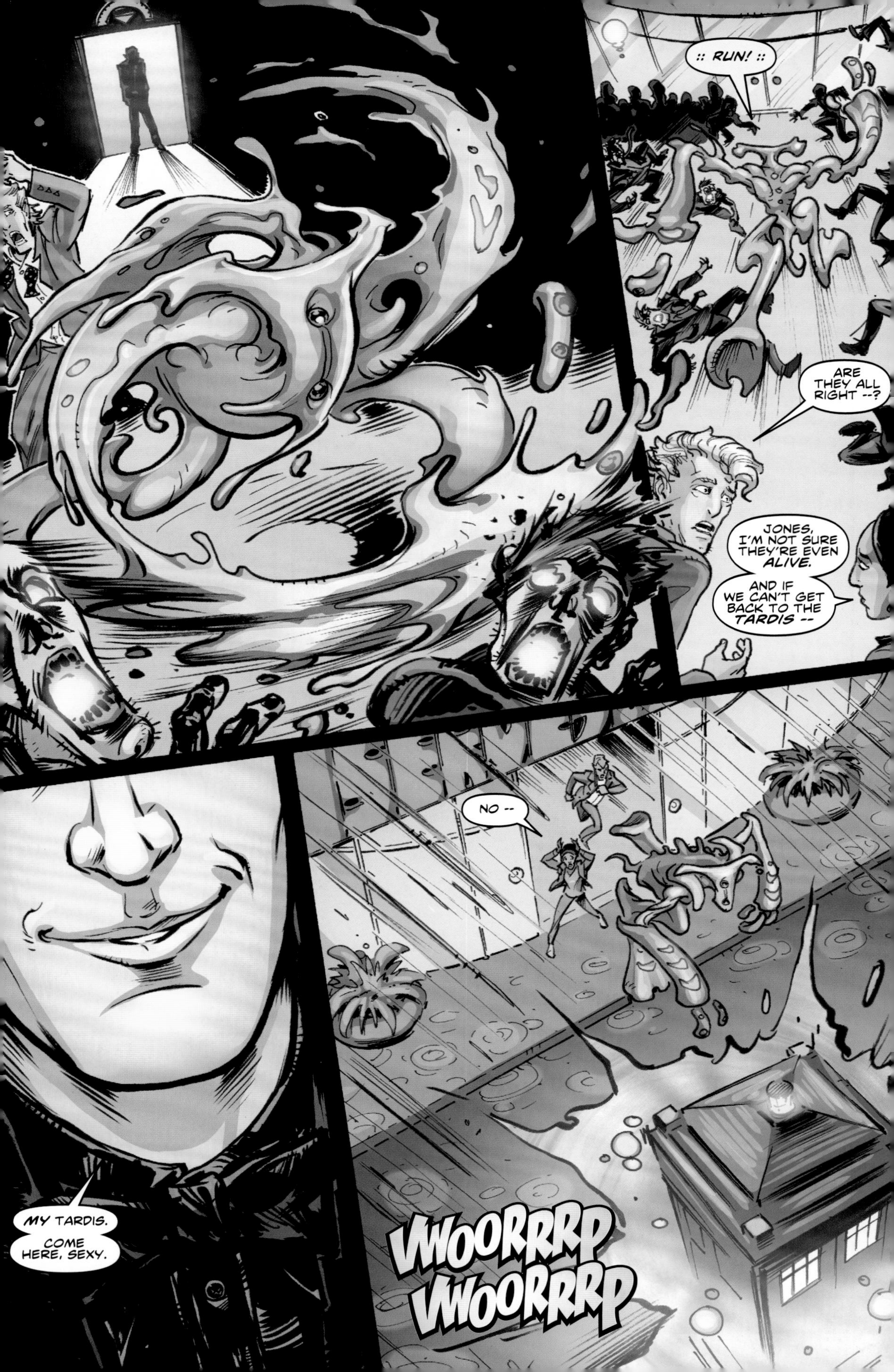
:: RUN! ::
ARE THEY ALL RIGHT --?
JONES, I'M NOT SURE THEY'RE EVEN ALIVE.
AND IF WE CAN'T GET BACK TO THE TARDIS --
MY TARDIS.
COME HERE, SEXY.
NO --
VWOORRRP
VWOORRRP

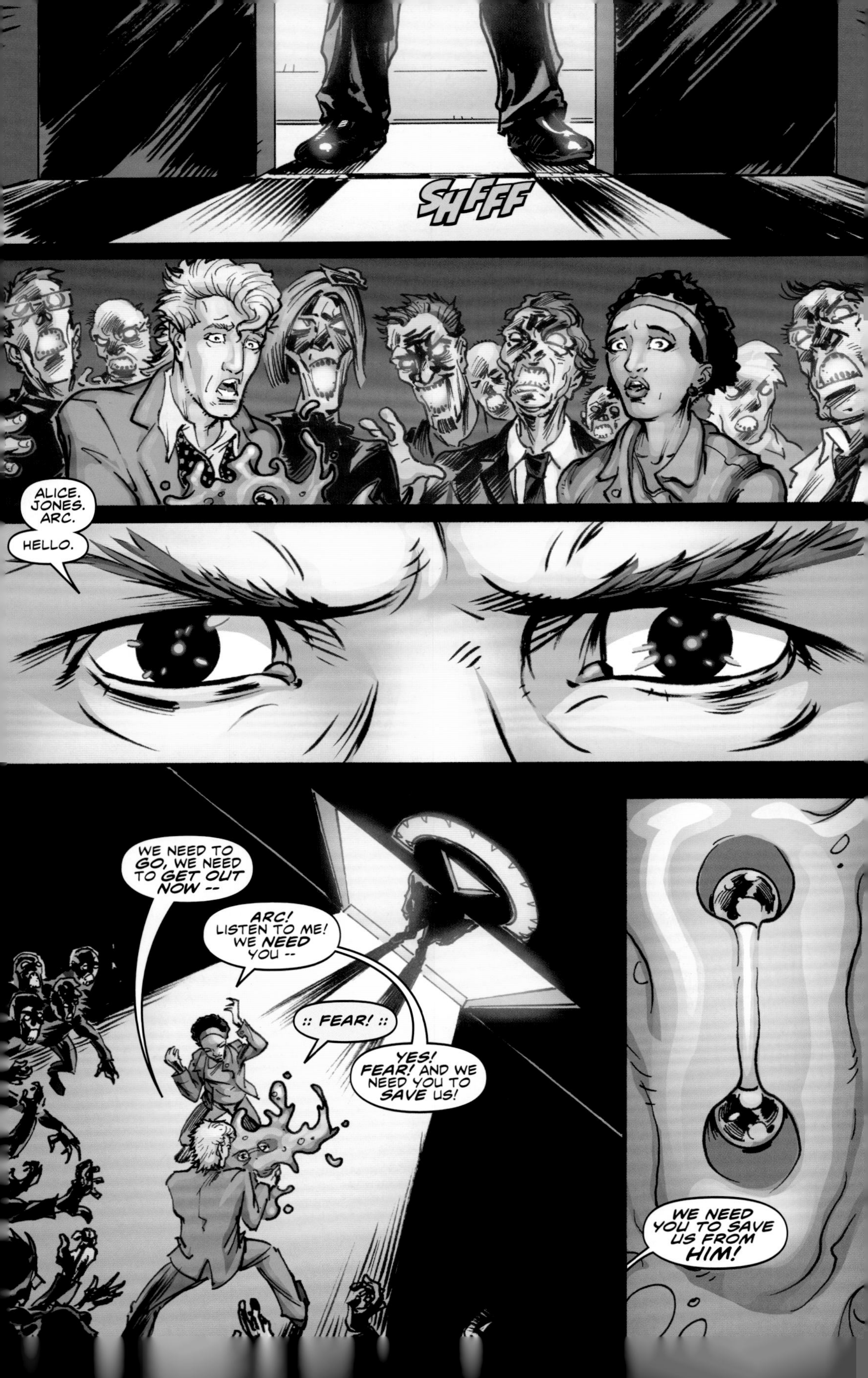
SHFFF
ALICE. JONES. ARC.
HELLO.
WE NEED TO GO, WE NEED TO GET OUT NOW --
ARC! LISTEN TO ME! WE NEED YOU --
:: FEAR! ::
YES! FEAR! AND WE NEED YOU TO SAVE US!
WE NEED YOU TO SAVE US FROM HIM!

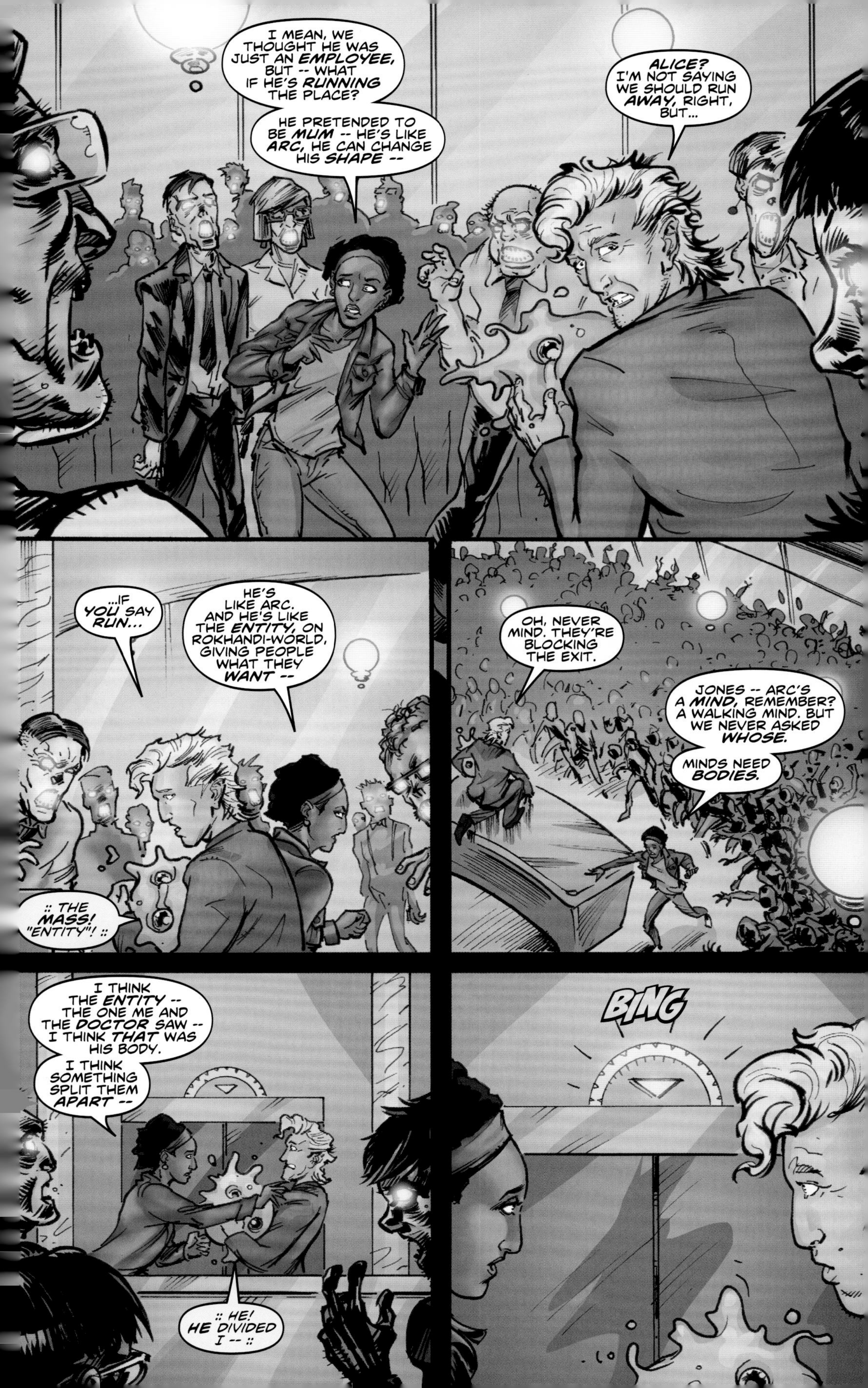
I MEAN, WE THOUGHT HE WAS JUST AN EMPLOYEE, BUT -- WHAT IF HE'S RUNNING THE PLACE?
HE PRETENDED TO BE MUM -- HE'S LIKE ARC, HE CAN CHANGE HIS SHAPE --
ALICE? I'M NOT SAYING WE SHOULD RUN AWAY, RIGHT, BUT...
...IF YOU SAY RUN...
HE'S LIKE ARC. AND HE'S LIKE THE ENTITY, ON ROKHANDI-WORLD, GIVING PEOPLE WHAT THEY WANT --
:: THE MASS! "ENTITY"! ::
OH, NEVER MIND. THEY'RE BLOCKING THE EXIT.
JONES -- ARC'S A MIND, REMEMBER? A WALKING MIND. BUT WE NEVER ASKED WHOSE.
MINDS NEED BODIES.
I THINK THE ENTITY -- THE ONE ME AND THE DOCTOR SAW -- I THINK THAT WAS HIS BODY.
I THINK SOMETHING SPLIT THEM APART --
:: HE! HE DIVIDED I -- ::
BING

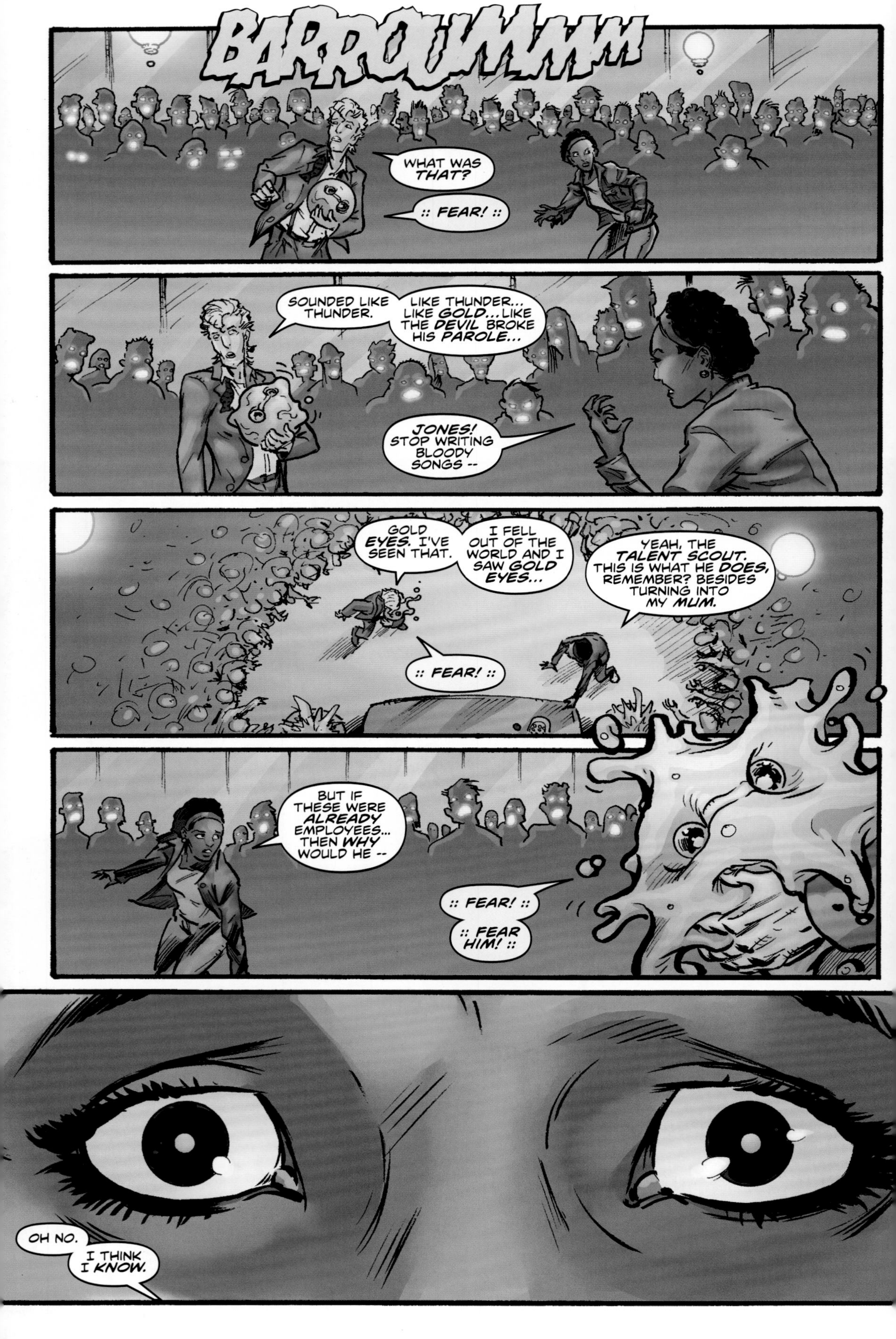
BARROUMMM
WHAT WAS THAT?
:: FEAR! ::
SOUNDED LIKE THUNDER.
LIKE THUNDER... LIKE GOLD... LIKE THE DEVIL BROKE HIS PAROLE...
JONES! STOP WRITING BLOODY SONGS --
GOLD EYES. I'VE SEEN THAT.
I FELL OUT OF THE WORLD AND I SAW GOLD EYES...
YEAH, THE TALENT SCOUT. THIS IS WHAT HE DOES, REMEMBER? BESIDES TURNING INTO MY MUM.
:: FEAR! ::
BUT IF THESE WERE ALREADY EMPLOYEES... THEN WHY WOULD HE --
:: FEAR! ::
:: FEAR HIM! ::
OH NO.
I THINK I KNOW.

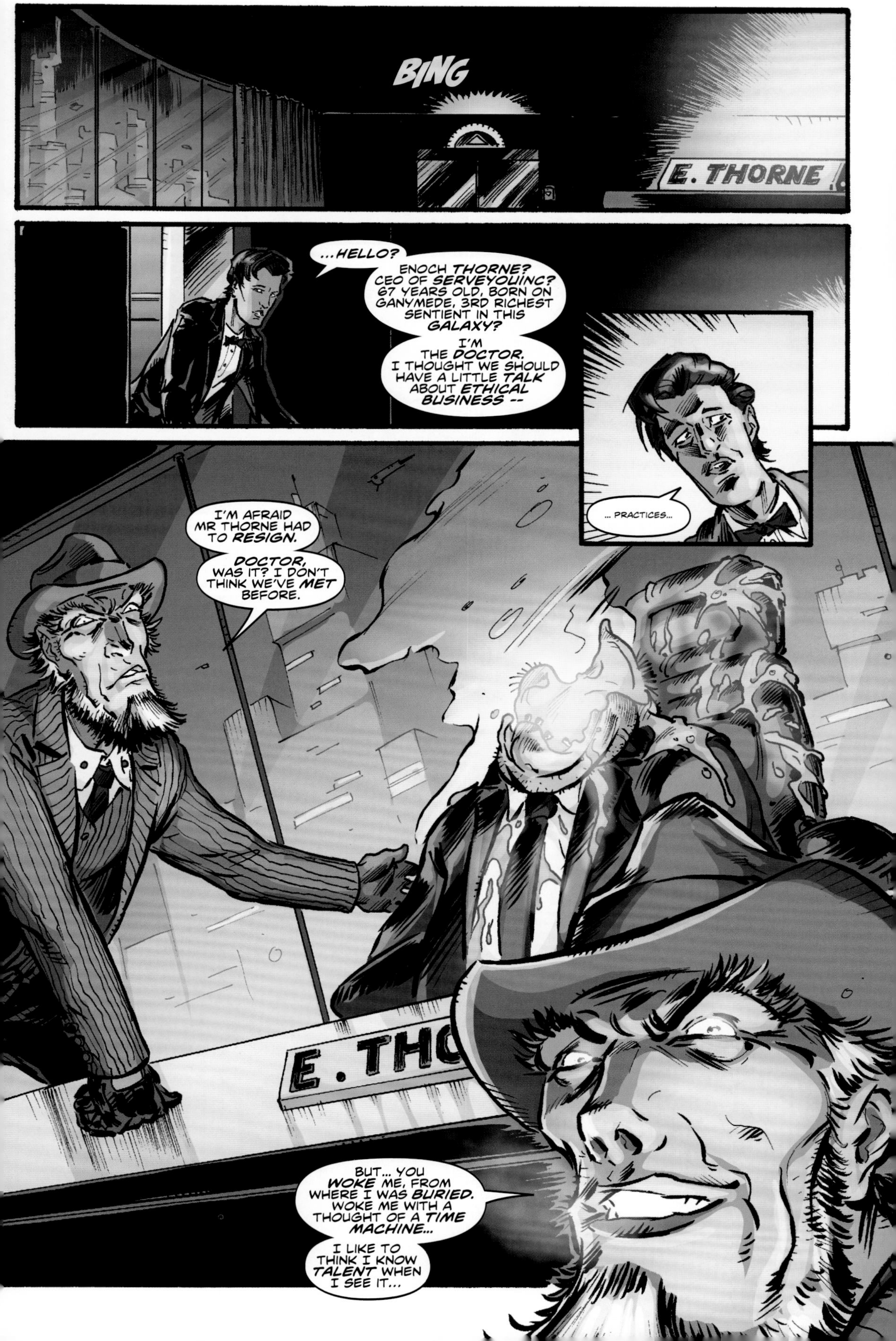
BING
E. THORNE
...HELLO?
ENOCH THORNE? CEO OF SERVEYOUINC? 67 YEARS OLD, BORN ON GANYMEDE, 3RD RICHEST SENTIENT IN THIS GALAXY?
I'M THE DOCTOR. I THOUGHT WE SHOULD HAVE A LITTLE TALK ABOUT ETHICAL BUSINESS --
... PRACTICES...
I'M AFRAID MR THORNE HAD TO RESIGN.
DOCTOR, WAS IT? I DON'T THINK WE'VE MET BEFORE.
E. THO
BUT... YOU WOKE ME, FROM WHERE I WAS BURIED. WOKE ME WITH A THOUGHT OF A TIME MACHINE...
I LIKE TO THINK I KNOW TALENT WHEN I SEE IT...

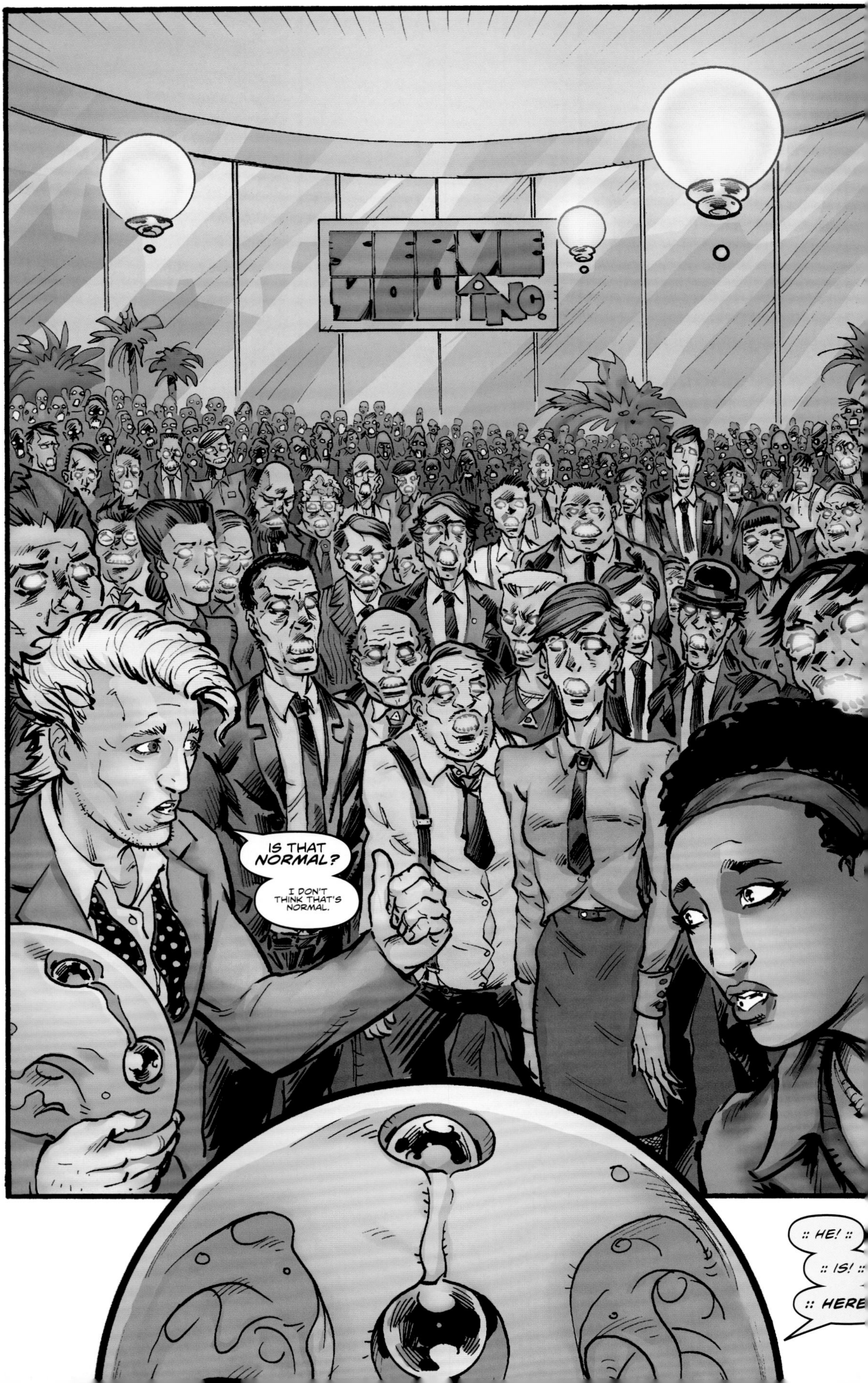
SERVE YOU INC.
IS THAT NORMAL?
I DON'T THINK THAT'S NORMAL.
:: HE! ::
:: IS! ::
:: HERE

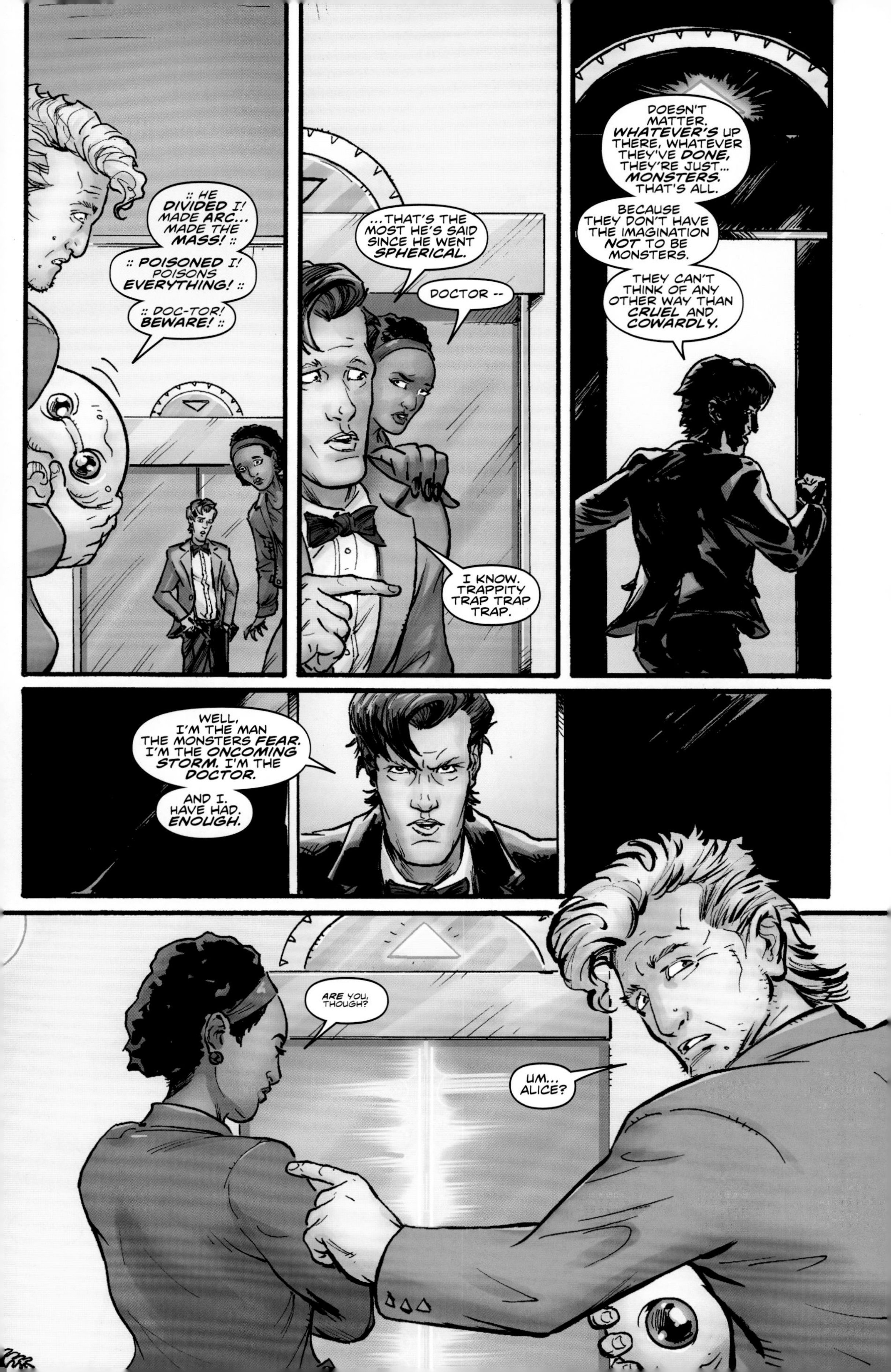
:: HE DIVIDED I! MADE ARC... MADE THE MASS! ::
:: POISONED I! POISONS EVERYTHING! ::
:: DOC-TOR! BEWARE! ::
...THAT'S THE MOST HE'S SAID SINCE HE WENT SPHERICAL.
DOCTOR --
I KNOW. TRAPPITY TRAP TRAP TRAP.
DOESN'T MATTER. WHATEVER'S UP THERE, WHATEVER THEY'VE DONE, THEY'RE JUST... MONSTERS. THAT'S ALL.
BECAUSE THEY DON'T HAVE THE IMAGINATION NOT TO BE MONSTERS.
THEY CAN'T THINK OF ANY OTHER WAY THAN CRUEL AND COWARDLY.
WELL, I'M THE MAN THE MONSTERS FEAR. I'M THE ONCOMING STORM. I'M THE DOCTOR.
AND I. HAVE HAD. ENOUGH.
ARE YOU, THOUGH?
UM... ALICE?

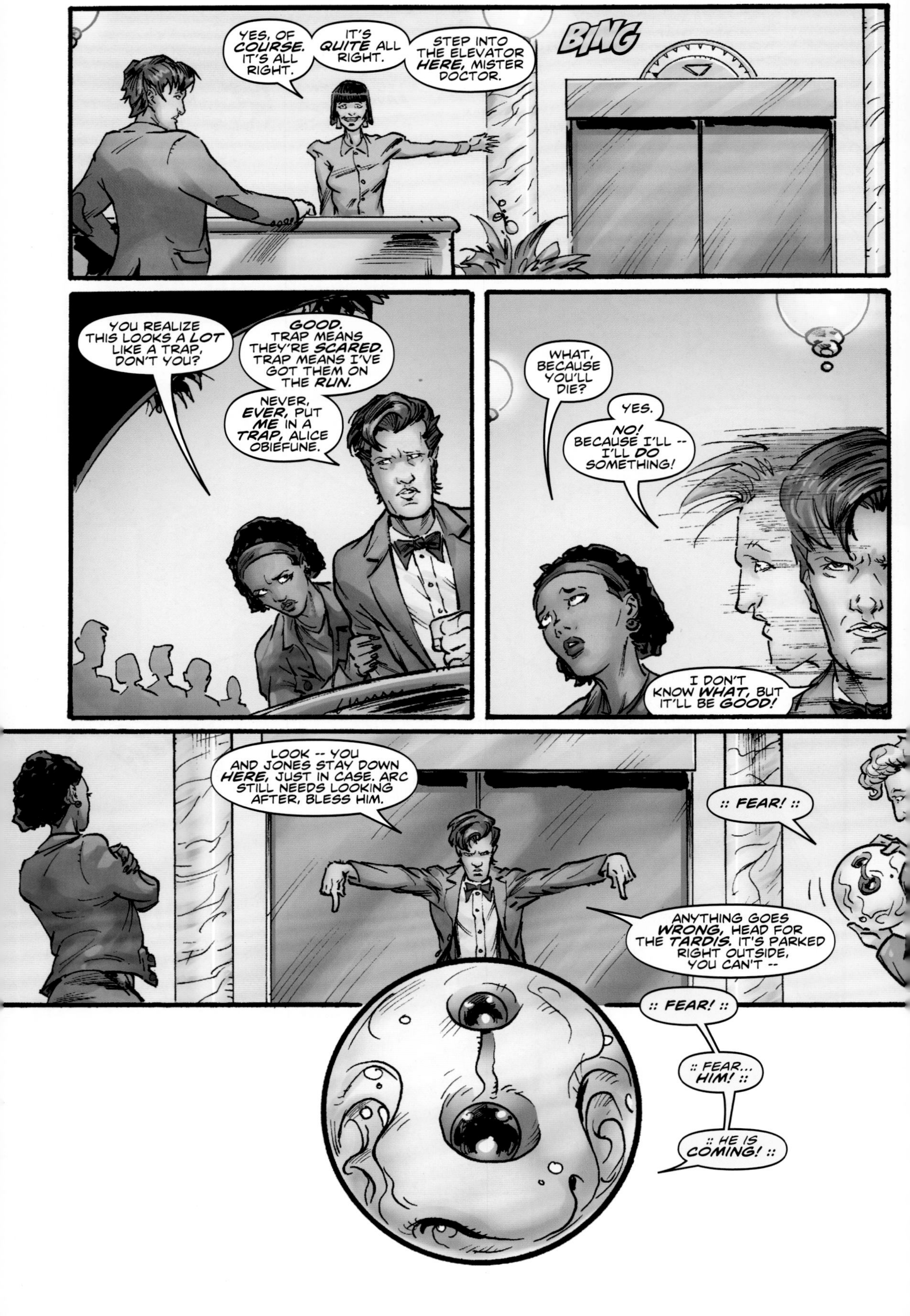
YES, OF COURSE. IT'S ALL RIGHT.
IT'S QUITE ALL RIGHT.
STEP INTO THE ELEVATOR HERE, MISTER DOCTOR.
BING
YOU REALIZE THIS LOOKS A LOT LIKE A TRAP, DON'T YOU?
GOOD. TRAP MEANS THEY'RE SCARED. TRAP MEANS I'VE GOT THEM ON THE RUN.
NEVER, EVER, PUT ME IN A TRAP, ALICE OBIEFUNE.
WHAT, BECAUSE YOU'LL DIE?
YES.
NO! BECAUSE I'LL -- I'LL DO SOMETHING!
I DON'T KNOW WHAT, BUT IT'LL BE GOOD!
LOOK -- YOU AND JONES STAY DOWN HERE, JUST IN CASE. ARC STILL NEEDS LOOKING AFTER, BLESS HIM.
:: FEAR! ::
ANYTHING GOES WRONG, HEAD FOR THE TARDIS. IT'S PARKED RIGHT OUTSIDE, YOU CAN'T --
:: FEAR! ::
:: FEAR... HIM! ::
:: HE IS COMING! ::

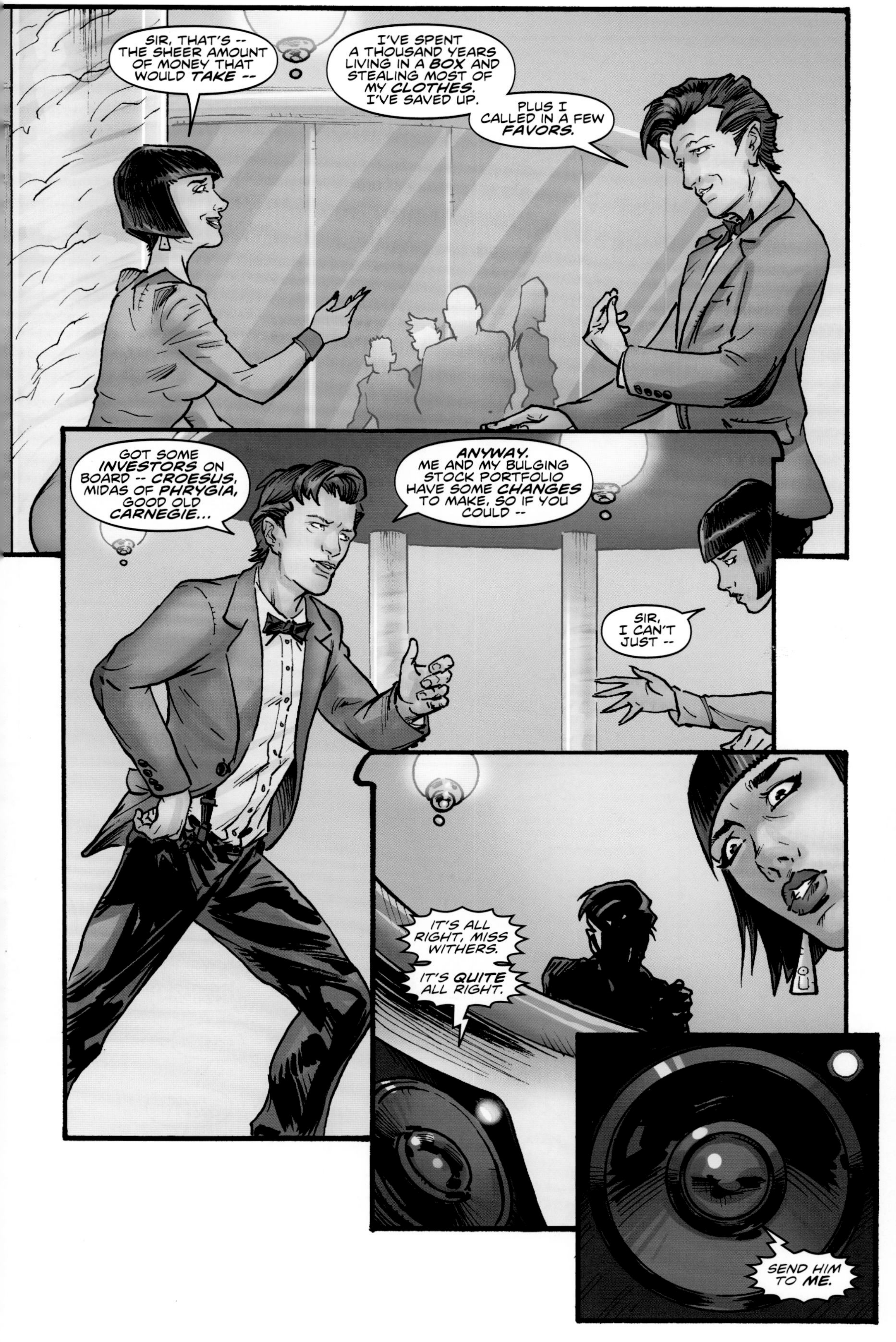

SIR, THAT'S -- THE SHEER AMOUNT OF MONEY THAT WOULD TAKE --
I'VE SPENT A THOUSAND YEARS LIVING IN A BOX AND STEALING MOST OF MY CLOTHES. I'VE SAVED UP.
PLUS I CALLED IN A FEW FAVORS.
GOT SOME INVESTORS ON BOARD -- CROESUS, MIDAS OF PHRYGIA, GOOD OLD CARNEGIE...
ANYWAY. ME AND MY BULGING STOCK PORTFOLIO HAVE SOME CHANGES TO MAKE, SO IF YOU COULD --
SIR, I CAN'T JUST --
IT'S ALL RIGHT, MISS WITHERS.
IT'S QUITE ALL RIGHT.
SEND HIM TO ME.

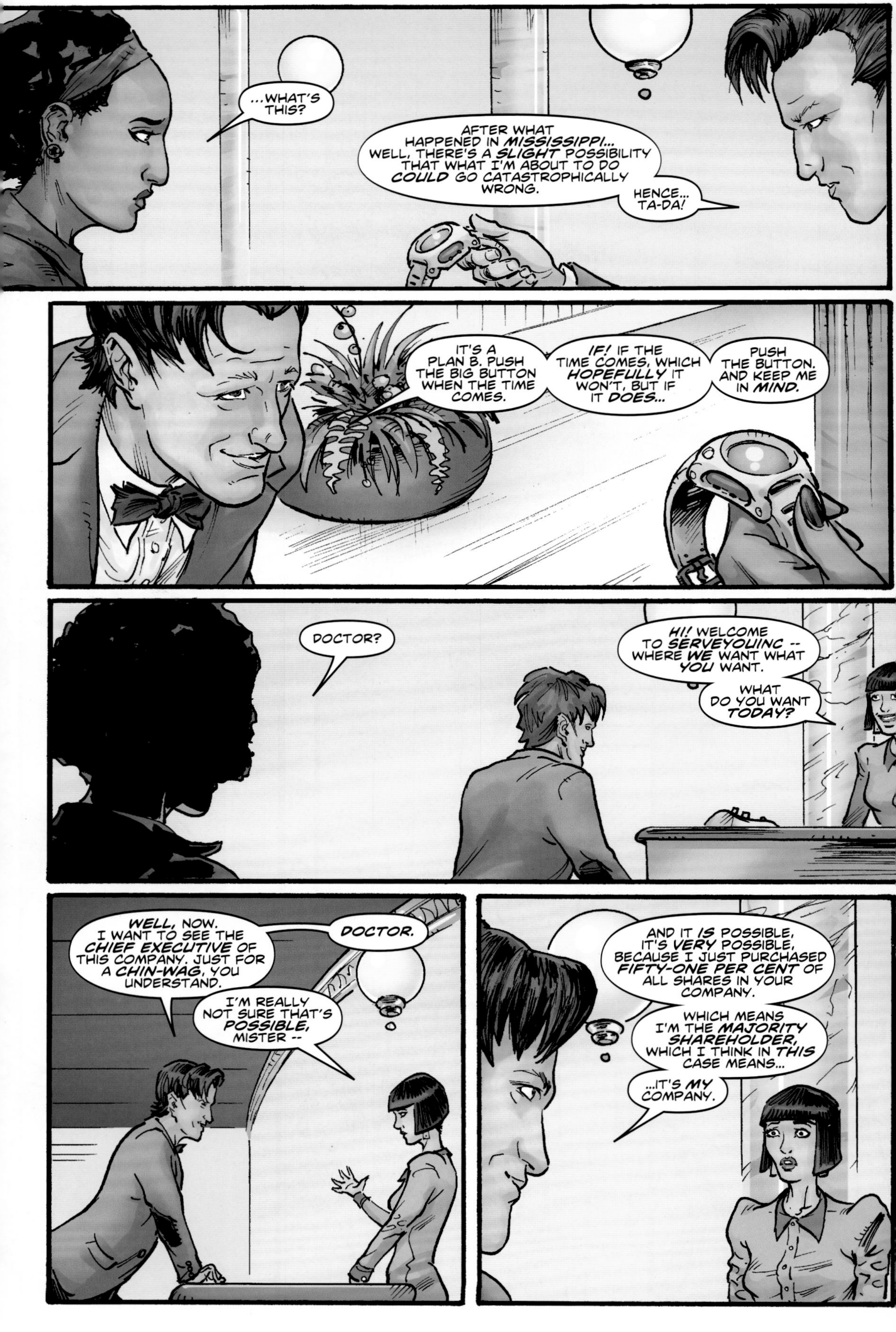
...WHAT'S THIS?
AFTER WHAT HAPPENED IN MISSISSIPPI... WELL, THERE'S A SLIGHT POSSIBILITY THAT WHAT I'M ABOUT TO DO COULD GO CATASTROPHICALLY WRONG.
HENCE... TA-DA!
IT'S A PLAN B. PUSH THE BIG BUTTON WHEN THE TIME COMES.
IF! IF THE TIME COMES, WHICH HOPEFULLY IT WON'T, BUT IF IT DOES...
PUSH THE BUTTON. AND KEEP ME IN MIND.
DOCTOR?
HI! WELCOME TO SERVEYOUINC -- WHERE WE WANT WHAT YOU WANT.
WHAT DO YOU WANT TODAY?
WELL, NOW. I WANT TO SEE THE CHIEF EXECUTIVE OF THIS COMPANY. JUST FOR A CHIN-WAG, YOU UNDERSTAND.
DOCTOR.
I'M REALLY NOT SURE THAT'S POSSIBLE, MISTER --
AND IT IS POSSIBLE, IT'S VERY POSSIBLE, BECAUSE I JUST PURCHASED FIFTY-ONE PER CENT OF ALL SHARES IN YOUR COMPANY.
WHICH MEANS I'M THE MAJORITY SHAREHOLDER, WHICH I THINK IN THIS CASE MEANS...
...IT'S MY COMPANY.

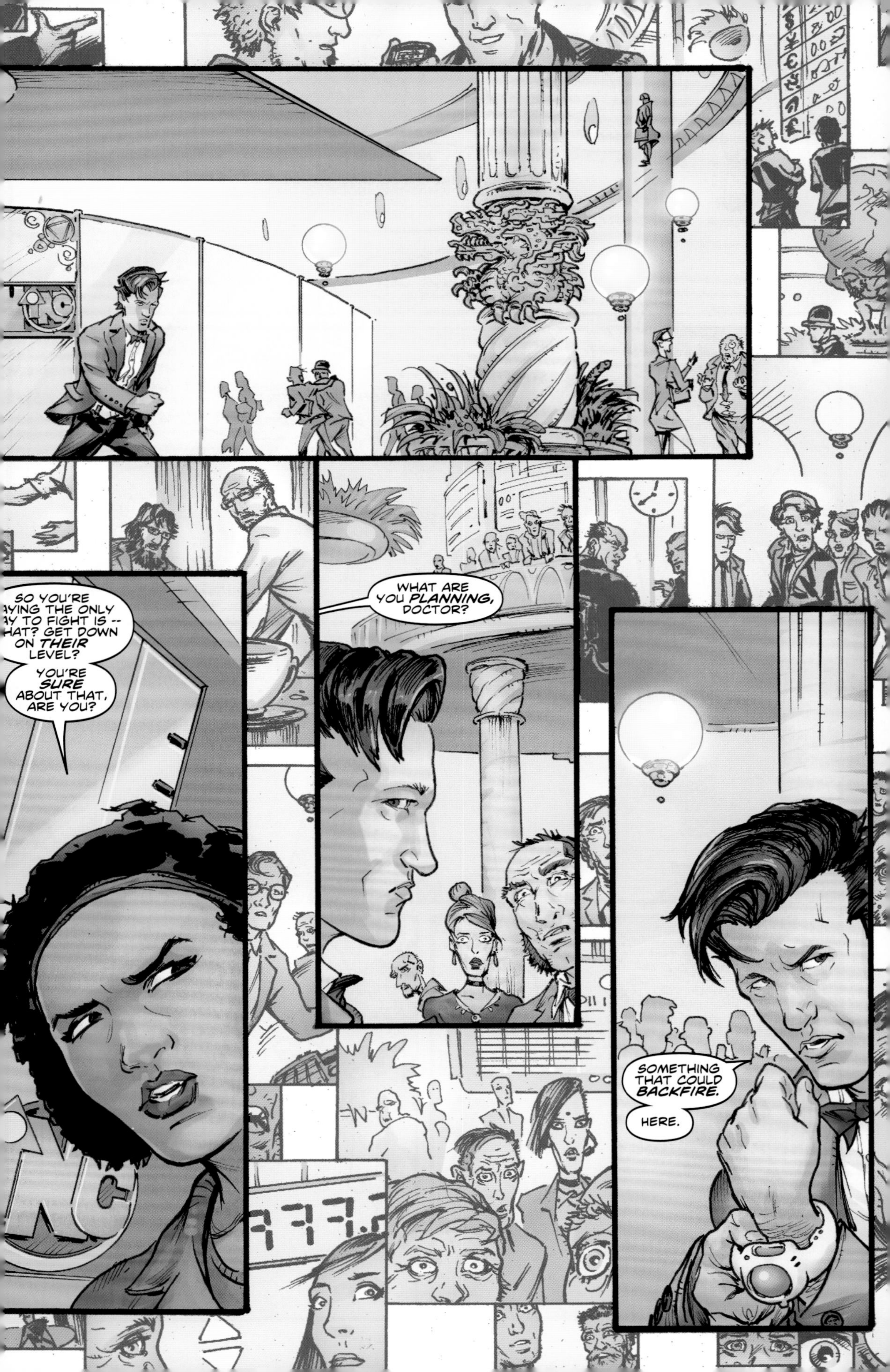

SO YOU'RE AYING THE ONLY AY TO FIGHT IS -- HAT? GET DOWN ON *THEIR* LEVEL?
YOU'RE *SURE* ABOUT THAT, ARE YOU?
WHAT ARE YOU *PLANNING*, DOCTOR?
SOMETHING THAT COULD *BACKFIRE*.
HERE.

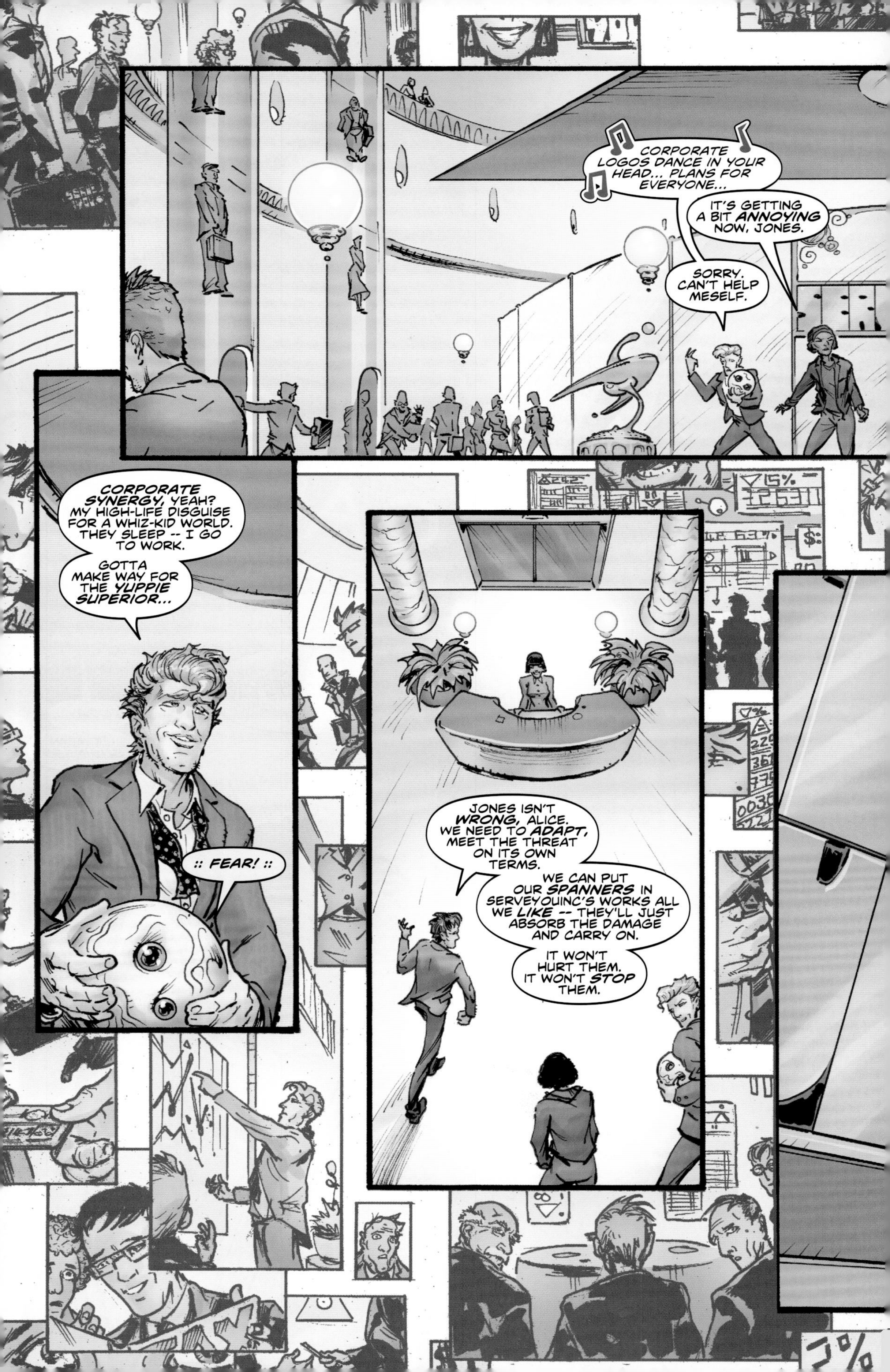
CORPORATE LOGOS DANCE IN YOUR HEAD... PLANS FOR EVERYONE...
IT'S GETTING A BIT ANNOYING NOW, JONES.
SORRY. CAN'T HELP MESELF.
CORPORATE SYNERGY, YEAH? MY HIGH-LIFE DISGUISE FOR A WHIZ-KID WORLD. THEY SLEEP -- I GO TO WORK.
GOTTA MAKE WAY FOR THE YUPPIE SUPERIOR...
:: FEAR! ::
JONES ISN'T WRONG, ALICE. WE NEED TO ADAPT, MEET THE THREAT ON ITS OWN TERMS.
WE CAN PUT OUR SPANNERS IN SERVEYOUINC'S WORKS ALL WE LIKE -- THEY'LL JUST ABSORB THE DAMAGE AND CARRY ON.
IT WON'T HURT THEM. IT WON'T STOP THEM.

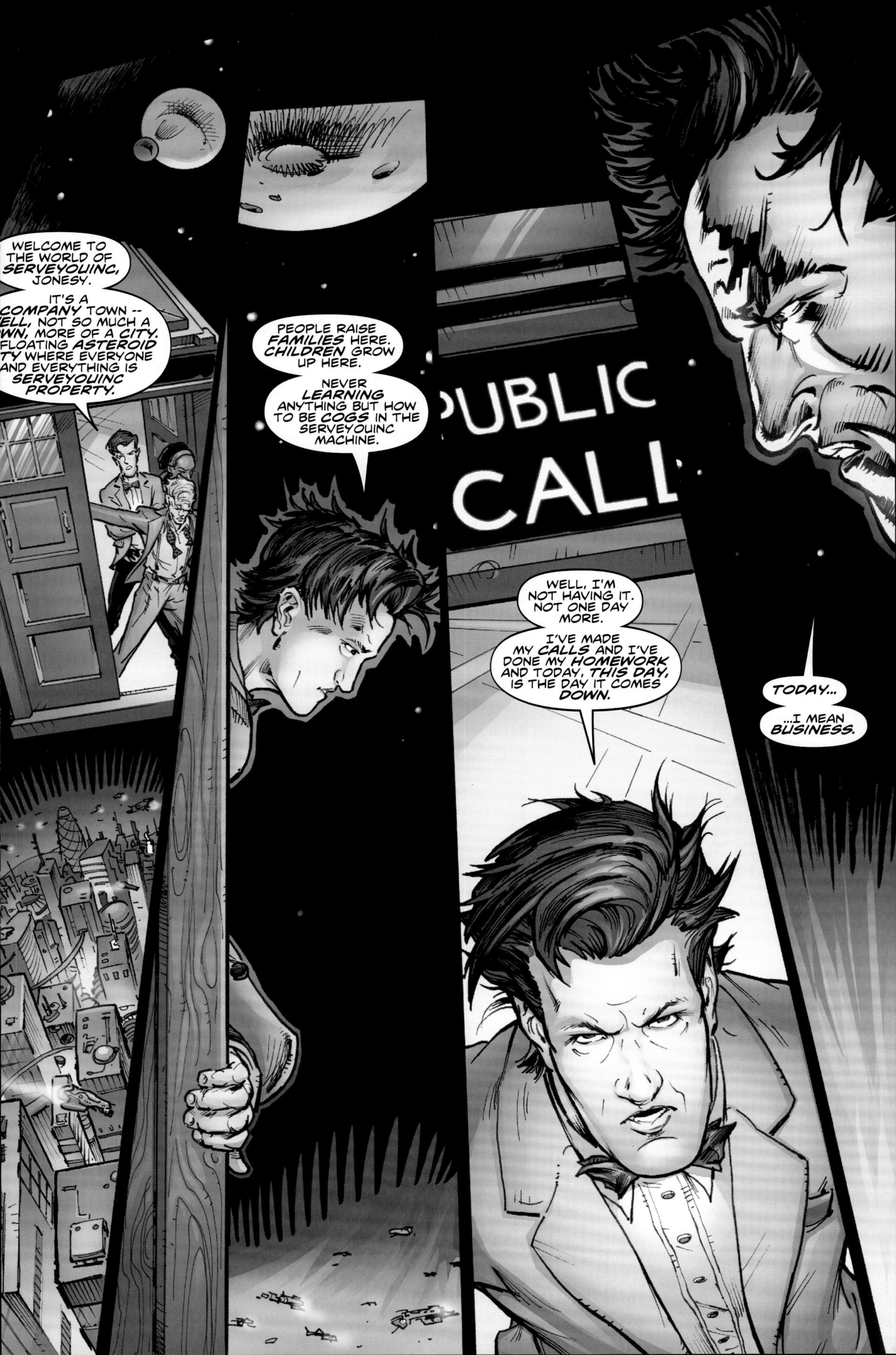
WELCOME TO THE WORLD OF SERVEYOUINC, JONESY.
IT'S A COMPANY TOWN -- WELL, NOT SO MUCH A WN, MORE OF A CITY. FLOATING ASTEROID TY WHERE EVERYONE AND EVERYTHING IS SERVEYOUINC PROPERTY.
PEOPLE RAISE FAMILIES HERE. CHILDREN GROW UP HERE.
NEVER LEARNING ANYTHING BUT HOW TO BE COGS IN THE SERVEYOUINC MACHINE.
PUBLIC
CALL
WELL, I'M NOT HAVING IT. NOT ONE DAY MORE.
I'VE MADE MY CALLS AND I'VE DONE MY HOMEWORK AND TODAY, THIS DAY, IS THE DAY IT COMES DOWN.
TODAY...
...I MEAN BUSINESS.

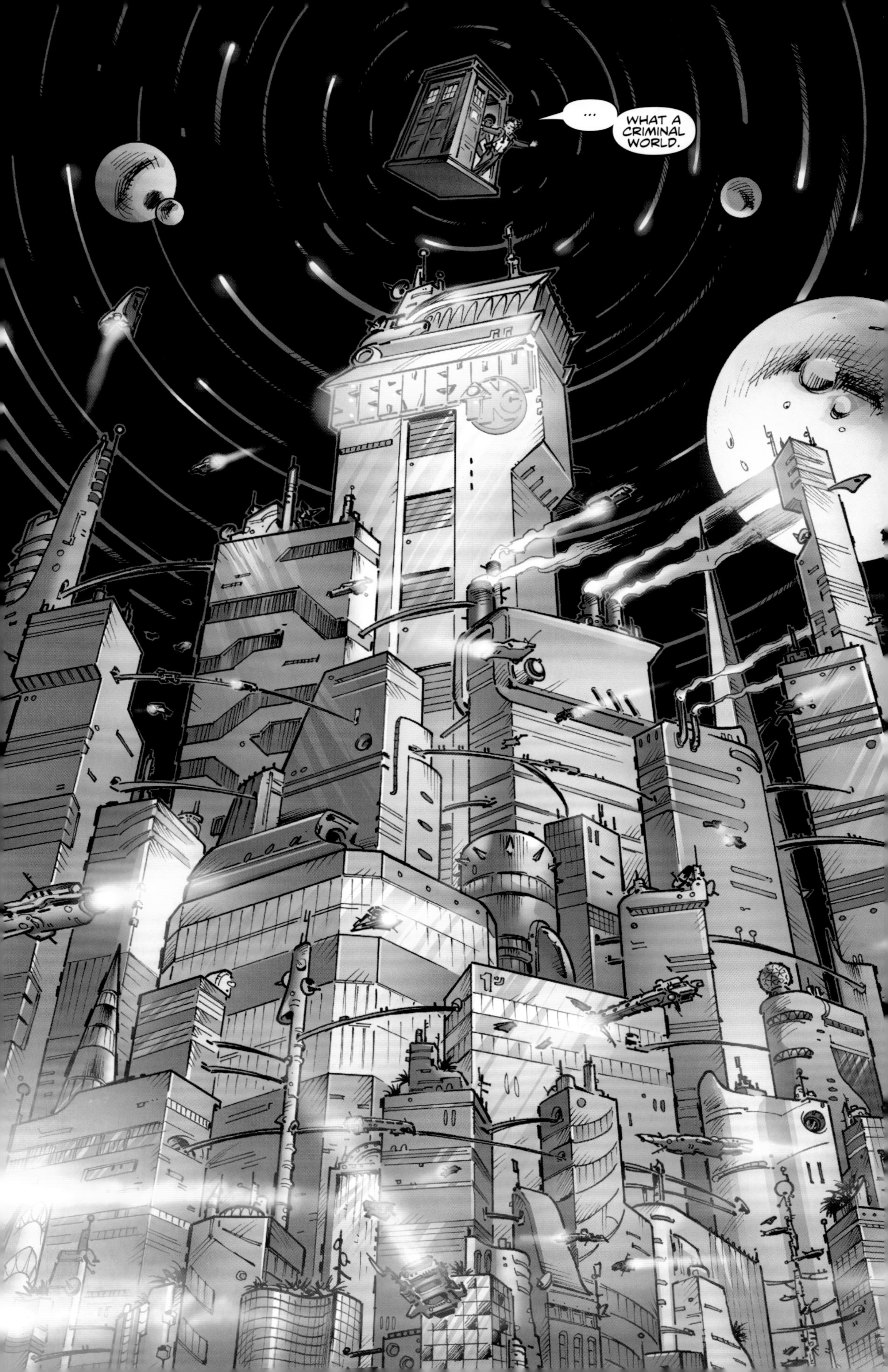
...
WHAT A CRIMINAL WORLD.

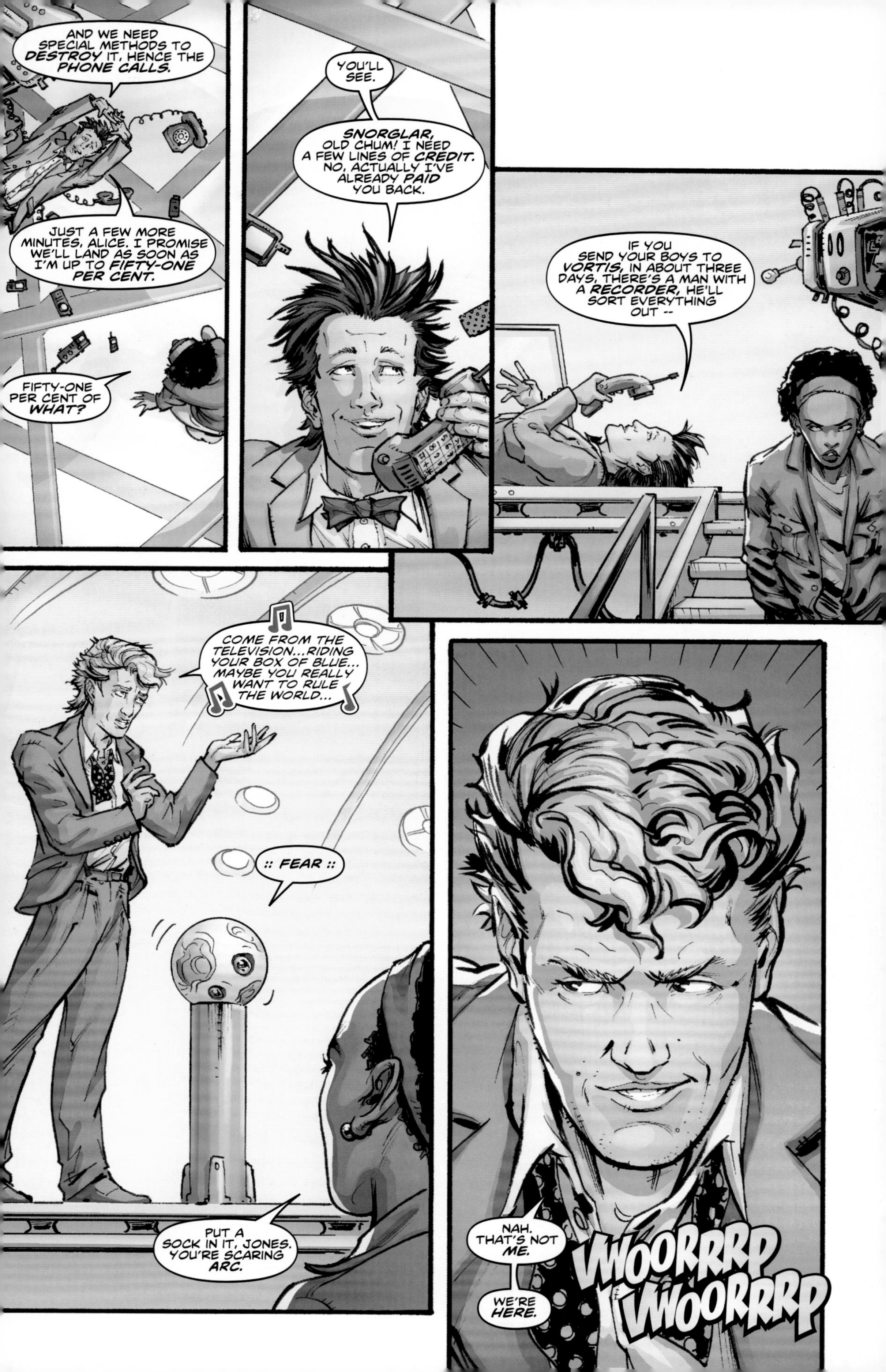
AND WE NEED SPECIAL METHODS TO DESTROY IT, HENCE THE PHONE CALLS.
JUST A FEW MORE MINUTES, ALICE. I PROMISE WE'LL LAND AS SOON AS I'M UP TO FIFTY-ONE PER CENT.
FIFTY-ONE PER CENT OF WHAT?
YOU'LL SEE.
SNORGLAR, OLD CHUM! I NEED A FEW LINES OF CREDIT. NO, ACTUALLY I'VE ALREADY PAID YOU BACK.
IF YOU SEND YOUR BOYS TO VORTIS, IN ABOUT THREE DAYS, THERE'S A MAN WITH A RECORDER, HE'LL SORT EVERYTHING OUT --
COME FROM THE TELEVISION...RIDING YOUR BOX OF BLUE... MAYBE YOU REALLY WANT TO RULE THE WORLD...
:: FEAR ::
PUT A SOCK IN IT, JONES. YOU'RE SCARING ARC.
NAH. THAT'S NOT ME.
WE'RE HERE.
VWOORRRP VWOORRRP

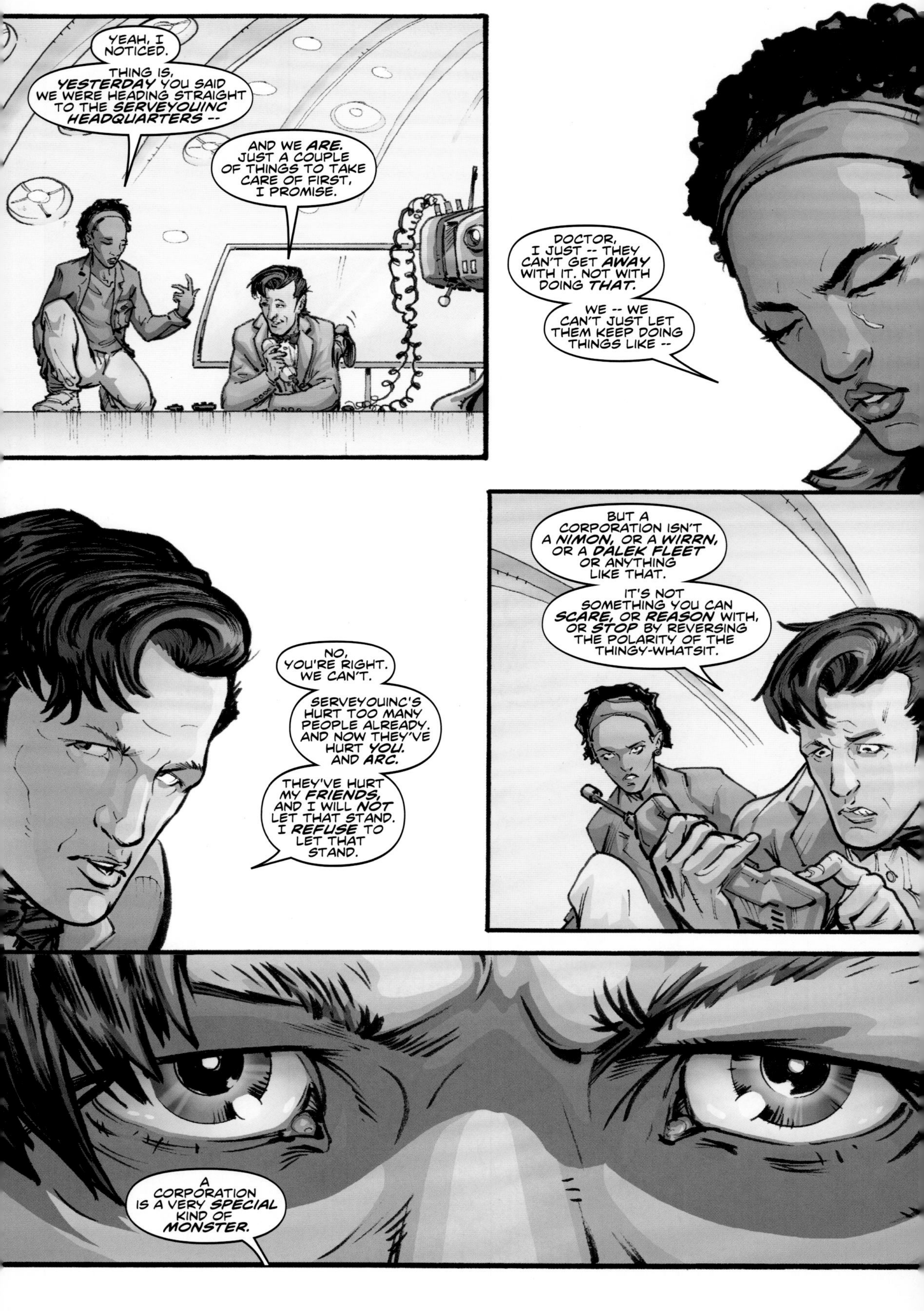
YEAH, I NOTICED.
THING IS, YESTERDAY YOU SAID WE WERE HEADING STRAIGHT TO THE SERVEYOUINC HEADQUARTERS --
AND WE ARE. JUST A COUPLE OF THINGS TO TAKE CARE OF FIRST, I PROMISE.
DOCTOR, I JUST -- THEY CAN'T GET AWAY WITH IT. NOT WITH DOING THAT.
WE -- WE CAN'T JUST LET THEM KEEP DOING THINGS LIKE --
NO, YOU'RE RIGHT. WE CAN'T.
SERVEYOUINC'S HURT TOO MANY PEOPLE ALREADY. AND NOW THEY'VE HURT YOU. AND ARC.
THEY'VE HURT MY FRIENDS, AND I WILL NOT LET THAT STAND. I REFUSE TO LET THAT STAND.
BUT A CORPORATION ISN'T A NIMON, OR A WIRRN, OR A DALEK FLEET OR ANYTHING LIKE THAT.
IT'S NOT SOMETHING YOU CAN SCARE, OR REASON WITH, OR STOP BY REVERSING THE POLARITY OF THE THINGY-WHATSIT.
A CORPORATION IS A VERY SPECIAL KIND OF MONSTER.

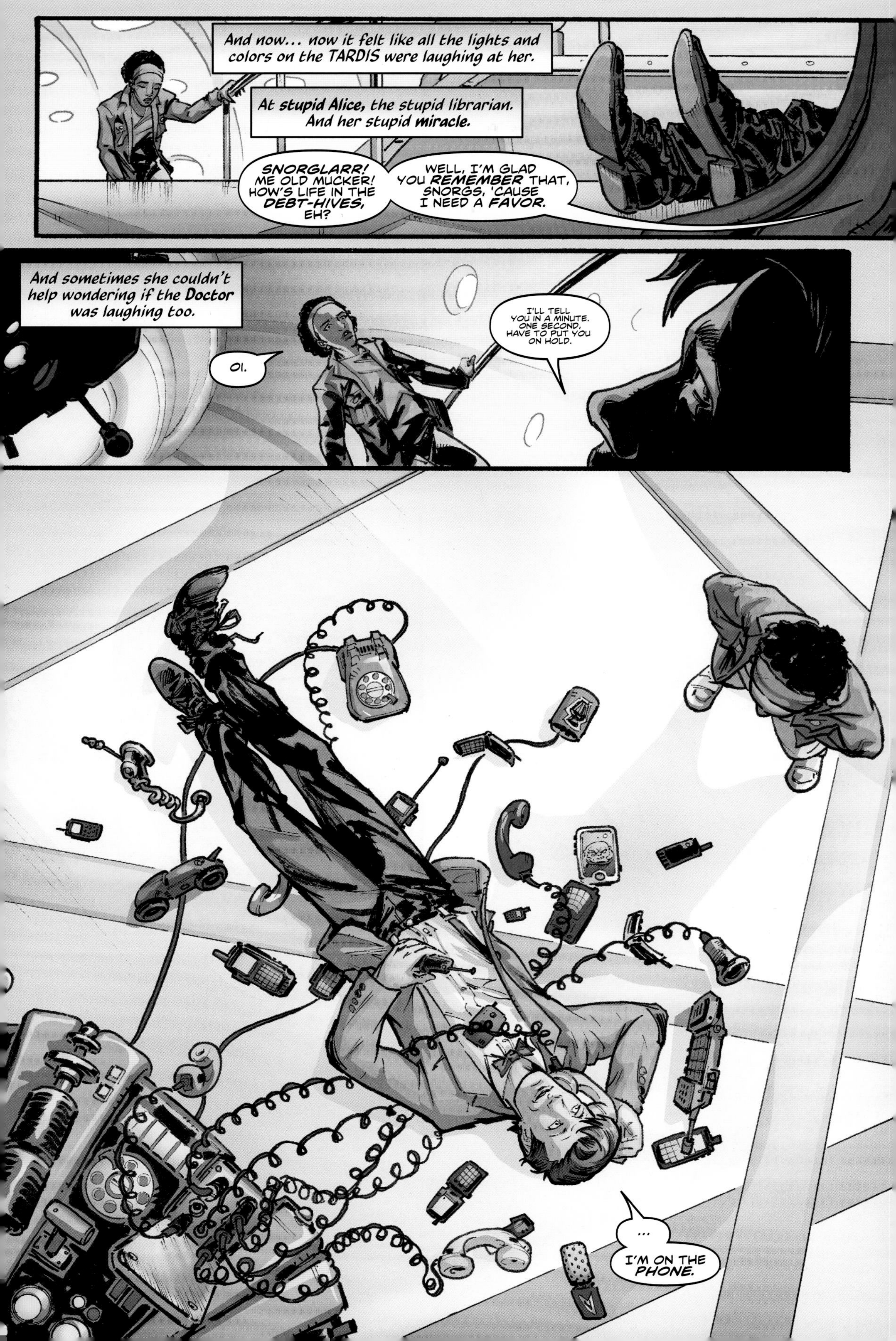
And now... now it felt like all the lights and colors on the TARDIS were laughing at her.
At stupid Alice, the stupid librarian. And her stupid miracle.
SNORGLARR! ME OLD MUCKER! HOW'S LIFE IN THE DEBT-HIVES, EH?
WELL, I'M GLAD YOU REMEMBER THAT, SNORGS, 'CAUSE I NEED A FAVOR.
And sometimes she couldn't help wondering if the Doctor was laughing too.
OI.
I'LL TELL YOU IN A MINUTE. ONE SECOND, HAVE TO PUT YOU ON HOLD.
... I'M ON THE PHONE.

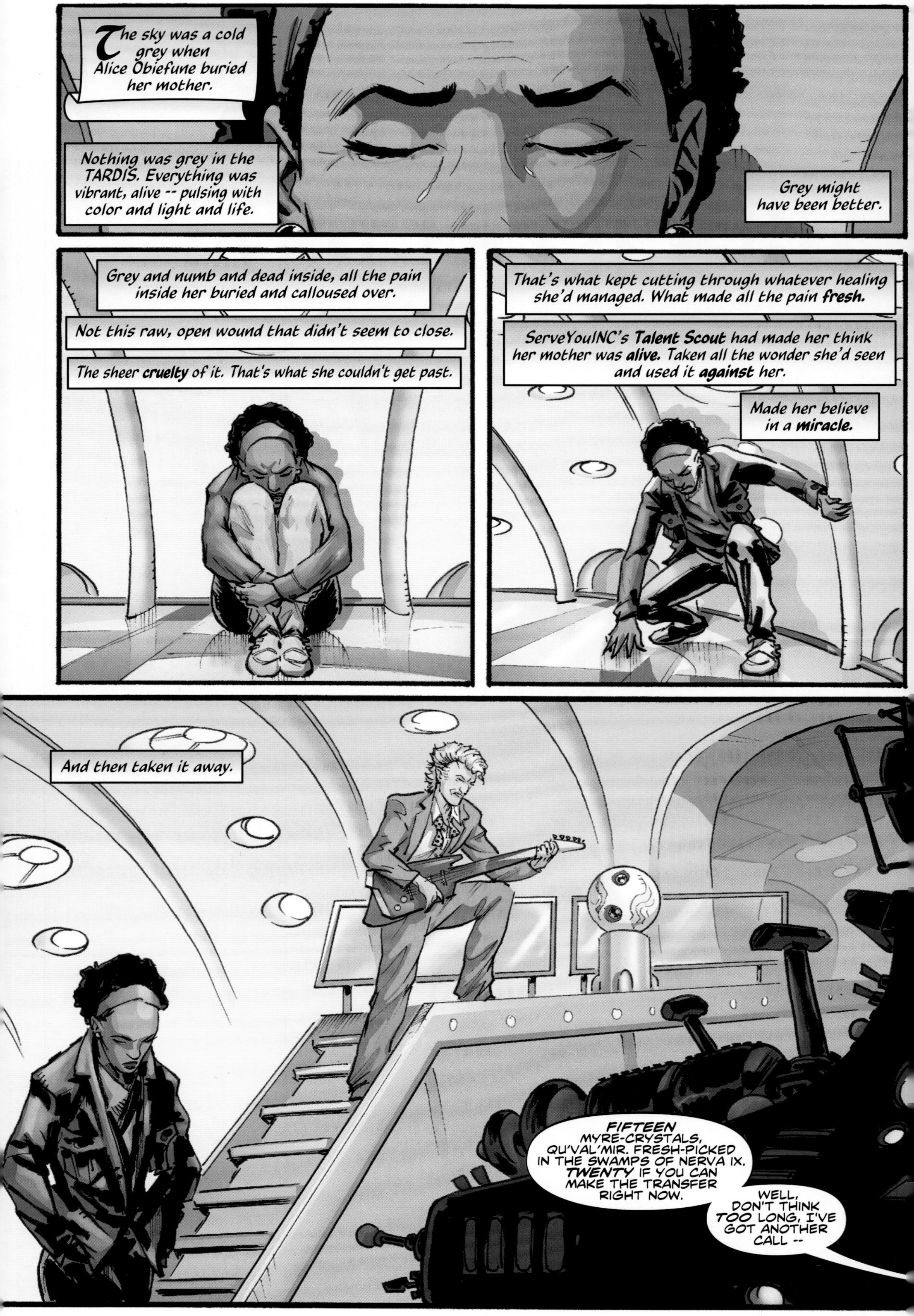
The sky was a cold grey when Alice Obiefune buried her mother.
Nothing was grey in the TARDIS. Everything was vibrant, alive -- pulsing with color and light and life.
Grey might have been better.
Grey and numb and dead inside, all the pain inside her buried and calloused over.
Not this raw, open wound that didn't seem to close.
The sheer **cruelty** of it. That's what she couldn't get past.
That's what kept cutting through whatever healing she'd managed. What made all the pain **fresh.**
ServeYouINC's **Talent Scout** had made her think her mother was **alive.** Taken all the wonder she'd seen and used it **against** her.
Made her believe in a **miracle.**
And then taken it away.
FIFTEEN MYRE-CRYSTALS, QU'VAL'MIR. FRESH-PICKED IN THE SWAMPS OF NERVA IX. ***TWENTY*** IF YOU CAN MAKE THE TRANSFER RIGHT NOW.
WELL, DON'T THINK ***TOO*** LONG, I'VE GOT ANOTHER CALL --

CHAPTER 9

THE RISE AND FALL

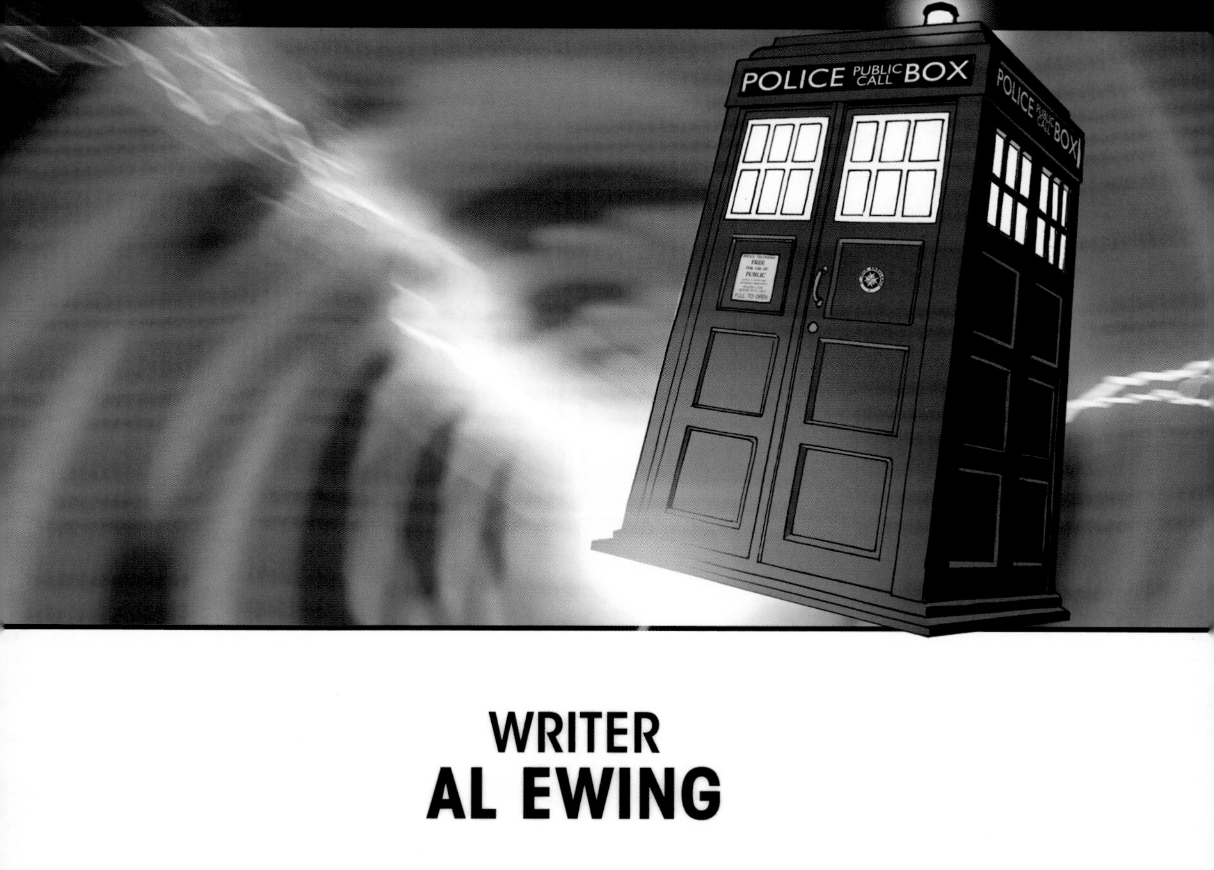
POLICE PUBLIC CALL BOX
POLICE PUBLIC CALL BOX

WRITER
AL EWING

ARTIST
BOO COOK

COLORIST
HI-FI

LETTERER
RICHARD STARKINGS AND COMICRAFT'S JIMMY BETANCOURT

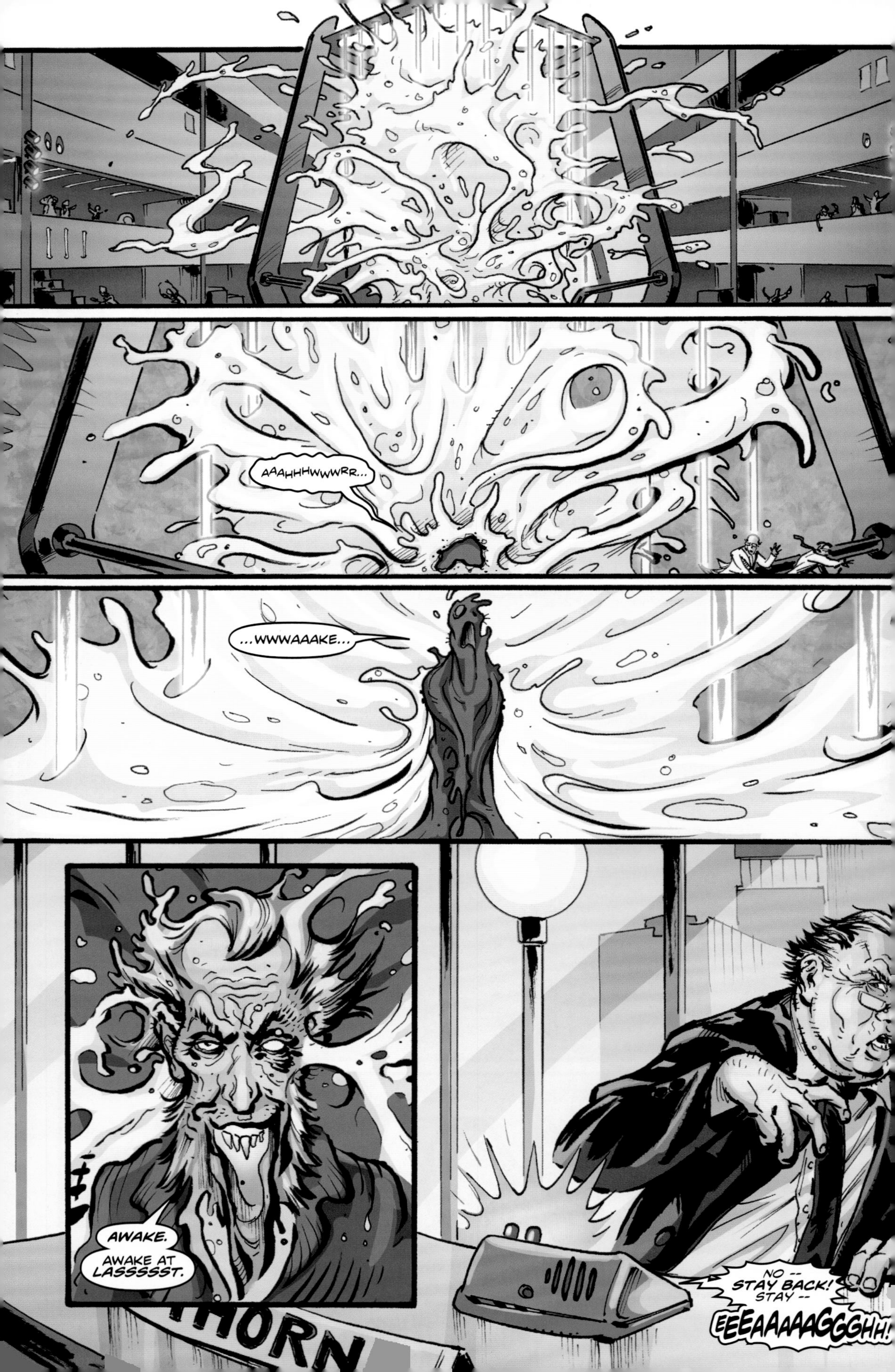
AAAHHHWWWRR...
...WWWAAAKE...
AWAKE.
AWAKE AT LASSSSST.
NO -- STAY BACK! STAY --
EEEAAAAAGGGHH!
THORN

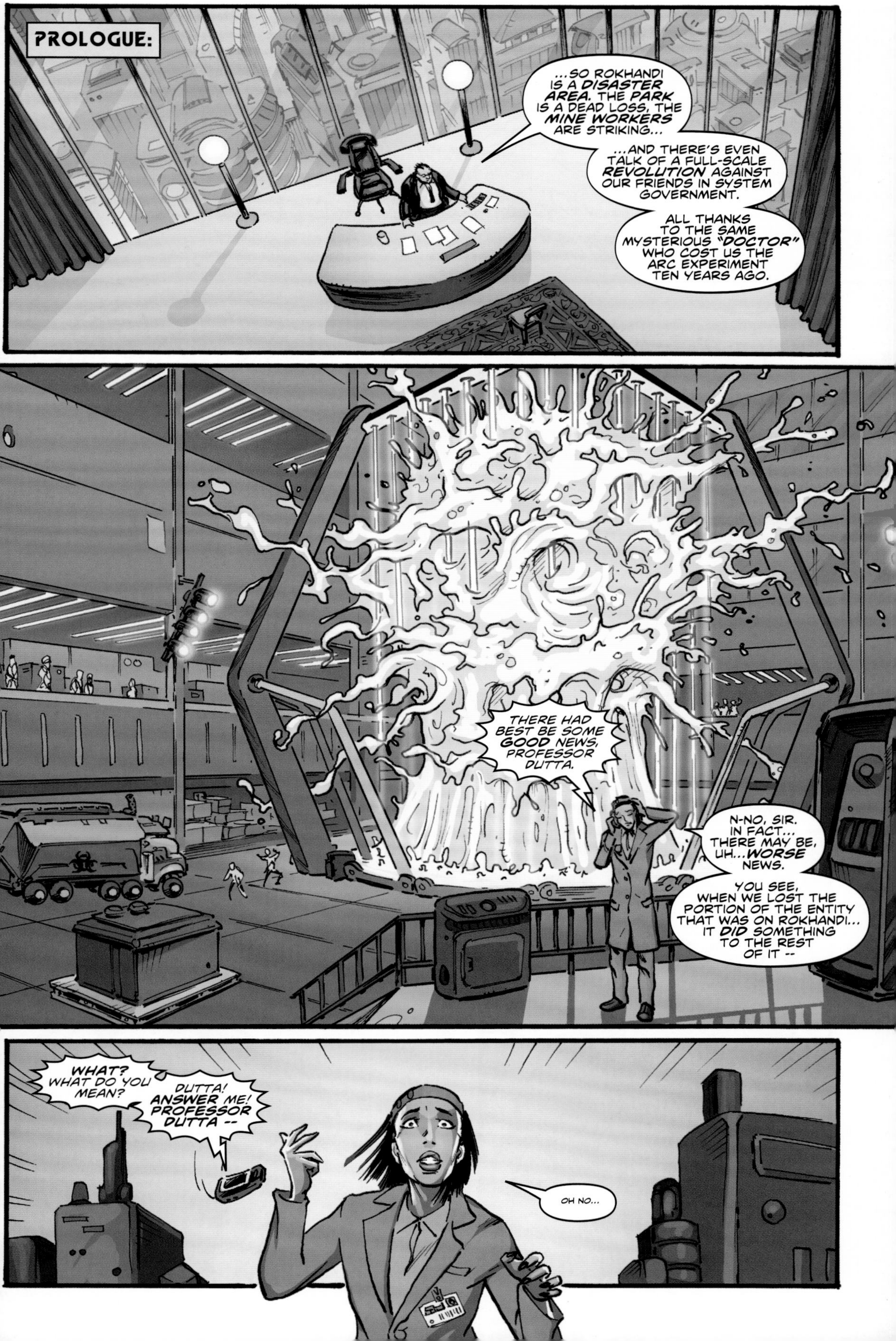
PROLOGUE:
...SO ROKHANDI IS A DISASTER AREA. THE PARK IS A DEAD LOSS, THE MINE WORKERS ARE STRIKING...
...AND THERE'S EVEN TALK OF A FULL-SCALE REVOLUTION AGAINST OUR FRIENDS IN SYSTEM GOVERNMENT.
ALL THANKS TO THE SAME MYSTERIOUS "DOCTOR" WHO COST US THE ARC EXPERIMENT TEN YEARS AGO.
THERE HAD BEST BE SOME GOOD NEWS, PROFESSOR DUTTA.
N-NO, SIR. IN FACT... THERE MAY BE, UH...WORSE NEWS.
YOU SEE, WHEN WE LOST THE PORTION OF THE ENTITY THAT WAS ON ROKHANDI... IT DID SOMETHING TO THE REST OF IT --
WHAT? WHAT DO YOU MEAN?
DUTTA! ANSWER ME! PROFESSOR DUTTA --
OH NO...

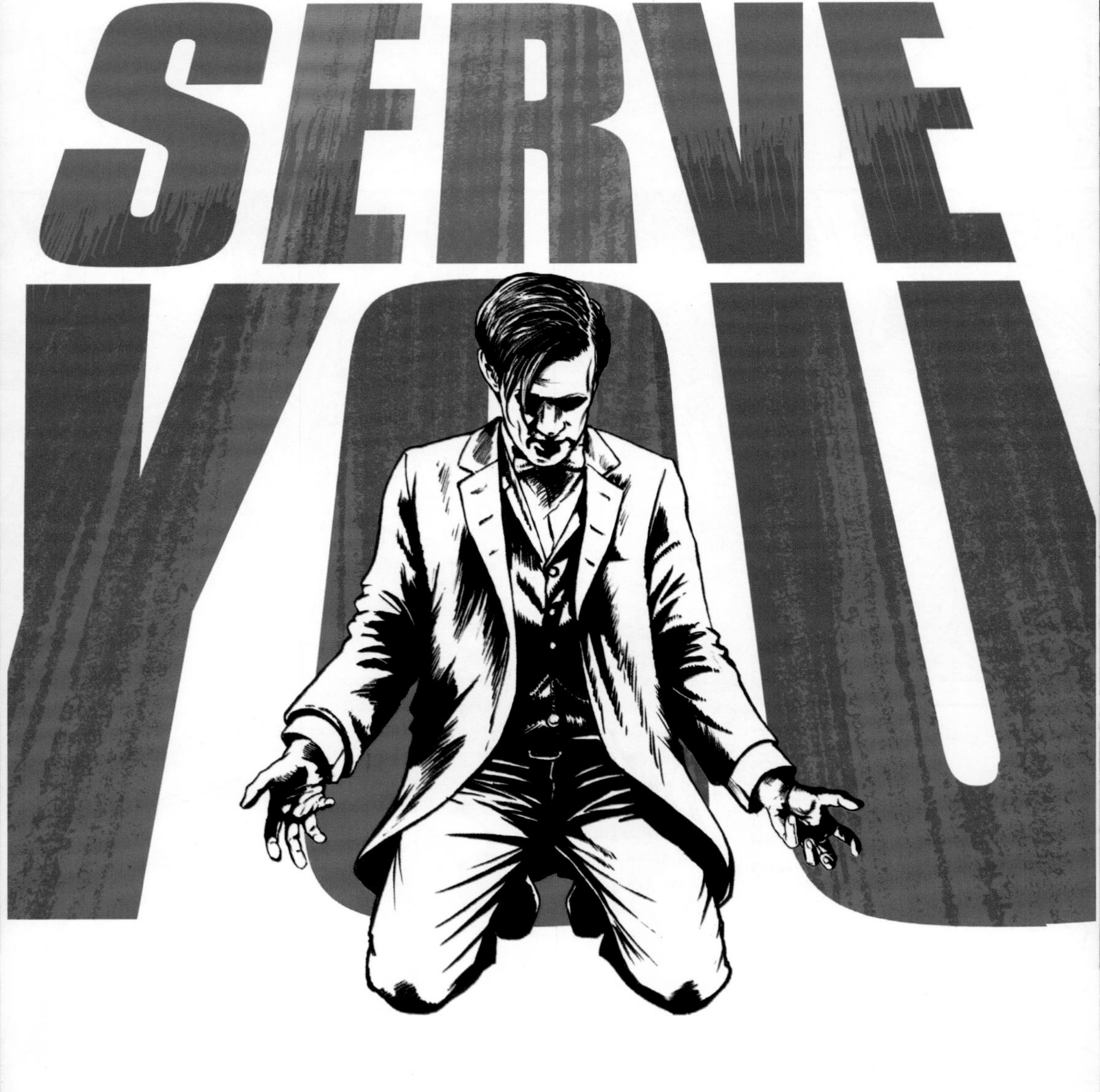

CHAPTER 9

Cover A: Brian Williamson

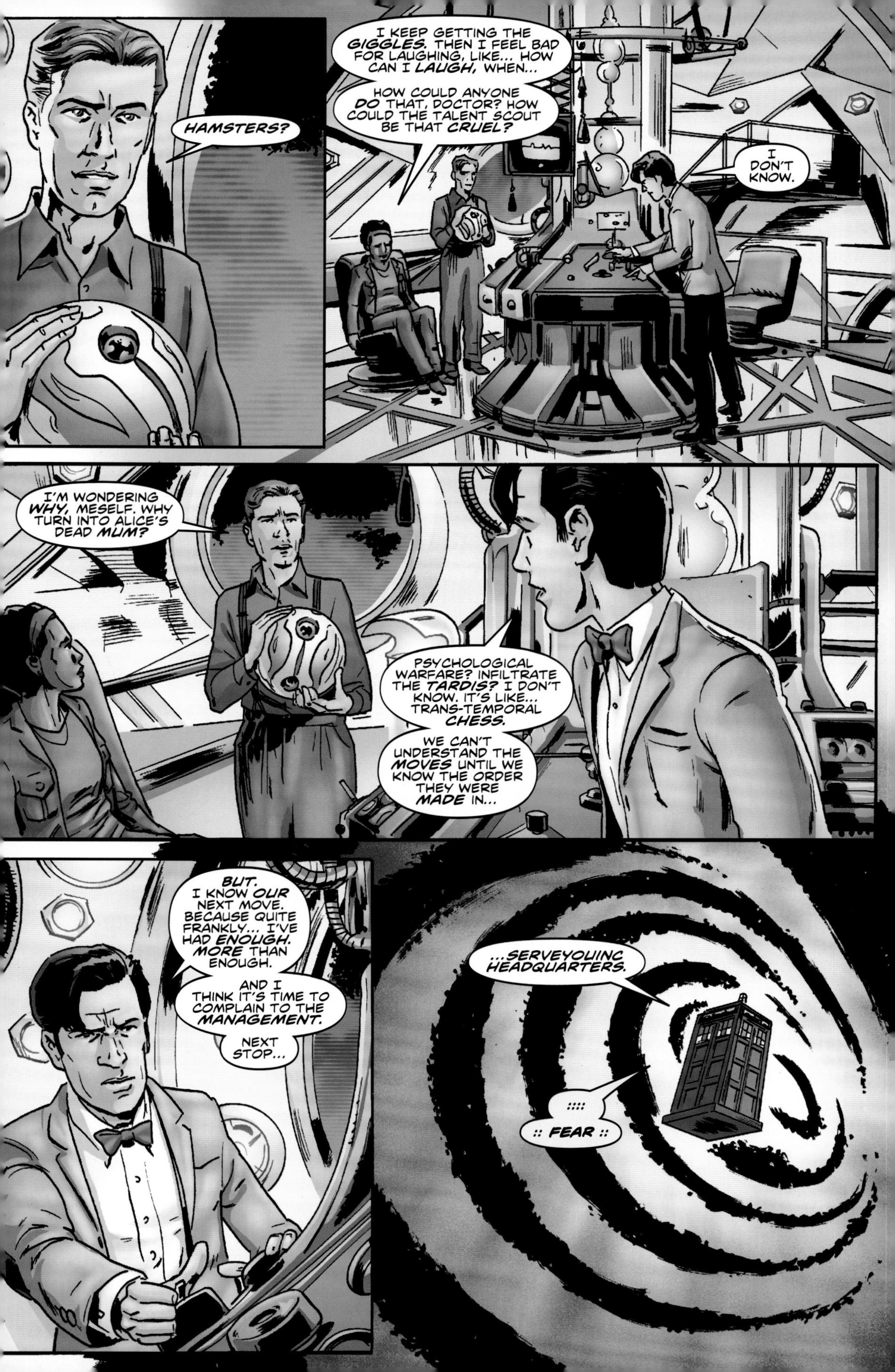
HAMSTERS?
I KEEP GETTING THE GIGGLES. THEN I FEEL BAD FOR LAUGHING, LIKE... HOW CAN I LAUGH, WHEN...
HOW COULD ANYONE DO THAT, DOCTOR? HOW COULD THE TALENT SCOUT BE THAT CRUEL?
I DON'T KNOW.
I'M WONDERING WHY, MESELF. WHY TURN INTO ALICE'S DEAD MUM?
PSYCHOLOGICAL WARFARE? INFILTRATE THE TARDIS? I DON'T KNOW. IT'S LIKE... TRANS-TEMPORAL CHESS.
WE CAN'T UNDERSTAND THE MOVES UNTIL WE KNOW THE ORDER THEY WERE MADE IN...
BUT. I KNOW OUR NEXT MOVE. BECAUSE QUITE FRANKLY... I'VE HAD ENOUGH. MORE THAN ENOUGH.
AND I THINK IT'S TIME TO COMPLAIN TO THE MANAGEMENT.
NEXT STOP...
...SERVEYOUINC HEADQUARTERS.
::::
:: FEAR ::

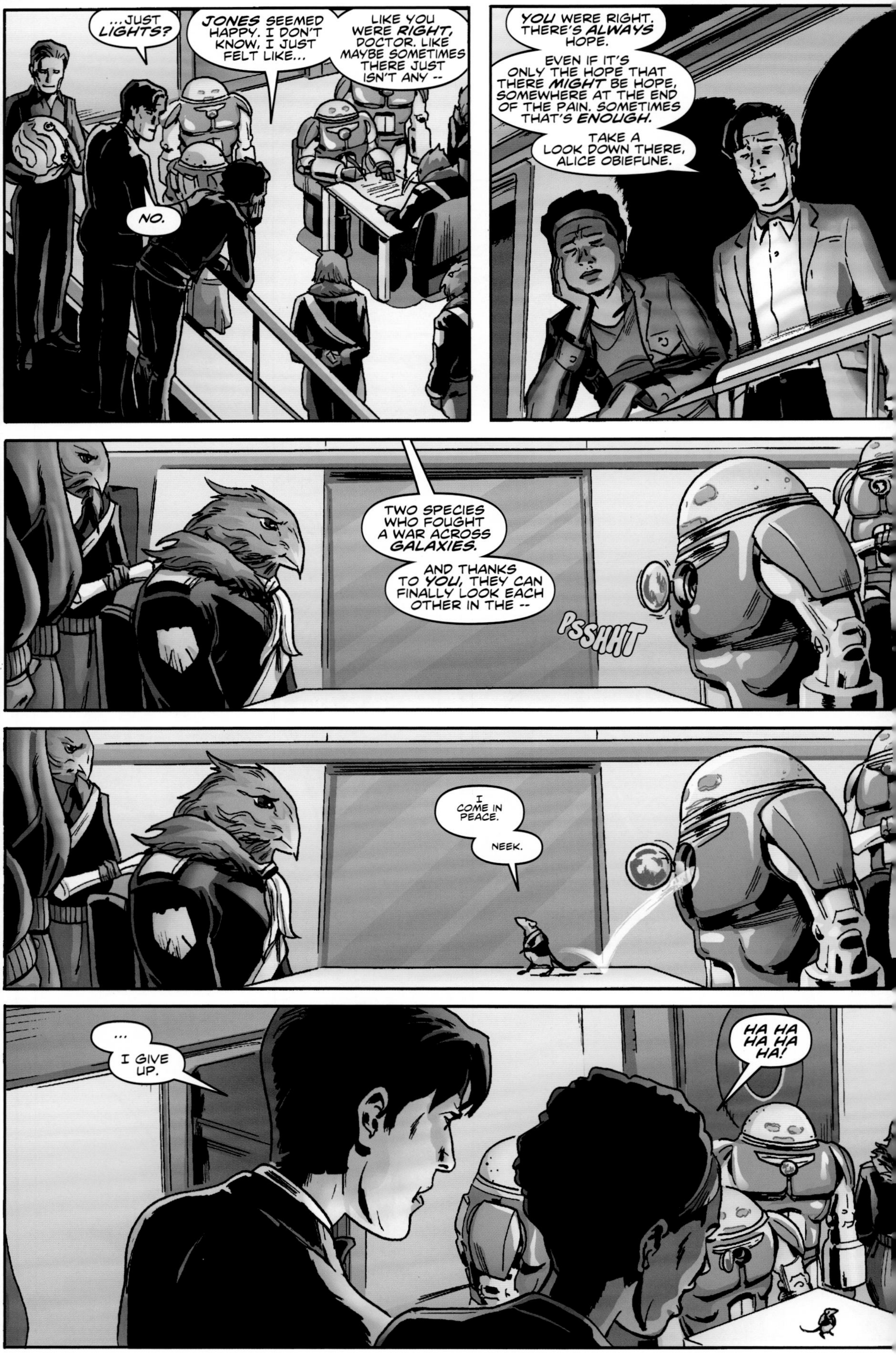
...JUST LIGHTS?
JONES SEEMED HAPPY. I DON'T KNOW, I JUST FELT LIKE...
LIKE YOU WERE RIGHT, DOCTOR. LIKE MAYBE SOMETIMES THERE JUST ISN'T ANY --
NO.
YOU WERE RIGHT. THERE'S ALWAYS HOPE.
EVEN IF IT'S ONLY THE HOPE THAT THERE MIGHT BE HOPE, SOMEWHERE AT THE END OF THE PAIN. SOMETIMES THAT'S ENOUGH.
TAKE A LOOK DOWN THERE, ALICE OBIEFUNE.
TWO SPECIES WHO FOUGHT A WAR ACROSS GALAXIES.
AND THANKS TO YOU, THEY CAN FINALLY LOOK EACH OTHER IN THE --
PSSHHT
I COME IN PEACE.
NEEK.
... I GIVE UP.
HA HA HA HA HA!

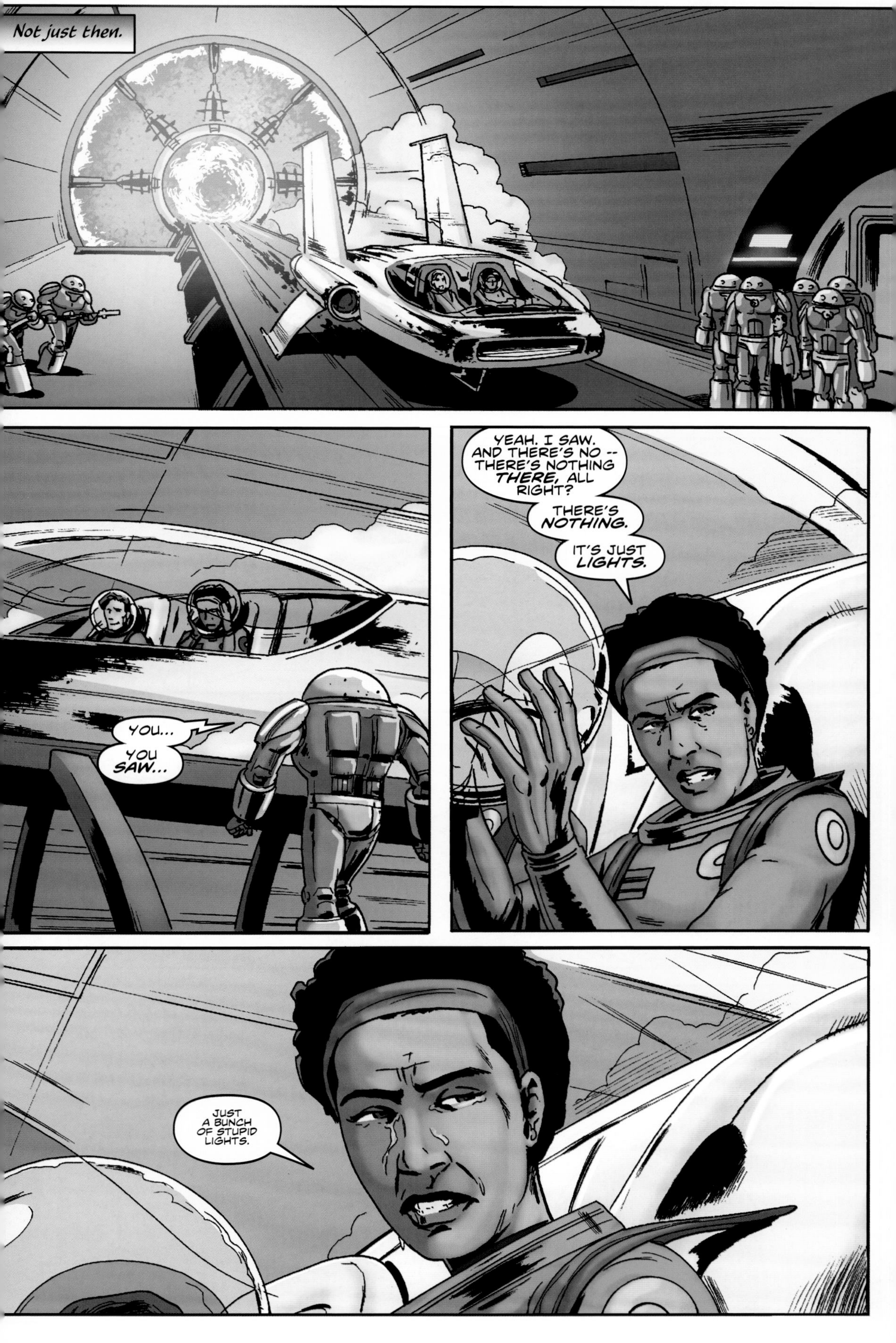
Not just then.
YOU...
YOU SAW...
YEAH. I SAW. AND THERE'S NO -- THERE'S NOTHING THERE, ALL RIGHT?
THERE'S NOTHING.
IT'S JUST LIGHTS.
JUST A BUNCH OF STUPID LIGHTS.

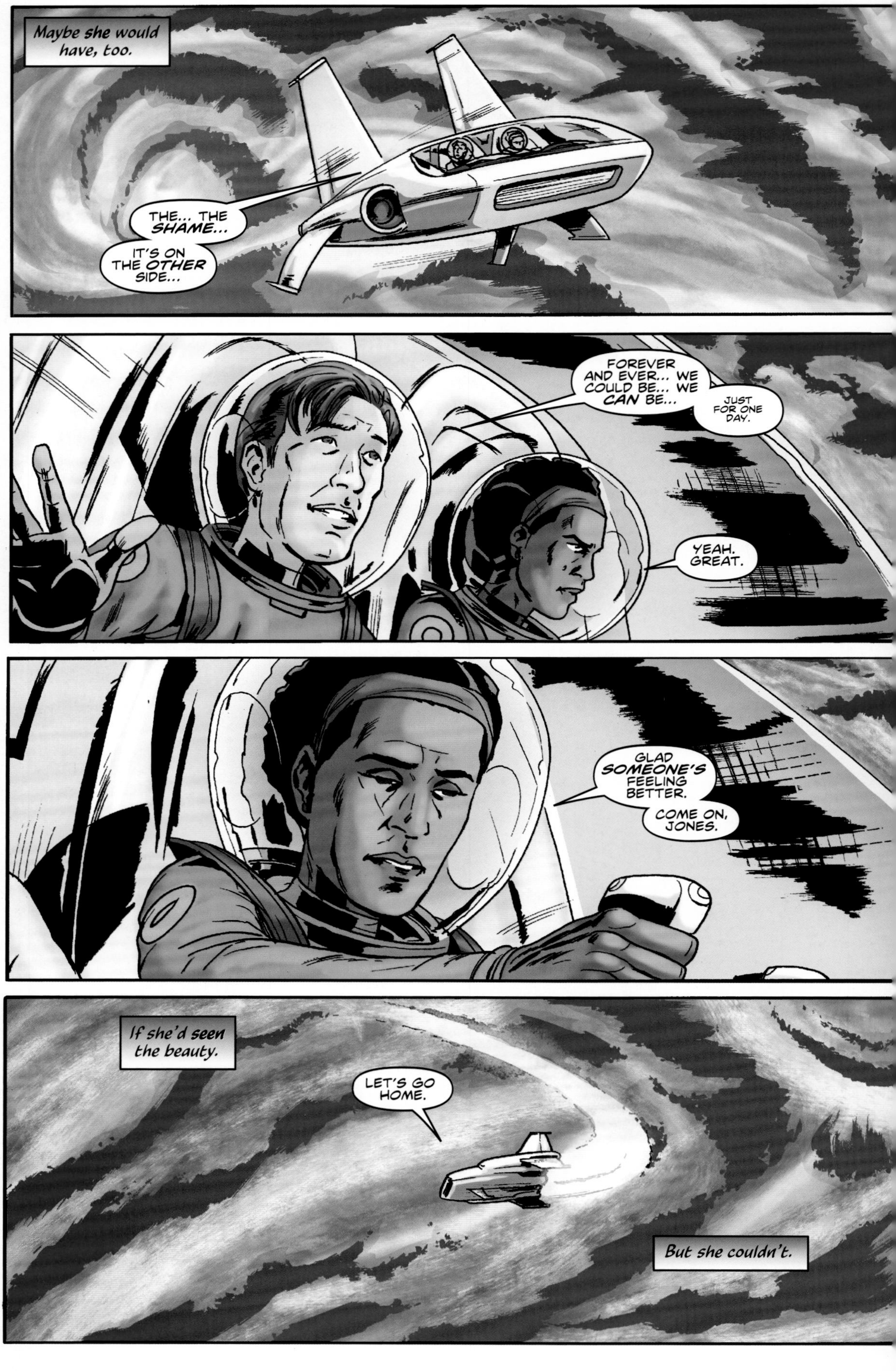
Maybe she would have, too.
THE... THE SHAME...
IT'S ON THE OTHER SIDE...
FOREVER AND EVER... WE COULD BE... WE CAN BE...
JUST FOR ONE DAY.
YEAH. GREAT.
GLAD SOMEONE'S FEELING BETTER.
COME ON, JONES.
If she'd seen the beauty.
LET'S GO HOME.
But she couldn't.

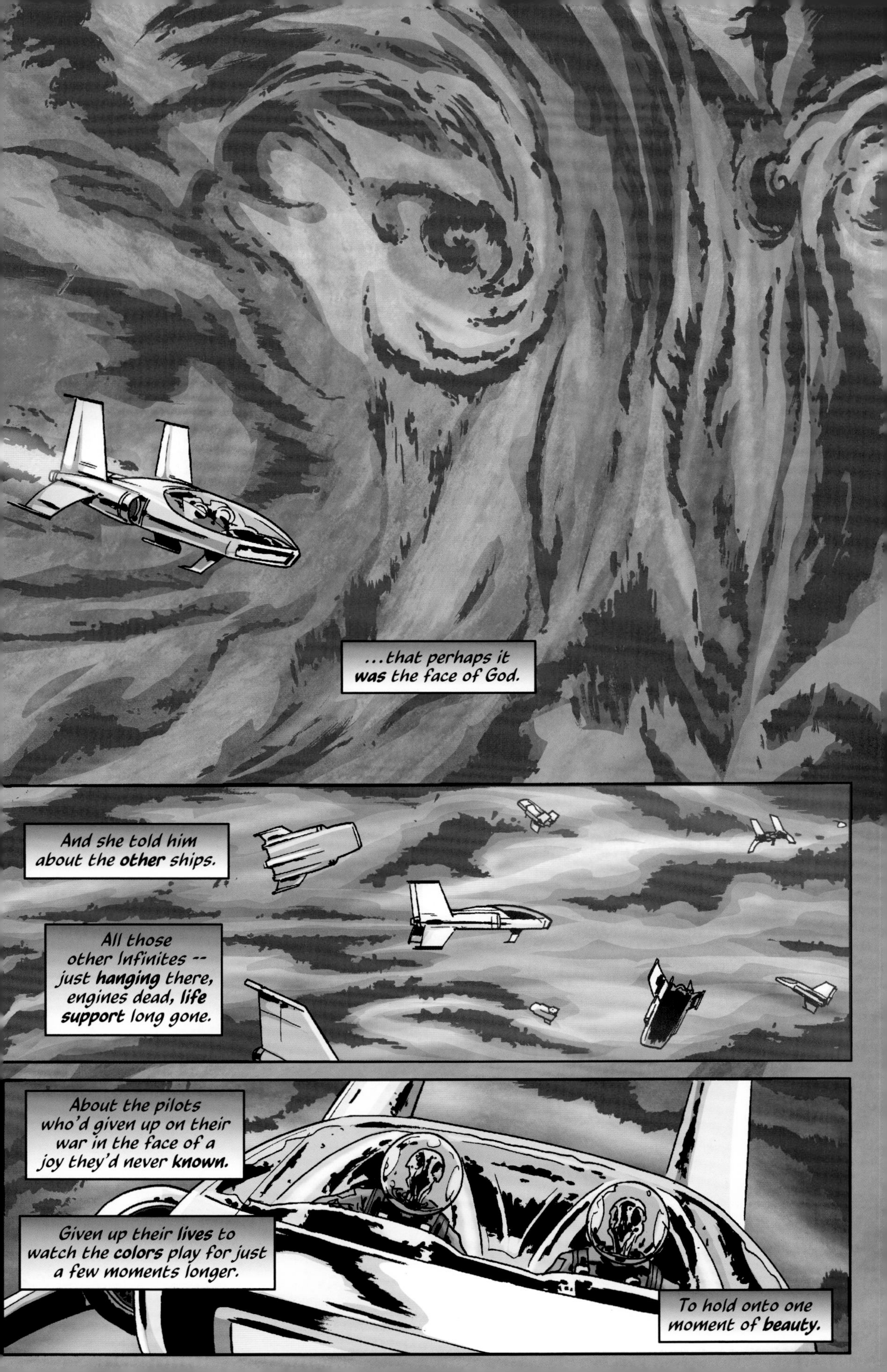
...that perhaps it was the face of God.
And she told him about the other ships.
All those other Infinites -- just hanging there, engines dead, life support long gone.
About the pilots who'd given up on their war in the face of a joy they'd never known.
Given up their lives to watch the colors play for just a few moments longer.
To hold onto one moment of beauty.

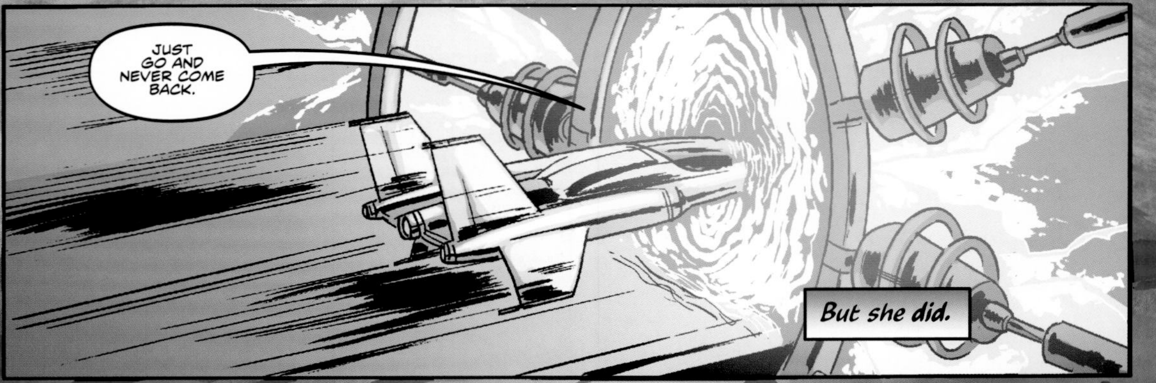
JUST GO AND NEVER COME BACK.
But she did.

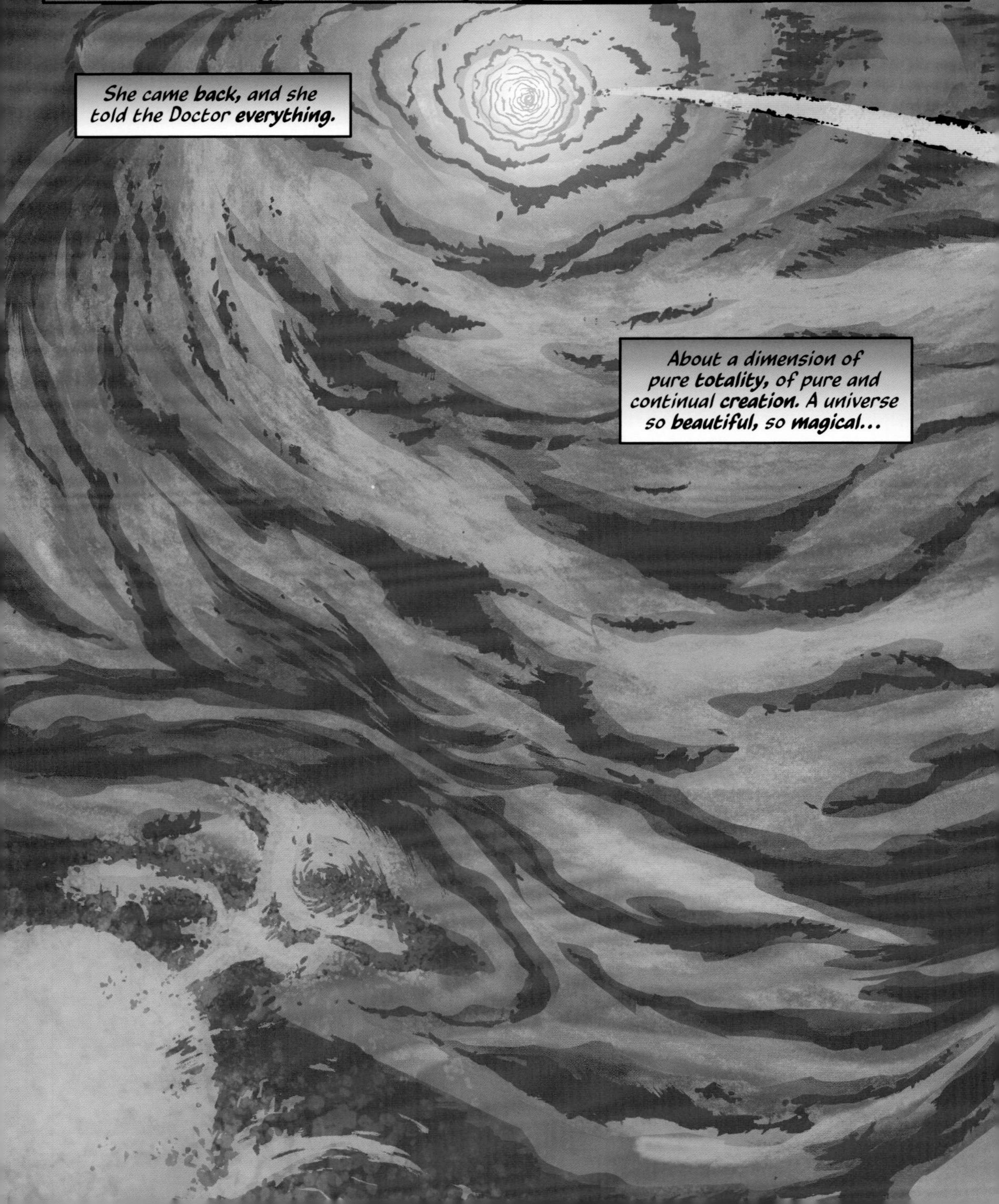
She came back, and she told the Doctor everything.
About a dimension of pure totality, of pure and continual creation. A universe so beautiful, so magical...

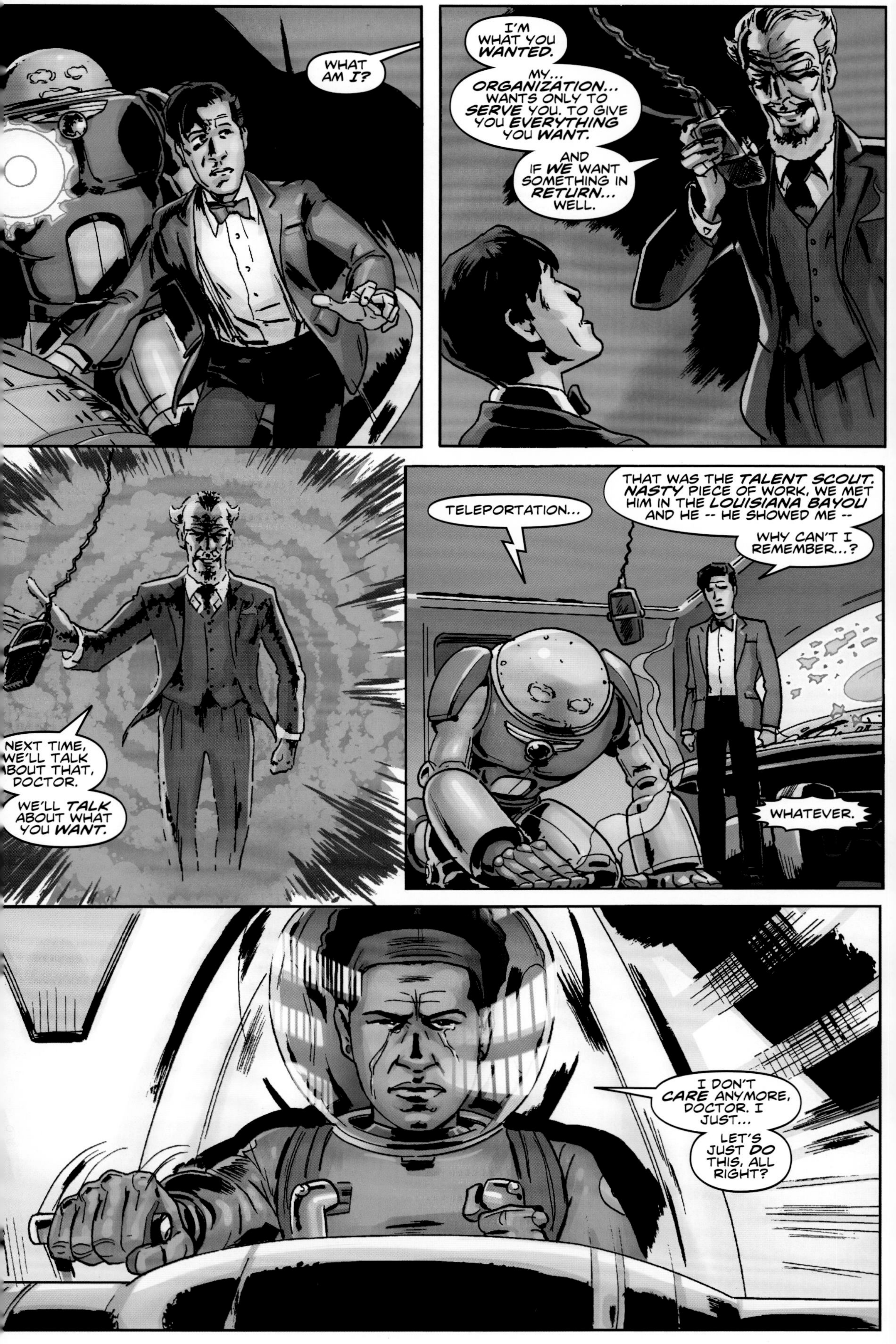

WHAT AM I?
I'M WHAT YOU WANTED.
MY... ORGANIZATION... WANTS ONLY TO SERVE YOU. TO GIVE YOU EVERYTHING YOU WANT.
AND IF WE WANT SOMETHING IN RETURN... WELL.
NEXT TIME, WE'LL TALK ABOUT THAT, DOCTOR.
WE'LL TALK ABOUT WHAT YOU WANT.
TELEPORTATION...
THAT WAS THE TALENT SCOUT. NASTY PIECE OF WORK, WE MET HIM IN THE LOUISIANA BAYOU AND HE -- HE SHOWED ME --
WHY CAN'T I REMEMBER...?
WHATEVER.
I DON'T CARE ANYMORE, DOCTOR. I JUST...
LET'S JUST DO THIS, ALL RIGHT?

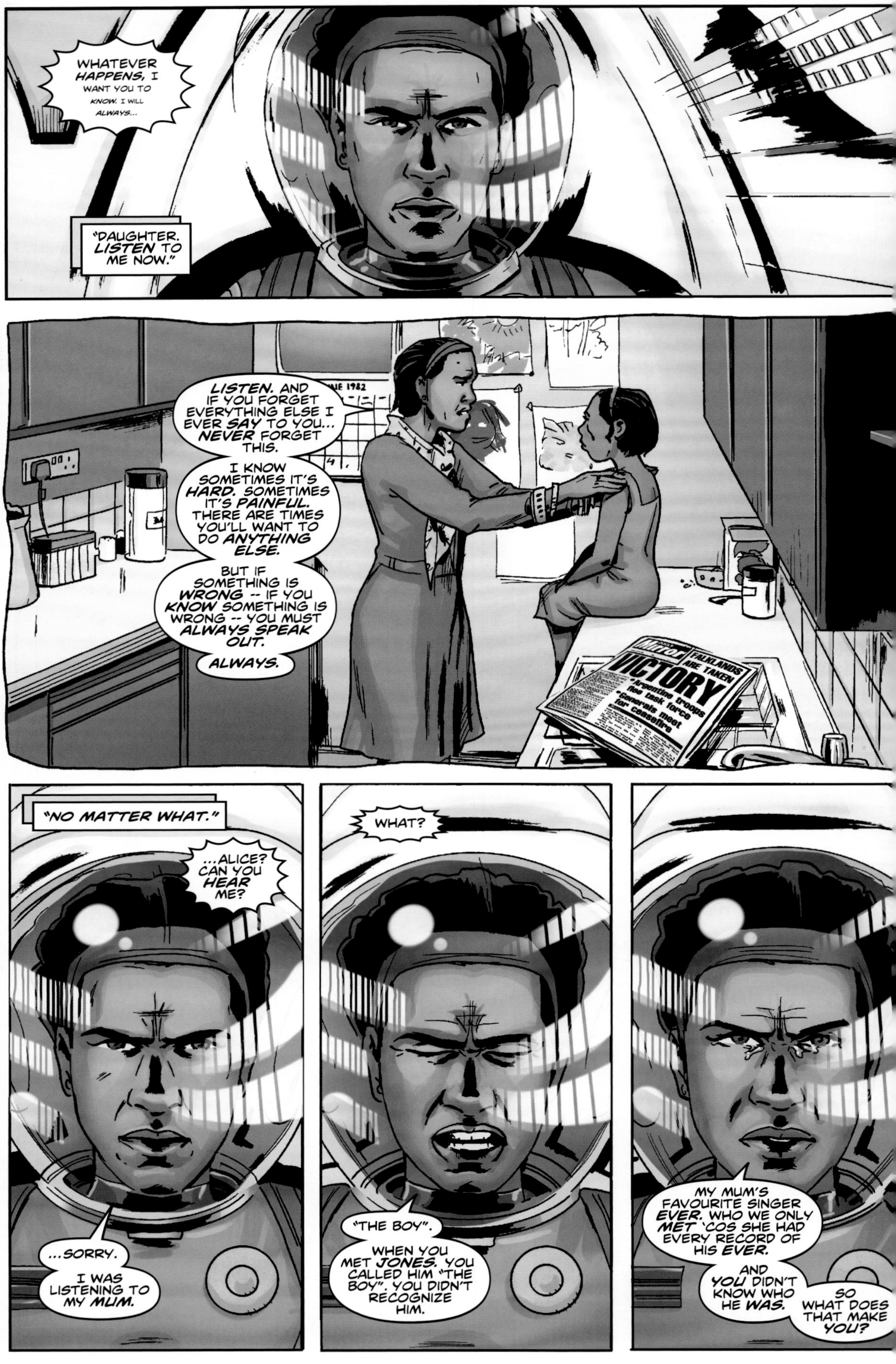

WHATEVER HAPPENS, I WANT YOU TO KNOW. I WILL ALWAYS...
"DAUGHTER. LISTEN TO ME NOW."
LISTEN. AND IF YOU FORGET EVERYTHING ELSE I EVER SAY TO YOU... NEVER FORGET THIS.
I KNOW SOMETIMES IT'S HARD. SOMETIMES IT'S PAINFUL. THERE ARE TIMES YOU'LL WANT TO DO ANYTHING ELSE.
BUT IF SOMETHING IS WRONG -- IF YOU KNOW SOMETHING IS WRONG -- YOU MUST ALWAYS SPEAK OUT.
ALWAYS.
FALKLANDS ARE TAKEN
VICTORY
"NO MATTER WHAT."
...ALICE? CAN YOU HEAR ME?
...SORRY.
I WAS LISTENING TO MY MUM.
WHAT?
"THE BOY".
WHEN YOU MET JONES, YOU CALLED HIM "THE BOY". YOU DIDN'T RECOGNIZE HIM.
MY MUM'S FAVOURITE SINGER EVER. WHO WE ONLY MET 'COS SHE HAD EVERY RECORD OF HIS EVER.
AND YOU DIDN'T KNOW WHO HE WAS.
SO WHAT DOES THAT MAKE YOU?

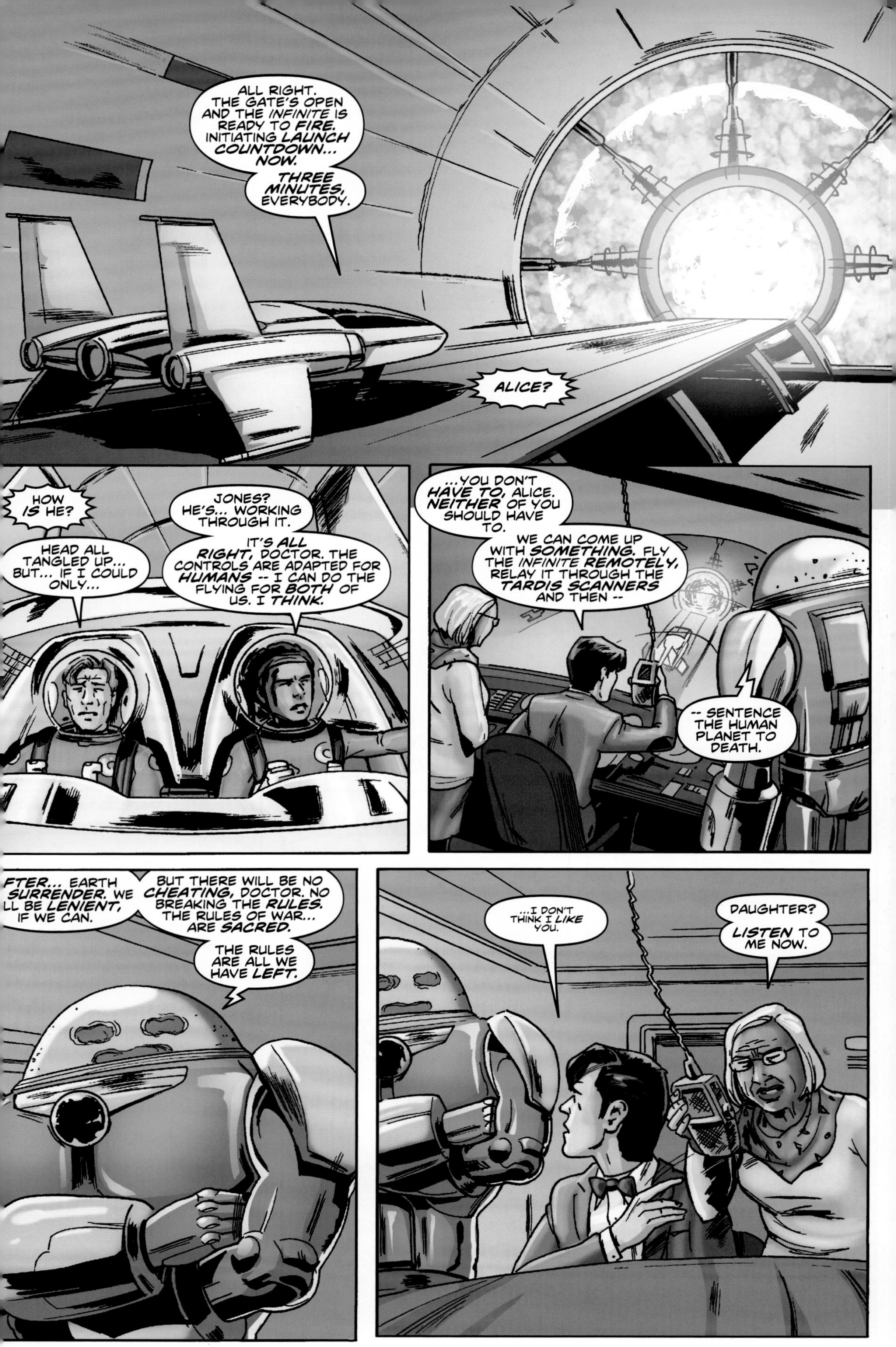
ALL RIGHT. THE GATE'S OPEN AND THE INFINITE IS READY TO FIRE. INITIATING LAUNCH COUNTDOWN... NOW.
THREE MINUTES, EVERYBODY.
ALICE?
HOW IS HE?
HEAD ALL TANGLED UP... BUT... IF I COULD ONLY...
JONES? HE'S... WORKING THROUGH IT.
IT'S ALL RIGHT, DOCTOR. THE CONTROLS ARE ADAPTED FOR HUMANS -- I CAN DO THE FLYING FOR BOTH OF US. I THINK.
...YOU DON'T HAVE TO, ALICE. NEITHER OF YOU SHOULD HAVE TO.
WE CAN COME UP WITH SOMETHING. FLY THE INFINITE REMOTELY, RELAY IT THROUGH THE TARDIS SCANNERS AND THEN --
-- SENTENCE THE HUMAN PLANET TO DEATH.
FTER... EARTH SURRENDER. WE LL BE LENIENT, IF WE CAN.
BUT THERE WILL BE NO CHEATING, DOCTOR. NO BREAKING THE RULES. THE RULES OF WAR... ARE SACRED.
THE RULES ARE ALL WE HAVE LEFT.
...I DON'T THINK I LIKE YOU.
DAUGHTER?
LISTEN TO ME NOW.

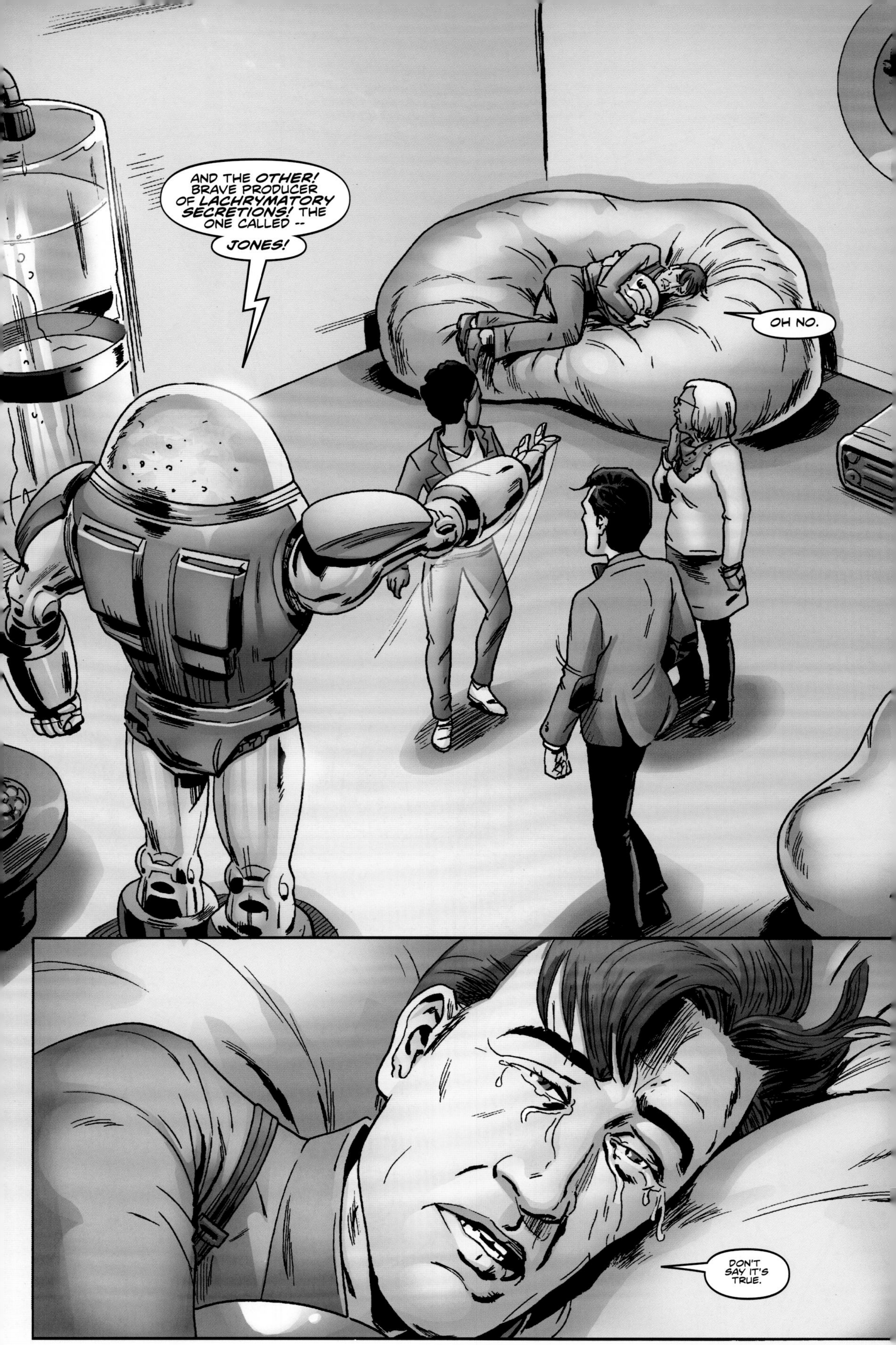
AND THE OTHER! BRAVE PRODUCER OF LACHRYMATORY SECRETIONS! THE ONE CALLED --
JONES!
OH NO.
DON'T SAY IT'S TRUE.

IT'S NOT *"THE TARDIS ASTRONAUT"*.

'SCUSE ME? DID YOU JUST MAKE A JOKE?

YOUR QUERY IS *IRRELEVANT.*

THE CRAFT MUST BE THE *INFINITE ITSELF,* OR A REPRODUCTION THEREOF. THE *SACRED CRAFT.* AND THE CANDIDATE MUST BE OF THE *CHALLENGING SPECIES.*

NO SECONDS. NO *OUTSIDERS,* DOCTOR.

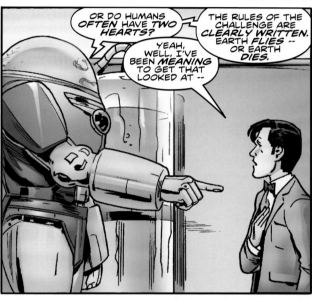

OR DO HUMANS OFTEN HAVE *TWO HEARTS?*

THE RULES OF THE CHALLENGE ARE *CLEARLY WRITTEN.* EARTH *FLIES* -- OR EARTH *DIES.*

YEAH, WELL, I'VE BEEN *MEANING* TO GET THAT LOOKED AT --

EARTH *DIES?* YOU DIDN'T HAPPEN TO *NOTICE* THAT BIT?

THEY WERE GOING TO *KILL YOU!* I DIDN'T HAVE *TIME* FOR THE *SMALL PRINT!*

OH DEAR.

TWO PILOTS!

TWO WARRIOR *EARTHLINGS!* TWO TO SEE THE FACE OF GOD AND *SAVE THEIR WORLD!*

THE ONE CALLED *ALICE OBIEFUNE...*

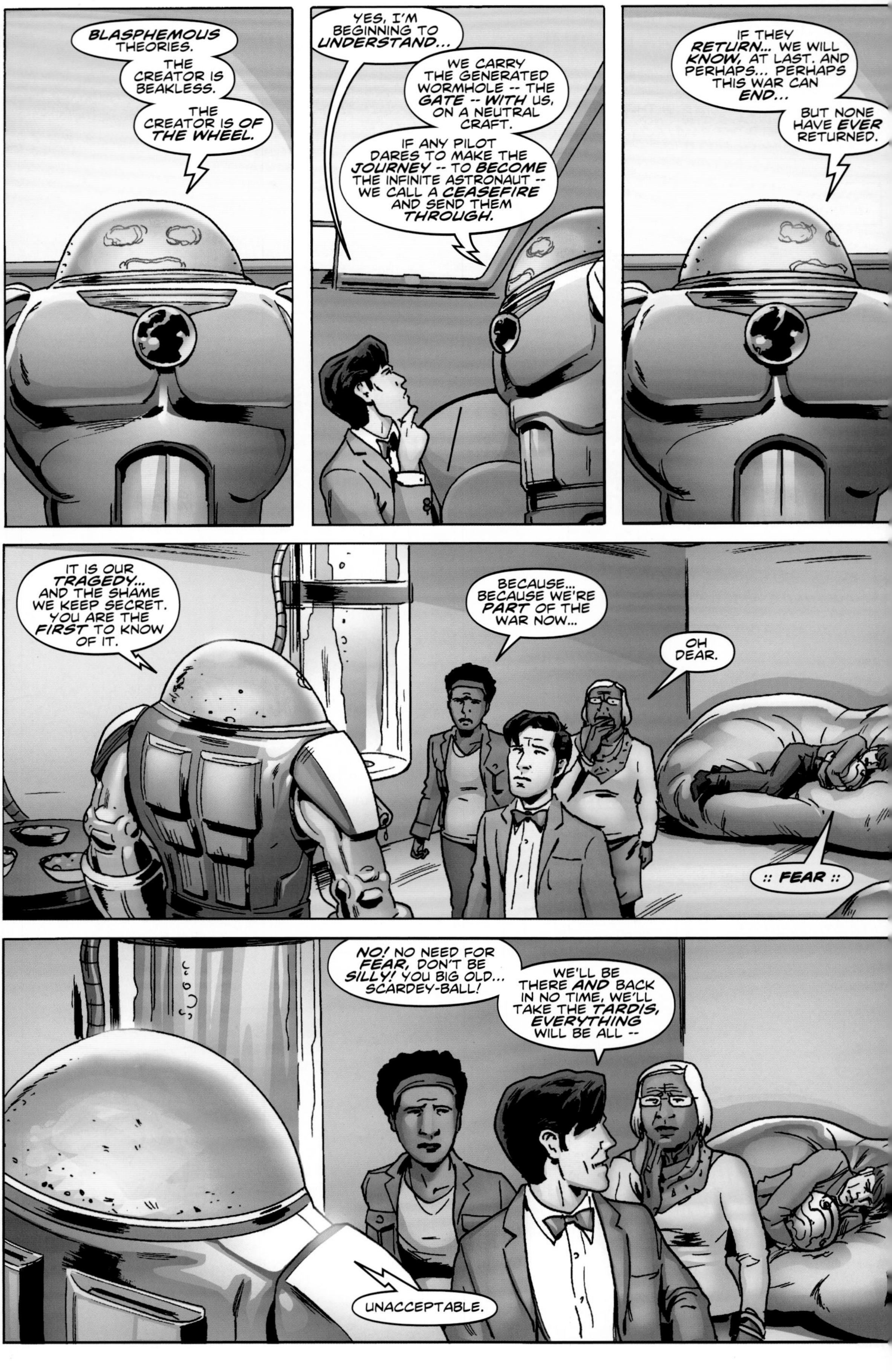
BLASPHEMOUS THEORIES.
THE CREATOR IS BEAKLESS.
THE CREATOR IS OF THE WHEEL.
YES, I'M BEGINNING TO UNDERSTAND...
WE CARRY THE GENERATED WORMHOLE -- THE GATE -- WITH US, ON A NEUTRAL CRAFT.
IF ANY PILOT DARES TO MAKE THE JOURNEY -- TO BECOME THE INFINITE ASTRONAUT -- WE CALL A CEASEFIRE AND SEND THEM THROUGH.
IF THEY RETURN... WE WILL KNOW, AT LAST. AND PERHAPS... PERHAPS THIS WAR CAN END...
BUT NONE HAVE EVER RETURNED.
IT IS OUR TRAGEDY... AND THE SHAME WE KEEP SECRET. YOU ARE THE FIRST TO KNOW OF IT.
BECAUSE... BECAUSE WE'RE PART OF THE WAR NOW...
OH DEAR.
:: FEAR ::
NO! NO NEED FOR FEAR, DON'T BE SILLY! YOU BIG OLD... SCARDEY-BALL!
WE'LL BE THERE AND BACK IN NO TIME, WE'LL TAKE THE TARDIS, EVERYTHING WILL BE ALL --
UNACCEPTABLE.

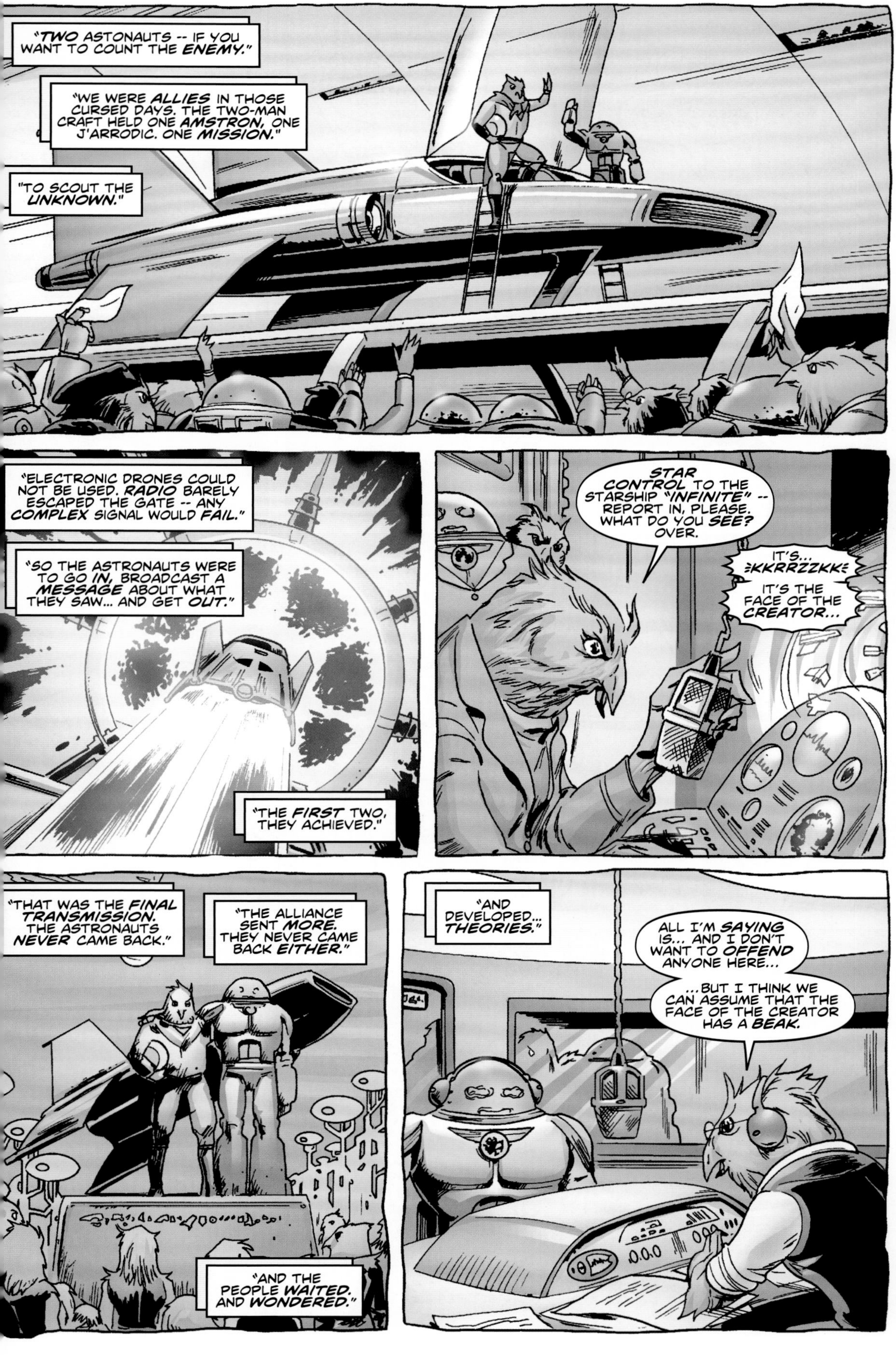
"TWO ASTONAUTS -- IF YOU WANT TO COUNT THE ENEMY."
"WE WERE ALLIES IN THOSE CURSED DAYS. THE TWO-MAN CRAFT HELD ONE AMSTRON, ONE J'ARRODIC. ONE MISSION."
"TO SCOUT THE UNKNOWN."
"ELECTRONIC DRONES COULD NOT BE USED. RADIO BARELY ESCAPED THE GATE -- ANY COMPLEX SIGNAL WOULD FAIL."
"SO THE ASTRONAUTS WERE TO GO IN, BROADCAST A MESSAGE ABOUT WHAT THEY SAW... AND GET OUT."
"THE FIRST TWO, THEY ACHIEVED."
STAR CONTROL TO THE STARSHIP "INFINITE" -- REPORT IN, PLEASE. WHAT DO YOU SEE? OVER.
IT'S... KKRRZZKK IT'S THE FACE OF THE CREATOR...
"THAT WAS THE FINAL TRANSMISSION. THE ASTRONAUTS NEVER CAME BACK."
"THE ALLIANCE SENT MORE. THEY NEVER CAME BACK EITHER."
"AND THE PEOPLE WAITED. AND WONDERED."
"AND DEVELOPED... THEORIES."
ALL I'M SAYING IS... AND I DON'T WANT TO OFFEND ANYONE HERE...
...BUT I THINK WE CAN ASSUME THAT THE FACE OF THE CREATOR HAS A BEAK.

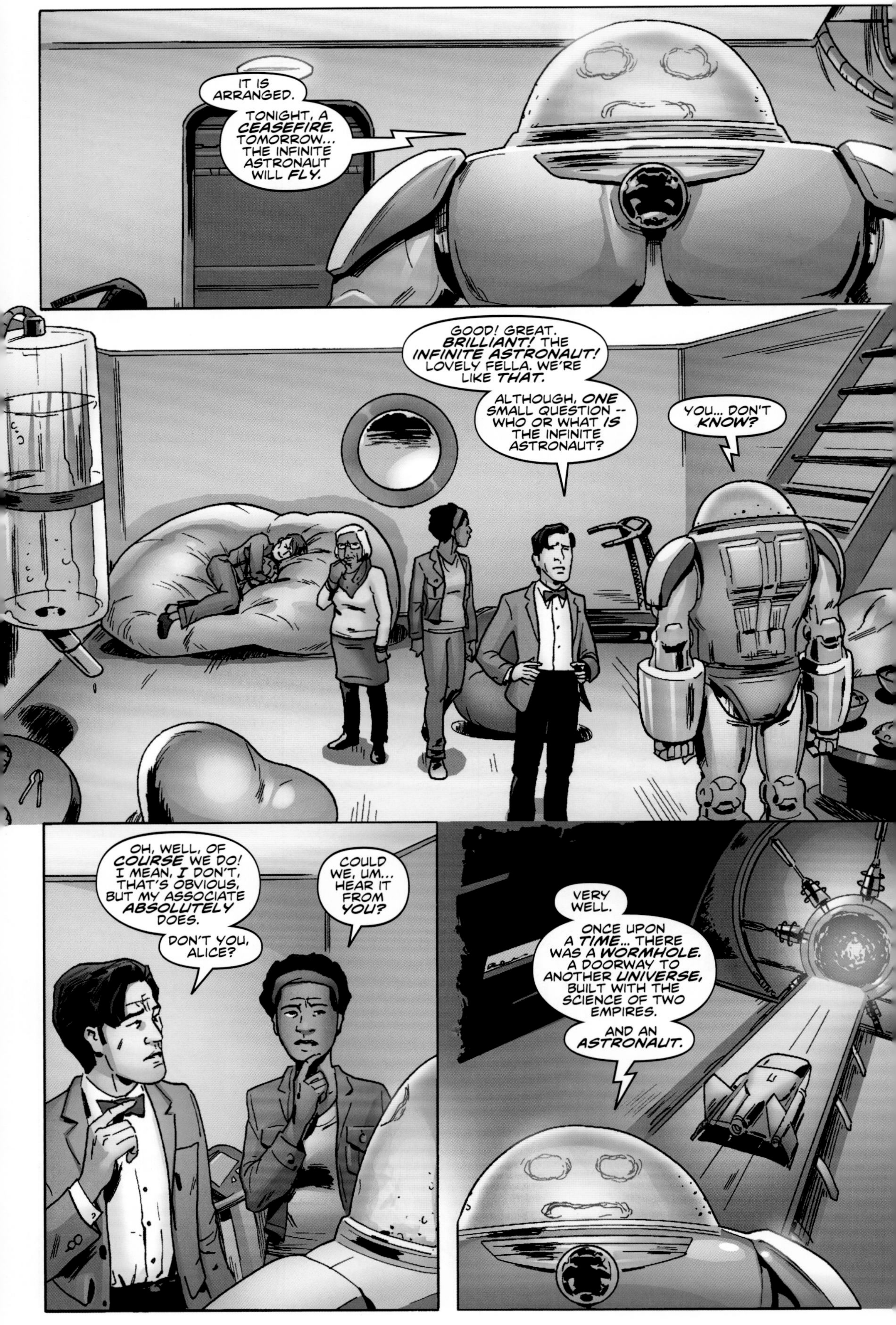
IT IS ARRANGED.
TONIGHT, A CEASEFIRE. TOMORROW... THE INFINITE ASTRONAUT WILL FLY.
GOOD! GREAT. BRILLIANT! THE INFINITE ASTRONAUT! LOVELY FELLA. WE'RE LIKE THAT.
ALTHOUGH, ONE SMALL QUESTION -- WHO OR WHAT IS THE INFINITE ASTRONAUT?
YOU... DON'T KNOW?
OH, WELL, OF COURSE WE DO! I MEAN, I DON'T, THAT'S OBVIOUS, BUT MY ASSOCIATE ABSOLUTELY DOES.
DON'T YOU, ALICE?
COULD WE, UM... HEAR IT FROM YOU?
VERY WELL.
ONCE UPON A TIME... THERE WAS A WORMHOLE. A DOORWAY TO ANOTHER UNIVERSE, BUILT WITH THE SCIENCE OF TWO EMPIRES.
AND AN ASTRONAUT.

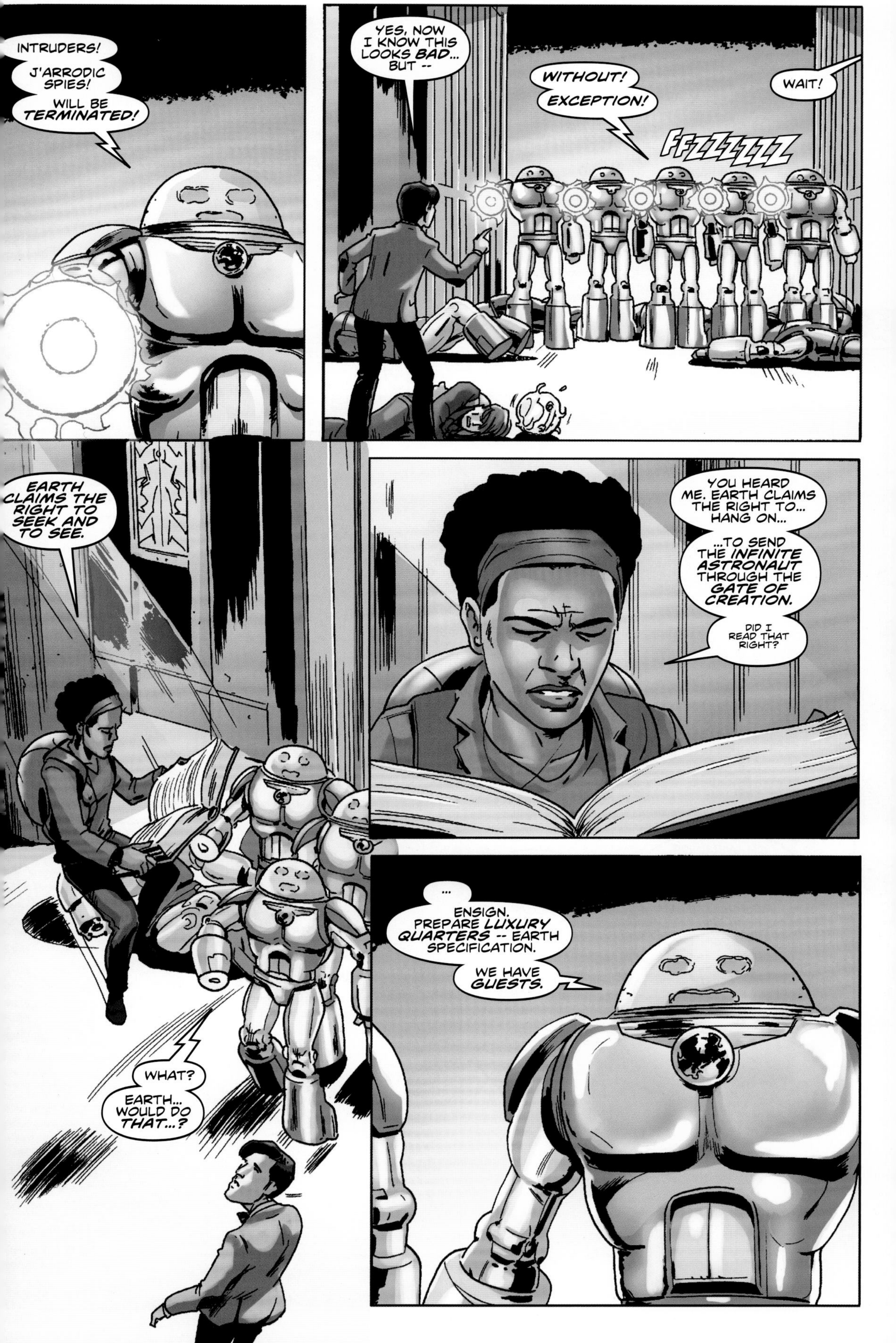
INTRUDERS!
J'ARRODIC SPIES!
WILL BE TERMINATED!
YES, NOW I KNOW THIS LOOKS BAD... BUT --
WITHOUT!
EXCEPTION!
WAIT!
FFZZZZZZZ
EARTH CLAIMS THE RIGHT TO SEEK AND TO SEE.
YOU HEARD ME. EARTH CLAIMS THE RIGHT TO... HANG ON...
...TO SEND THE INFINITE ASTRONAUT THROUGH THE GATE OF CREATION.
DID I READ THAT RIGHT?
WHAT?
EARTH... WOULD DO THAT...?
...
ENSIGN. PREPARE LUXURY QUARTERS -- EARTH SPECIFICATION.
WE HAVE GUESTS.

:: HURTS ::

:: FEAR ::

FEAR, IS IT? THAT WHAT CAME OVER YOU BEFORE? DOES TEND TO MAKE PEOPLE VIOLENT.

YOU SAID SOMETHING ABOUT...

:: FEAR! ::

:: HELP ARC, DOC-TORR! ::

:: HELP JONES! ::

WHEN IT'S GOOD... IT'S REALLY GOOD...

BUT WHEN IT'S BAD... I GO... I GO TO PIECES...

LIKE A... A P-P-PORTRAIT IN FLESH...

JONES, THE HUMAN CHAMELEON. HE'S MIRRORING YOUR FEAR, ARC? YOUR PAIN? AND YOU'RE FEELING HIS SICKNESS?

LIKE A FEEDBACK LOOP, EACH OF YOU REINFORCING THE OTHER --

DOCTOR?

NOT NOW, MRS OBIEFUNE --

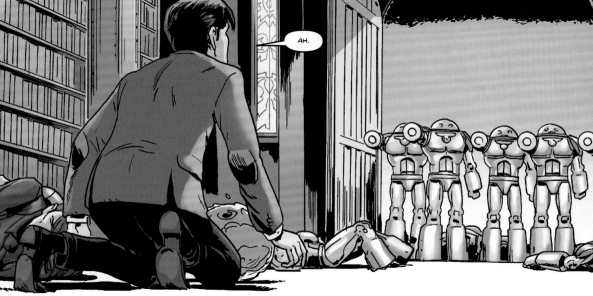

AH.

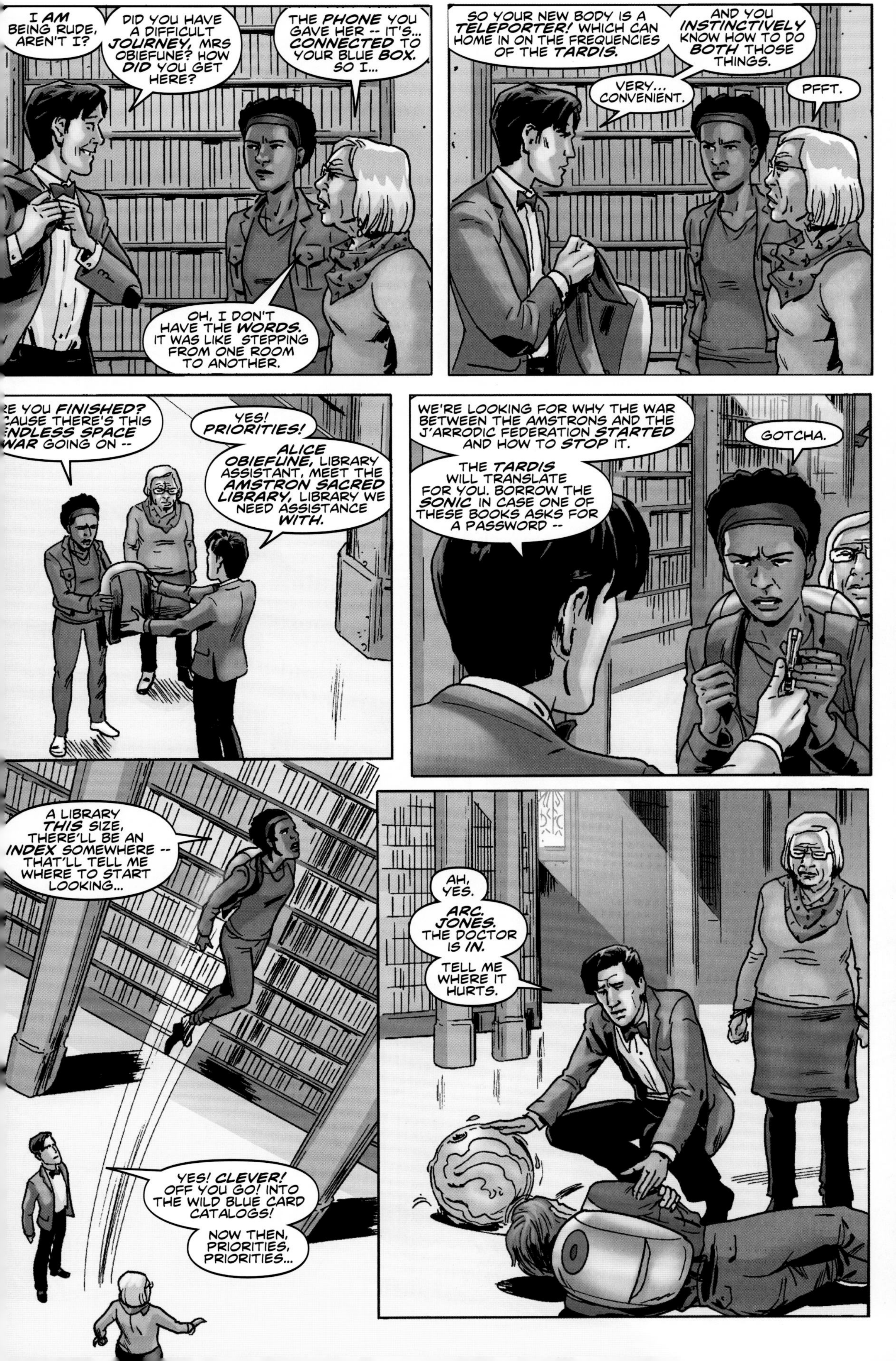
I AM BEING RUDE, AREN'T I?
DID YOU HAVE A DIFFICULT JOURNEY, MRS OBIEFUNE? HOW DID YOU GET HERE?
THE PHONE YOU GAVE HER -- IT'S... CONNECTED TO YOUR BLUE BOX. SO I...
OH, I DON'T HAVE THE WORDS. IT WAS LIKE STEPPING FROM ONE ROOM TO ANOTHER.
SO YOUR NEW BODY IS A TELEPORTER! WHICH CAN HOME IN ON THE FREQUENCIES OF THE TARDIS.
AND YOU INSTINCTIVELY KNOW HOW TO DO BOTH THOSE THINGS.
VERY... CONVENIENT.
PFFT.
RE YOU FINISHED? CAUSE THERE'S THIS NDLESS SPACE WAR GOING ON --
YES! PRIORITIES!
ALICE OBIEFUNE, LIBRARY ASSISTANT, MEET THE AMSTRON SACRED LIBRARY, LIBRARY WE NEED ASSISTANCE WITH.
WE'RE LOOKING FOR WHY THE WAR BETWEEN THE AMSTRONS AND THE J'ARRODIC FEDERATION STARTED AND HOW TO STOP IT.
THE TARDIS WILL TRANSLATE FOR YOU. BORROW THE SONIC IN CASE ONE OF THESE BOOKS ASKS FOR A PASSWORD --
GOTCHA.
A LIBRARY THIS SIZE, THERE'LL BE AN INDEX SOMEWHERE -- THAT'LL TELL ME WHERE TO START LOOKING...
YES! CLEVER! OFF YOU GO! INTO THE WILD BLUE CARD CATALOGS!
NOW THEN, PRIORITIES, PRIORITIES...
AH, YES.
ARC. JONES. THE DOCTOR IS IN.
TELL ME WHERE IT HURTS.

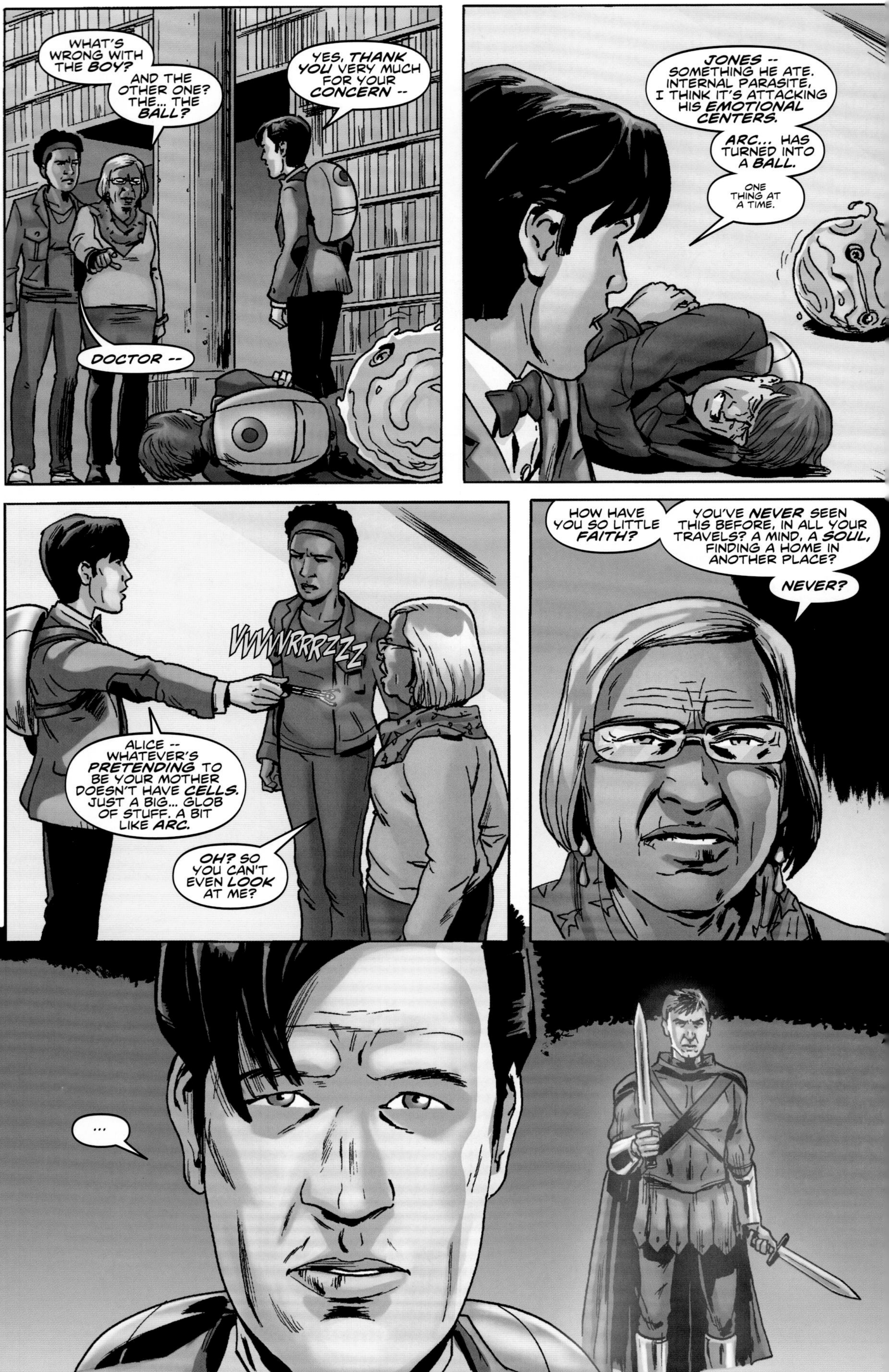
WHAT'S WRONG WITH THE BOY?
AND THE OTHER ONE? THE... THE BALL?
YES, THANK YOU VERY MUCH FOR YOUR CONCERN --
DOCTOR --
JONES -- SOMETHING HE ATE. INTERNAL PARASITE, I THINK IT'S ATTACKING HIS EMOTIONAL CENTERS.
ARC... HAS TURNED INTO A BALL.
ONE THING AT A TIME.
VVVVRRRZZZ
ALICE -- WHATEVER'S PRETENDING TO BE YOUR MOTHER DOESN'T HAVE CELLS. JUST A BIG... GLOB OF STUFF. A BIT LIKE ARC.
OH? SO YOU CAN'T EVEN LOOK AT ME?
HOW HAVE YOU SO LITTLE FAITH?
YOU'VE NEVER SEEN THIS BEFORE, IN ALL YOUR TRAVELS? A MIND, A SOUL, FINDING A HOME IN ANOTHER PLACE?
NEVER?
...

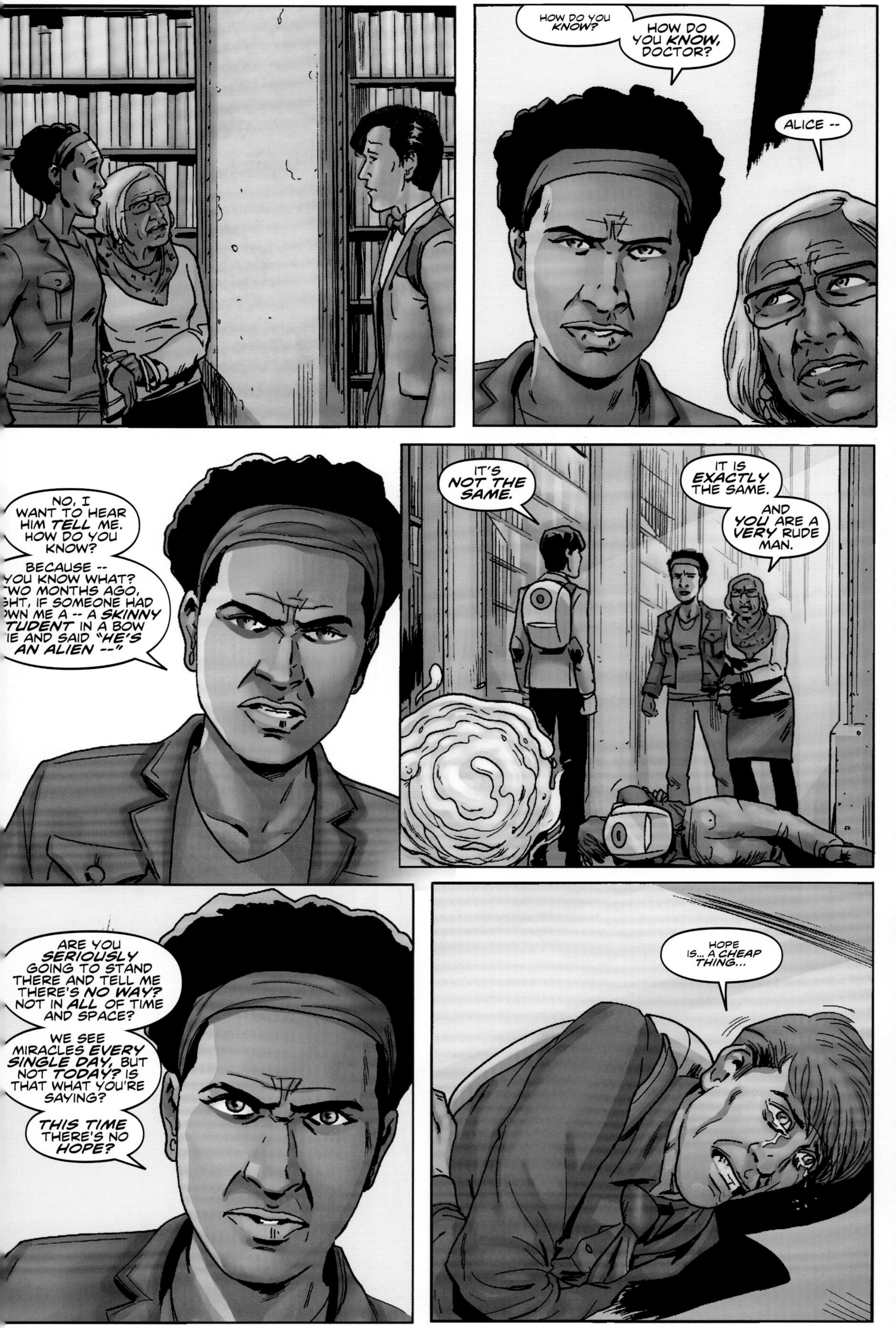

HOW DO YOU KNOW?
HOW DO YOU KNOW, DOCTOR?
ALICE --
NO, I WANT TO HEAR HIM TELL ME. HOW DO YOU KNOW?
BECAUSE -- YOU KNOW WHAT? TWO MONTHS AGO, GHT, IF SOMEONE HAD OWN ME A -- A SKINNY TUDENT IN A BOW TIE AND SAID "HE'S AN ALIEN --"
IT'S NOT THE SAME.
IT IS EXACTLY THE SAME.
AND YOU ARE A VERY RUDE MAN.
ARE YOU SERIOUSLY GOING TO STAND THERE AND TELL ME THERE'S NO WAY? NOT IN ALL OF TIME AND SPACE?
WE SEE MIRACLES EVERY SINGLE DAY, BUT NOT TODAY? IS THAT WHAT YOU'RE SAYING?
THIS TIME THERE'S NO HOPE?
HOPE IS... A CHEAP THING...

CHAPTER 8

THE INFINITE ASTRONAUT

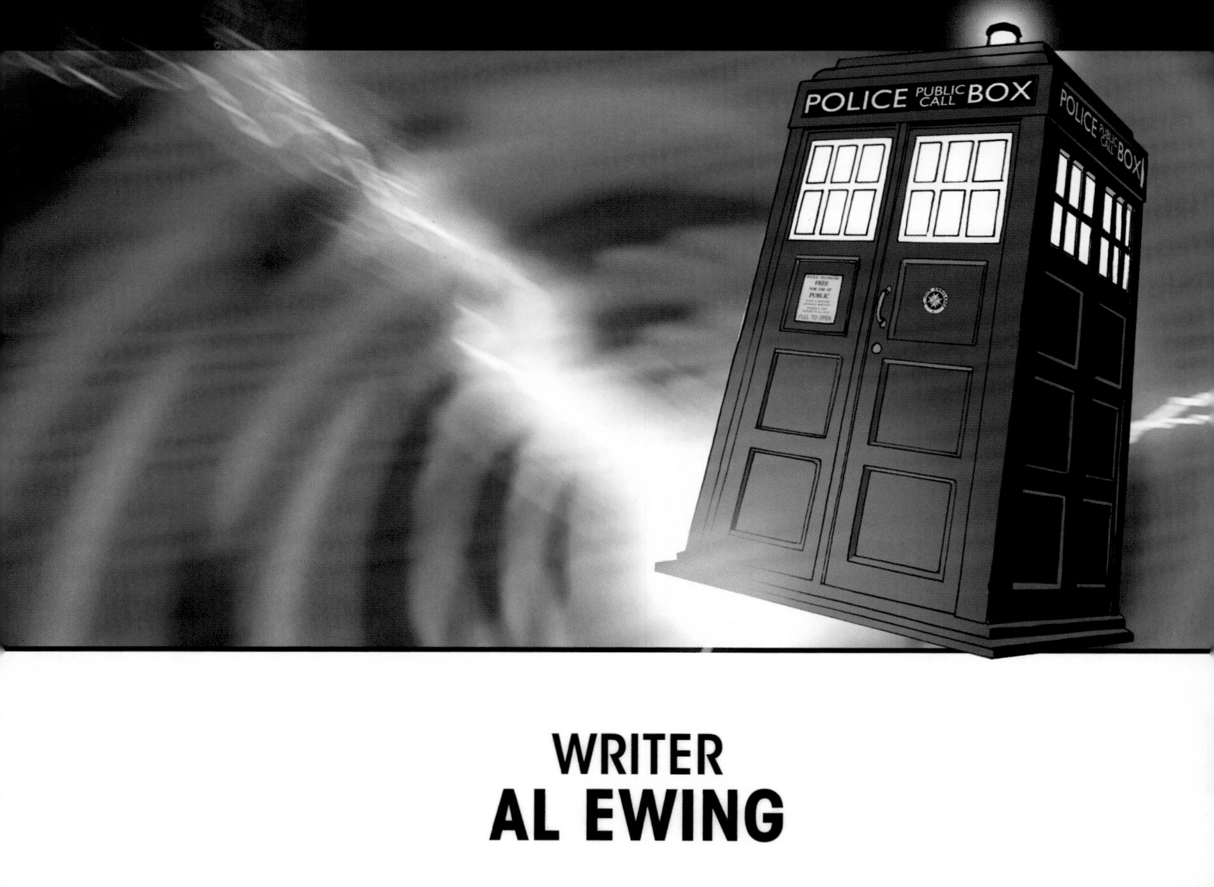
POLICE PUBLIC CALL BOX
POLICE PUBLIC CALL BOX

WRITER
AL EWING

ARTIST
WARREN PLEECE

COLORIST
HI-FI

LETTERER
RICHARD STARKINGS AND COMICRAFT'S JIMMY BETANCOURT

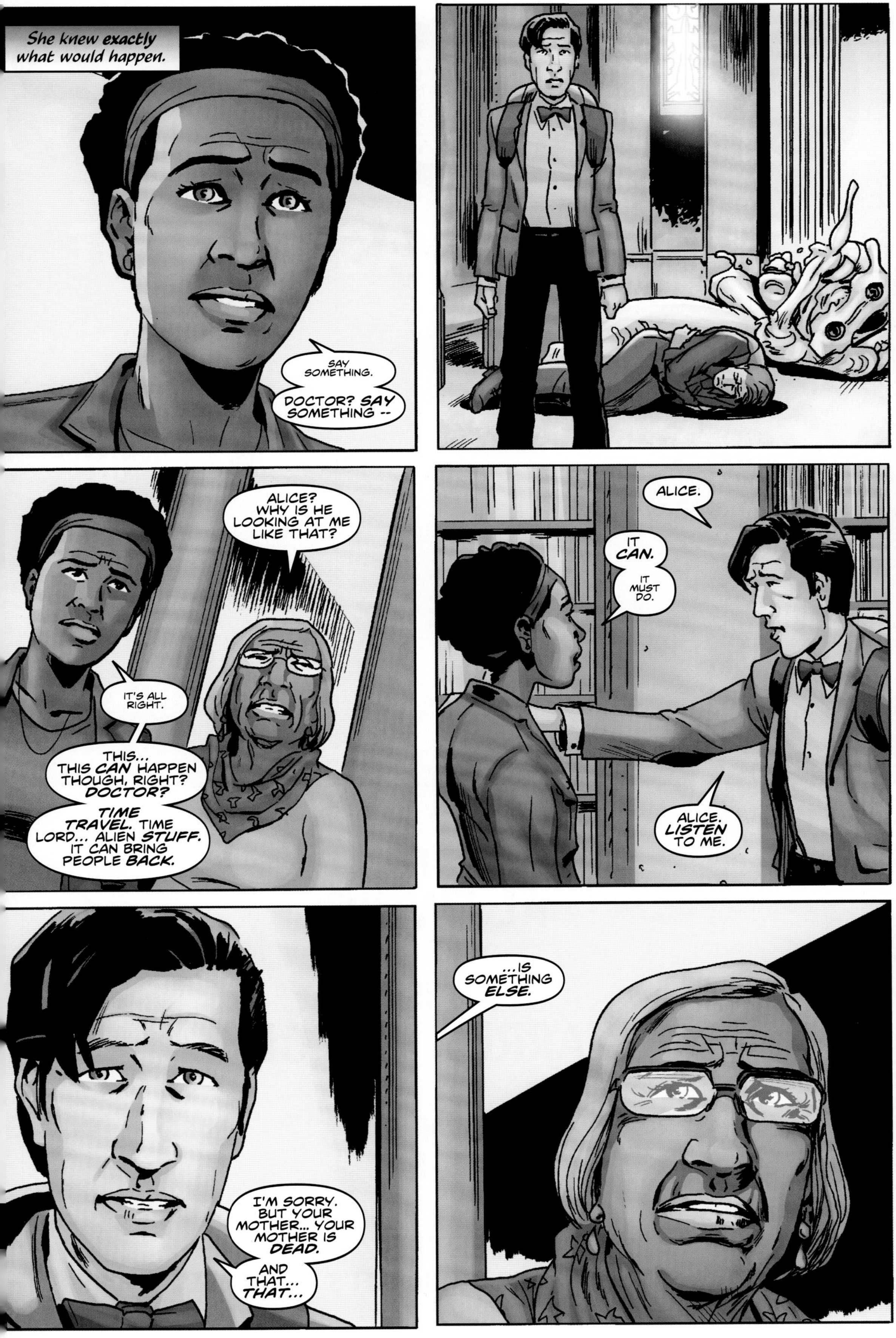
She knew exactly what would happen.
SAY SOMETHING.
DOCTOR? SAY SOMETHING --
ALICE? WHY IS HE LOOKING AT ME LIKE THAT?
IT'S ALL RIGHT.
THIS... THIS CAN HAPPEN THOUGH, RIGHT? DOCTOR?
TIME TRAVEL. TIME LORD... ALIEN STUFF. IT CAN BRING PEOPLE BACK.
ALICE.
IT CAN.
IT MUST DO.
ALICE. LISTEN TO ME.
I'M SORRY. BUT YOUR MOTHER... YOUR MOTHER IS DEAD.
AND THAT... THAT...
...IS SOMETHING ELSE.

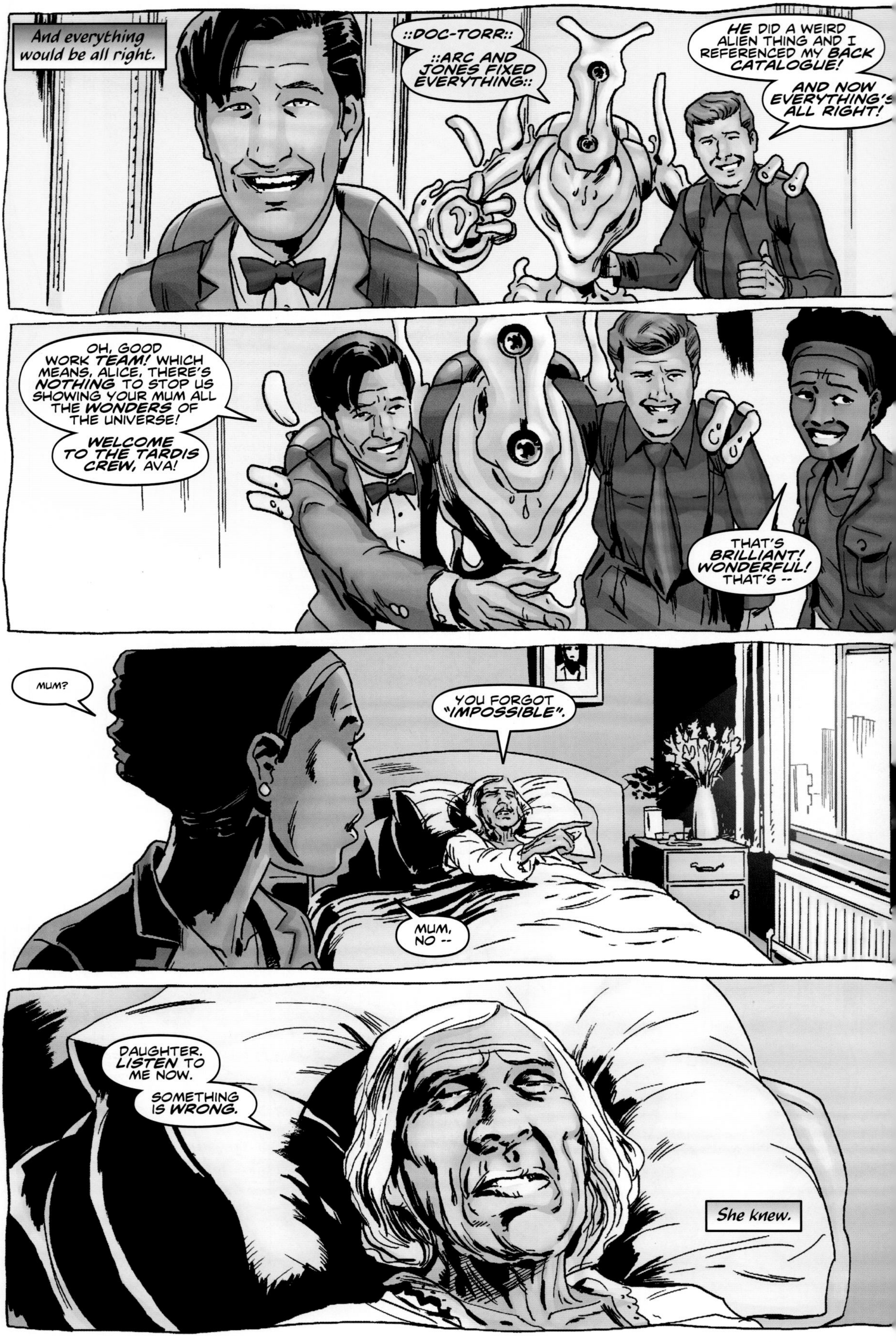
And everything would be all right.
::DOC-TORR::
::ARC AND JONES FIXED EVERYTHING::
HE DID A WEIRD ALIEN THING AND I REFERENCED MY BACK CATALOGUE!
AND NOW EVERYTHING'S ALL RIGHT!
OH, GOOD WORK TEAM! WHICH MEANS, ALICE, THERE'S NOTHING TO STOP US SHOWING YOUR MUM ALL THE WONDERS OF THE UNIVERSE!
WELCOME TO THE TARDIS CREW, AVA!
THAT'S BRILLIANT! WONDERFUL! THAT'S --
MUM?
YOU FORGOT "IMPOSSIBLE".
MUM, NO --
DAUGHTER. LISTEN TO ME NOW.
SOMETHING IS WRONG.
She knew.

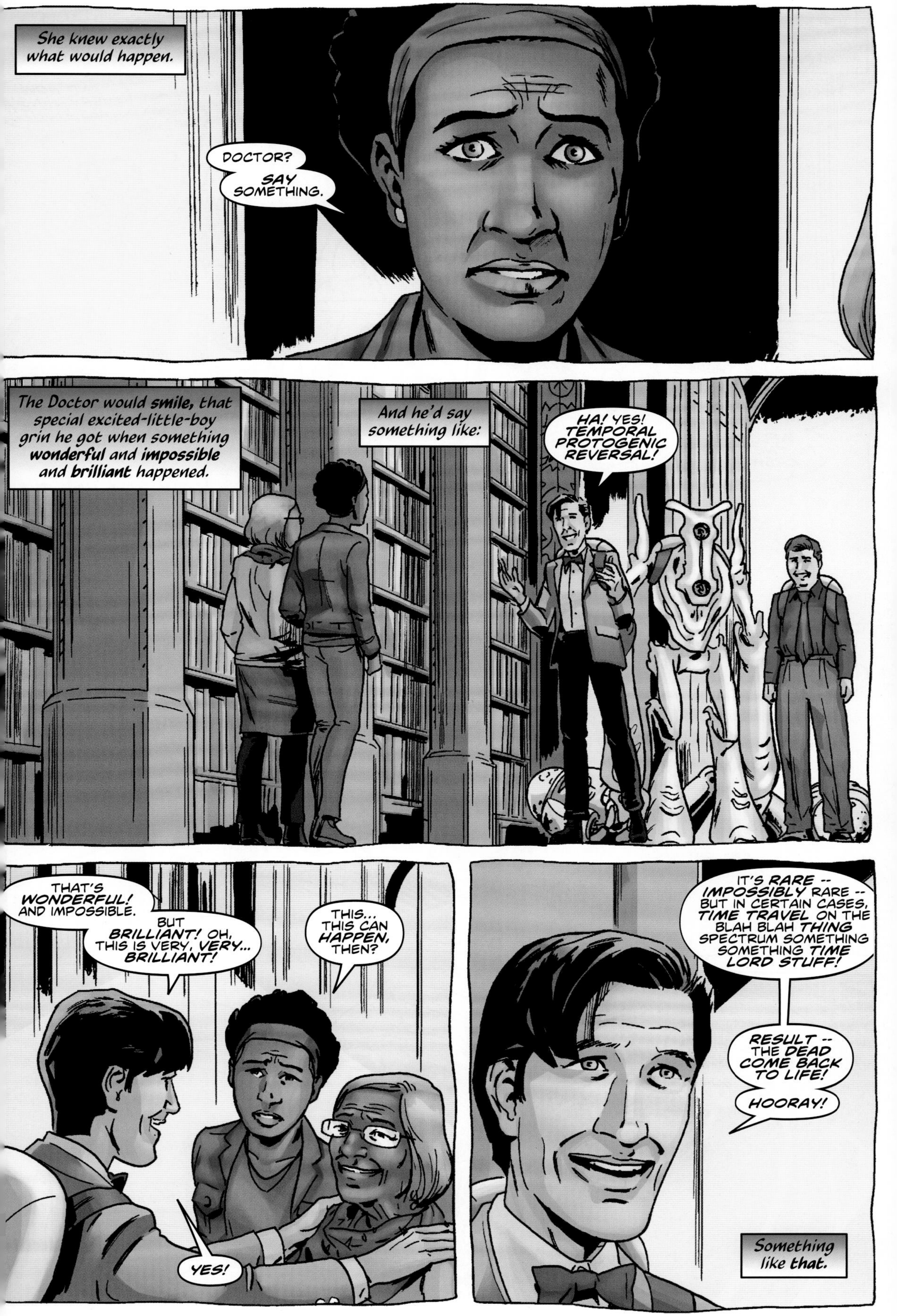
She knew exactly what would happen.
DOCTOR? SAY SOMETHING.
The Doctor would smile, that special excited-little-boy grin he got when something wonderful and impossible and brilliant happened.
And he'd say something like:
HA! YES! TEMPORAL PROTOGENIC REVERSAL!
THAT'S WONDERFUL! AND IMPOSSIBLE.
BUT BRILLIANT! OH, THIS IS VERY, VERY... BRILLIANT!
THIS... THIS CAN HAPPEN, THEN?
YES!
IT'S RARE -- IMPOSSIBLY RARE -- BUT IN CERTAIN CASES, TIME TRAVEL ON THE BLAH BLAH THING SPECTRUM SOMETHING SOMETHING TIME LORD STUFF!
RESULT -- THE DEAD COME BACK TO LIFE!
HOORAY!
Something like that.

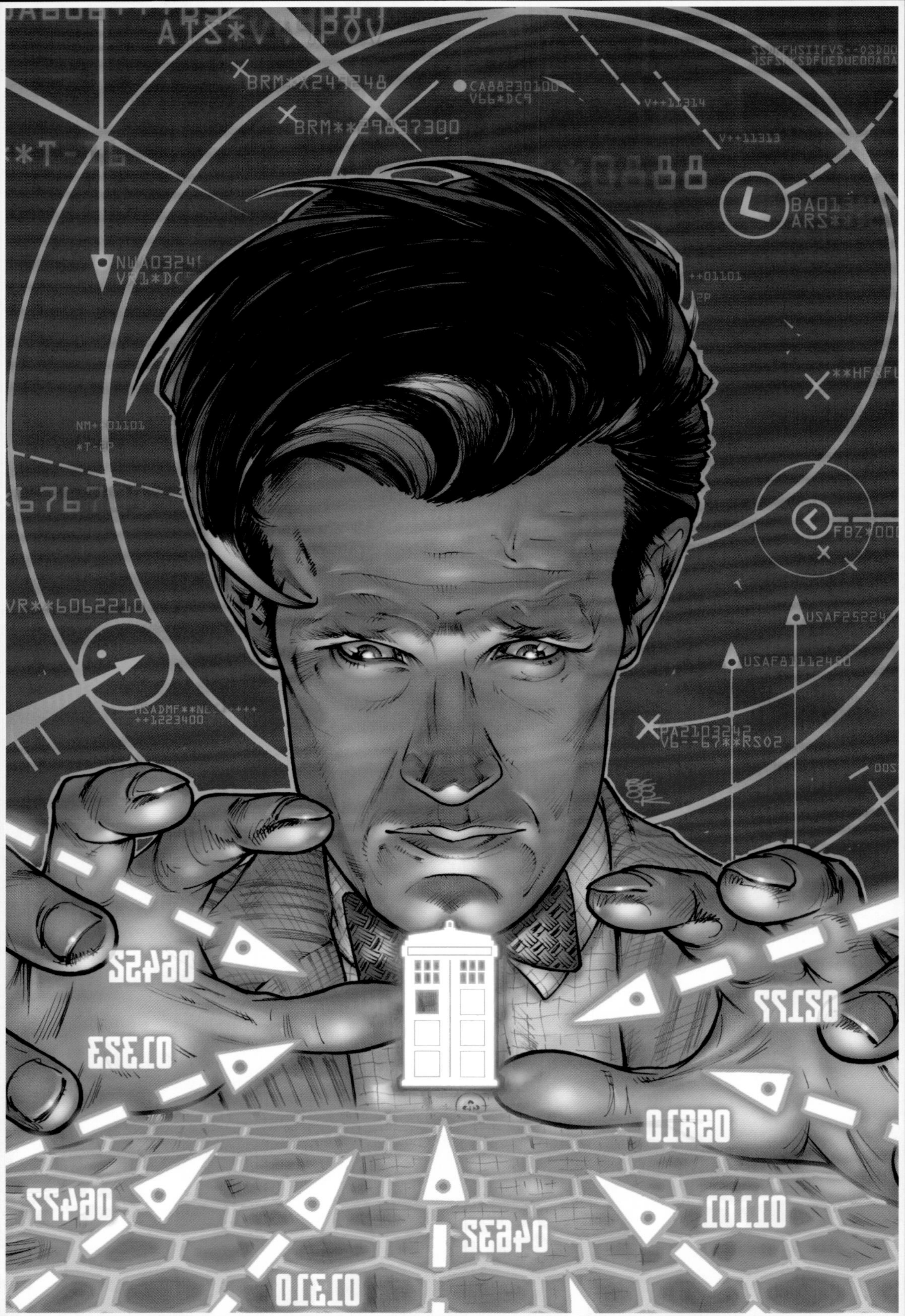

CHAPTER 8 Cover A: Boo Cook

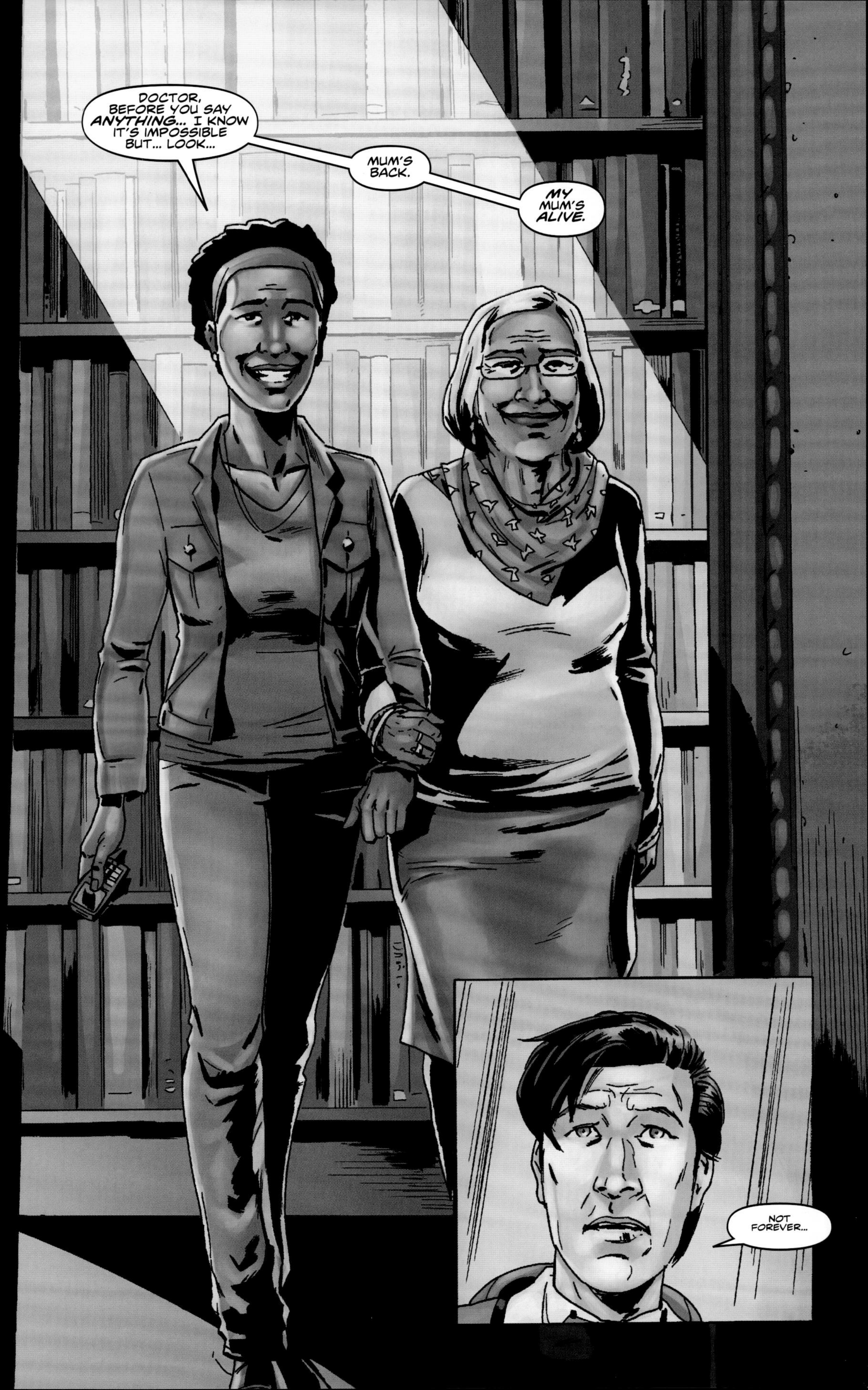
DOCTOR, BEFORE YOU SAY ANYTHING... I KNOW IT'S IMPOSSIBLE BUT... LOOK...
MUM'S BACK.
MY MUM'S ALIVE.
NOT FOREVER...

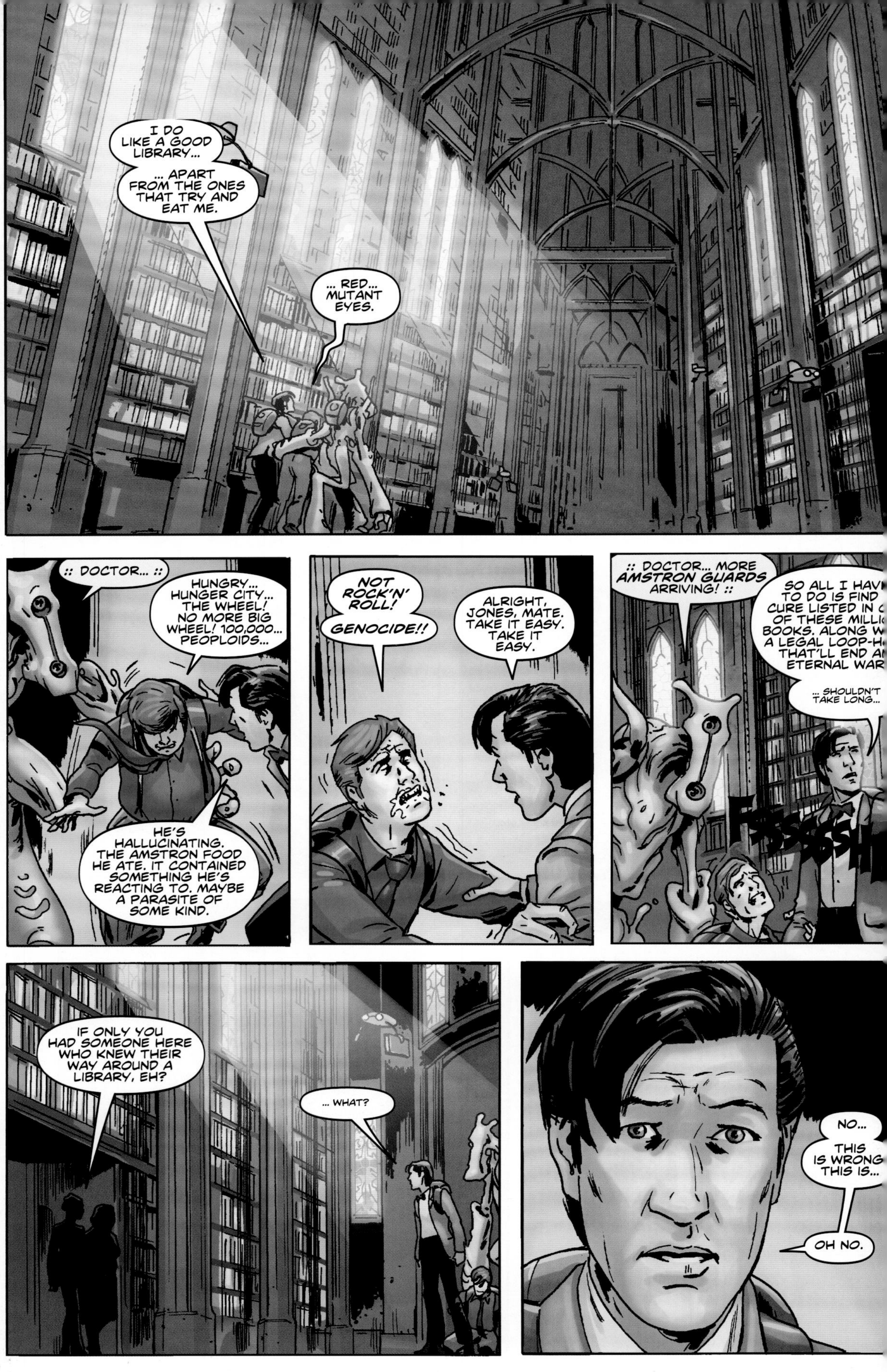
I DO LIKE A GOOD LIBRARY...
... APART FROM THE ONES THAT TRY AND EAT ME.
... RED... MUTANT EYES.
:: DOCTOR... ::
HUNGRY... HUNGER CITY... THE WHEEL! NO MORE BIG WHEEL! 100,000... PEOPLOIDS...
HE'S HALLUCINATING. THE AMSTRON FOOD HE ATE. IT CONTAINED SOMETHING HE'S REACTING TO. MAYBE A PARASITE OF SOME KIND.
NOT ROCK'N' ROLL!
GENOCIDE!!
ALRIGHT, JONES, MATE. TAKE IT EASY. TAKE IT EASY.
:: DOCTOR... MORE AMSTRON GUARDS ARRIVING! ::
SO ALL I HAV
TO DO IS FIND
CURE LISTED IN
OF THESE MILLI
BOOKS. ALONG W
A LEGAL LOOP-H
THAT'LL END A
ETERNAL WAR
... SHOULDN'T TAKE LONG...
IF ONLY YOU HAD SOMEONE HERE WHO KNEW THEIR WAY AROUND A LIBRARY, EH?
... WHAT?
NO...
THIS IS WRONG
THIS IS...
OH NO.

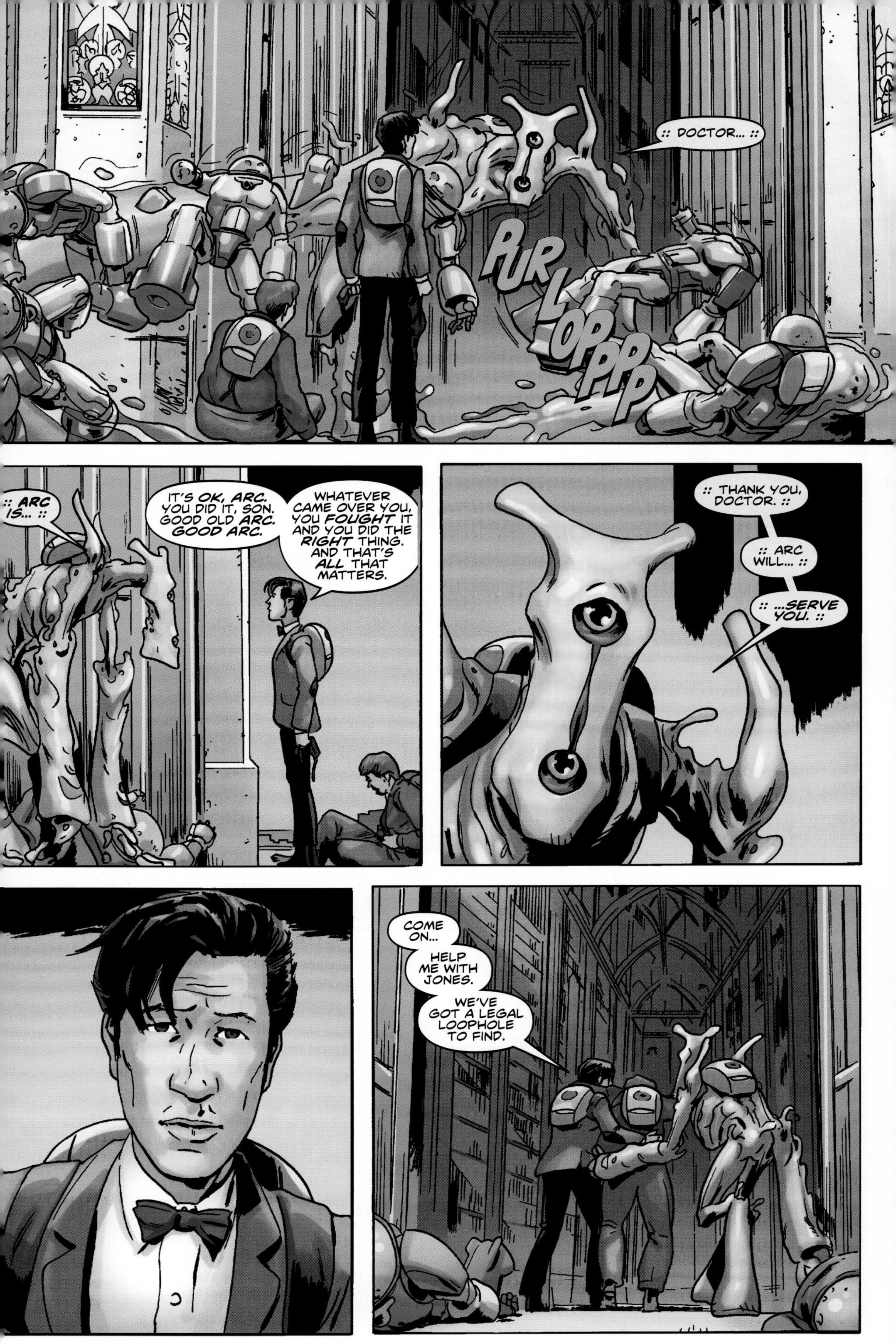
:: DOCTOR... ::
PURLOPPPP
:: ARC IS... ::
IT'S OK, ARC. YOU DID IT, SON. GOOD OLD ARC. GOOD ARC.
WHATEVER CAME OVER YOU, YOU FOUGHT IT AND YOU DID THE RIGHT THING. AND THAT'S ALL THAT MATTERS.
:: THANK YOU, DOCTOR. ::
:: ARC WILL... ::
:: ...SERVE YOU. ::
COME ON...
HELP ME WITH JONES.
WE'VE GOT A LEGAL LOOPHOLE TO FIND.

HE'S... NNNN... GROWING.

YES.. HIM AND YOU BOTH. I'M IMPOSING A TIGHT *TARDIS*-WIDE EXERCISE SCHEME FIRST THING TOMORROW.

IF WE SURVIVE...

:: ...WANT... ::

YOU KNOW WHAT, *ARC*?

RIGHT NOW I DON'T CARE WHAT YOU WANT.

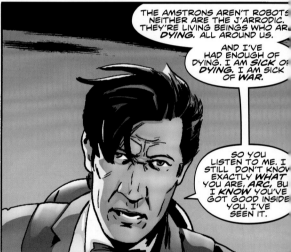

THE AMSTRONS AREN'T ROBOTS NEITHER ARE THE J'ARRODIC. THEY'RE LIVING BEINGS WHO AR*E* *DYING*. ALL AROUND US.

AND I'VE HAD ENOUGH OF DYING. I AM *SICK* O*F* *DYING*. I AM SICK OF *WAR*.

SO YOU LISTEN TO ME. I STILL DON'T KNOW EXACTLY *WHAT* YOU ARE, *ARC*, BUT I *KNOW* YOU'VE GOT GOOD INSIDE YOU. I'VE SEEN IT.

SO YOU SPIT OUT THE LIVING BEINGS INSIDE YOU *RIGHT NOW*.

:: HE... ::

:: ... IS COMING... ::

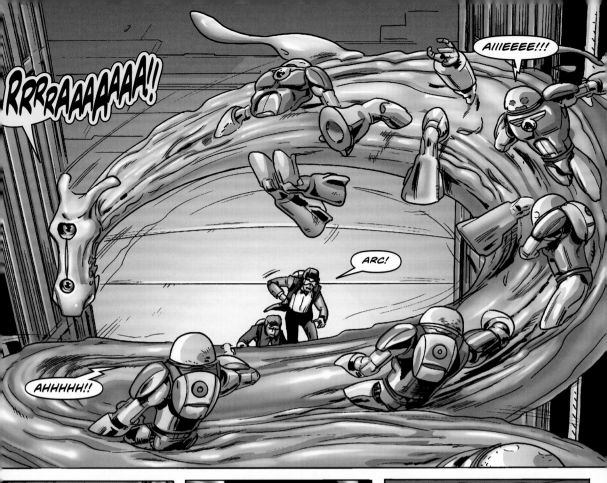

RRRRAAAAAAA!!

AIIIIEEEE!!!

ARC!

AHHHHH!!

NICELY DONE! THANKS FOR THE SAVE! MUCH APPRECIATED! YOU CAN KEEP THEIR GUNS BUT SPIT THEM OUT, EH?

COME ON. LET'S GET 'ONES INTO THE LAW MUSEUM AND...

DID YOU HEAR WHAT I SAID, ARC?

SPIT.

THEM.

OUT.

... ON THE BUS GOES ROUND AND ROUND. YES, YES. WE KNOW.

NOW. WE'RE THE AMSTRON LAW MUSEUM INSPECTORS. AND THIS IS A *FLASH* LAW MUSEUM INSPECTION. OHHH YES. UNEXPECTED!

THAT'S HOW WE ROLL IN THE AMSTRON LAW MUSEUM INSPECTION UNIT. *MAVERICKS!* OPEN UP AND LET'S HAVE A SHUFTY, EH?

J'ARRODIC WAR SPIES! THIS IS SACRED GROUND!

YOU WILL ALL BE GNAWED BENEATH THE WHEEL!

THE WHEEL...

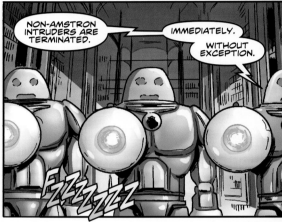

NON-AMSTRON INTRUDERS ARE TERMINATED.

IMMEDIATELY.

WITHOUT EXCEPTION.

ZZZZZZZ

AH...

FIRE!!

NNNNNN...

:: DOCTOR, PLEASE... ::

:: JONES HURTS. ::

COME ON, JONES! LET'S GET YOU INSIDE AND TAKE A LOOK AT YOU.

BEFORE WE ALL GETS BLOWN TO BITS.

ZZSSSHHHHKRAKKK

SOMETHING'S IN ME, DOCTOR. I CAN FEEL IT.

SOMETHING ALIEN.

I'M.... NNNNNNNNN... CHANGING.

ARC! GET THAT DOOR OPEN!

NOW!

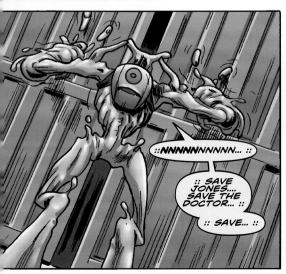

::NNNNNNNNNNN... ::

:: SAVE JONES.... SAVE THE DOCTOR... ::

:: SAVE... ::

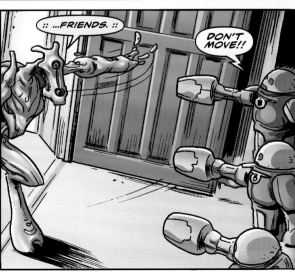

:: ...FRIENDS. ::

DON'T MOVE!!

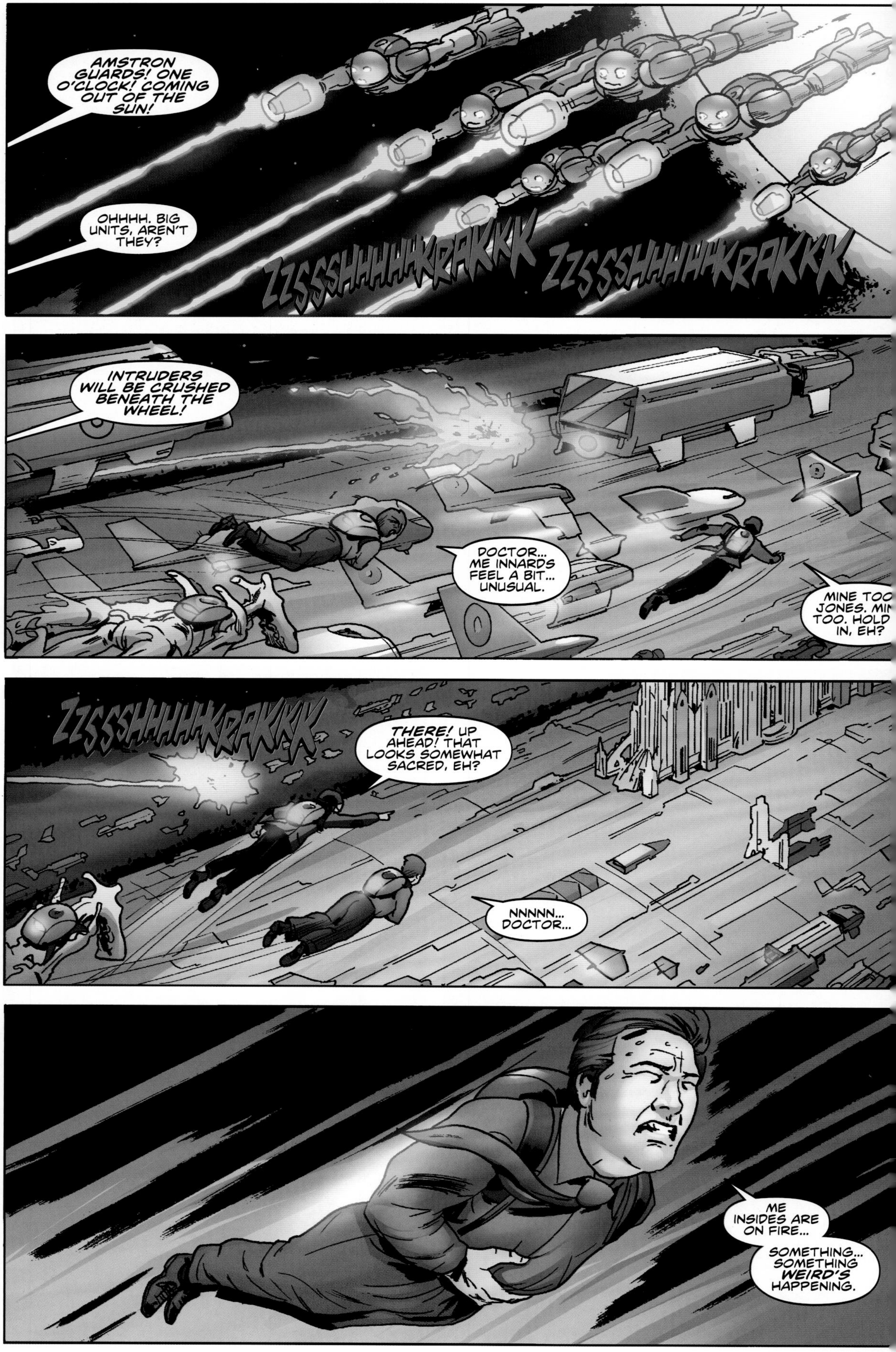

AMSTRON GUARDS! ONE O'CLOCK! COMING OUT OF THE SUN!
OHHHH. BIG UNITS, AREN'T THEY?
ZZSSSHHHHHKRAKKK
ZZSSSHHHHHKRAKKK
INTRUDERS WILL BE CRUSHED BENEATH THE WHEEL!
DOCTOR... ME INNARDS FEEL A BIT... UNUSUAL.
MINE TOO JONES. MIN TOO. HOLD IN, EH?
ZZSSSHHHHHKRAKKK
THERE! UP AHEAD! THAT LOOKS SOMEWHAT SACRED, EH?
NNNNN... DOCTOR...
ME INSIDES ARE ON FIRE...
SOMETHING... SOMETHING WEIRD'S HAPPENING.

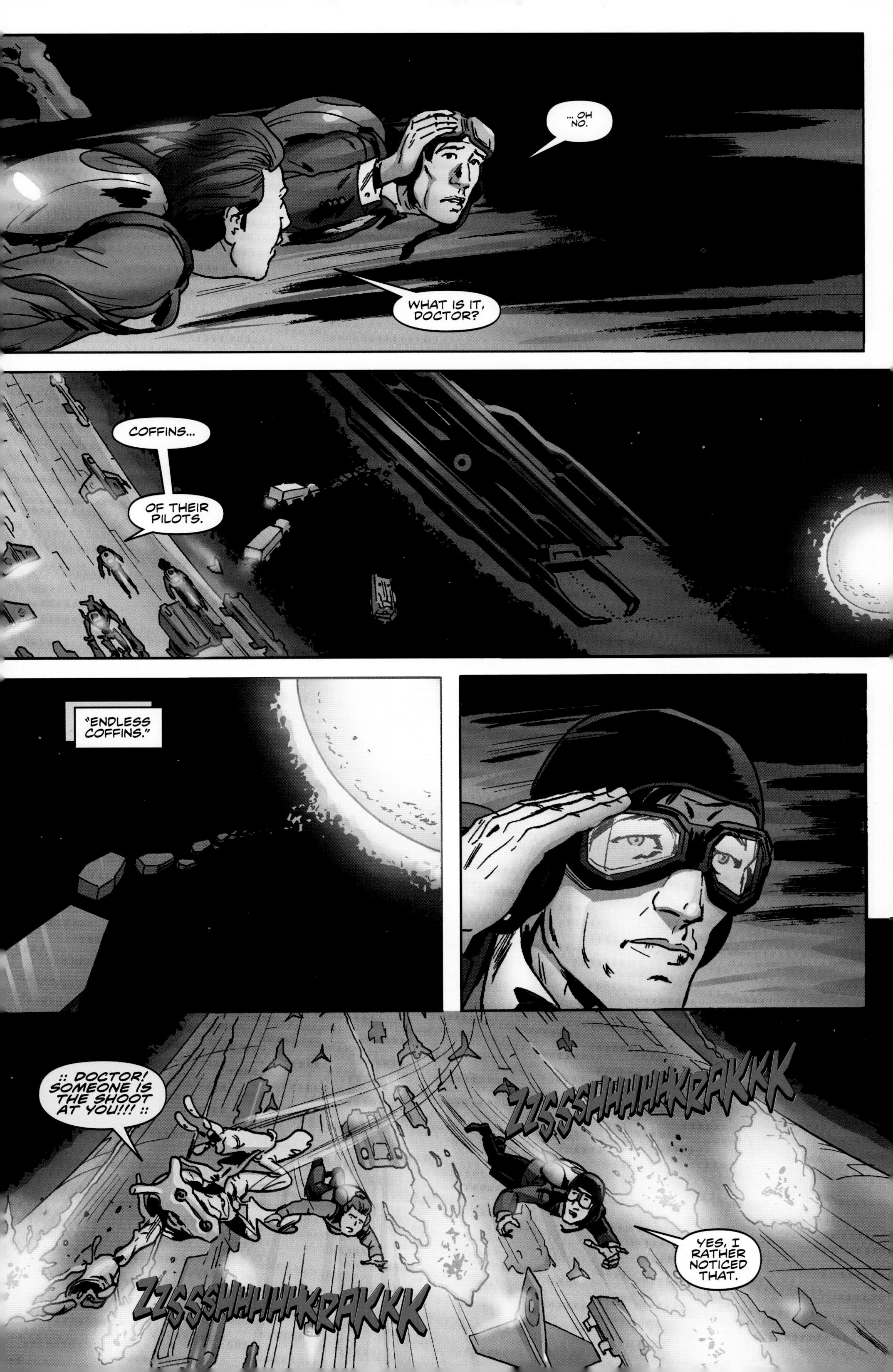
...OH NO.
WHAT IS IT, DOCTOR?
COFFINS...
OF THEIR PILOTS.
"ENDLESS COFFINS."
:: DOCTOR! SOMEONE IS THE SHOOT AT YOU!!! ::
ZZSSSHHHHHKRAKKK
ZZSSSHHHHHKRAKKK
YES, I RATHER NOTICED THAT.

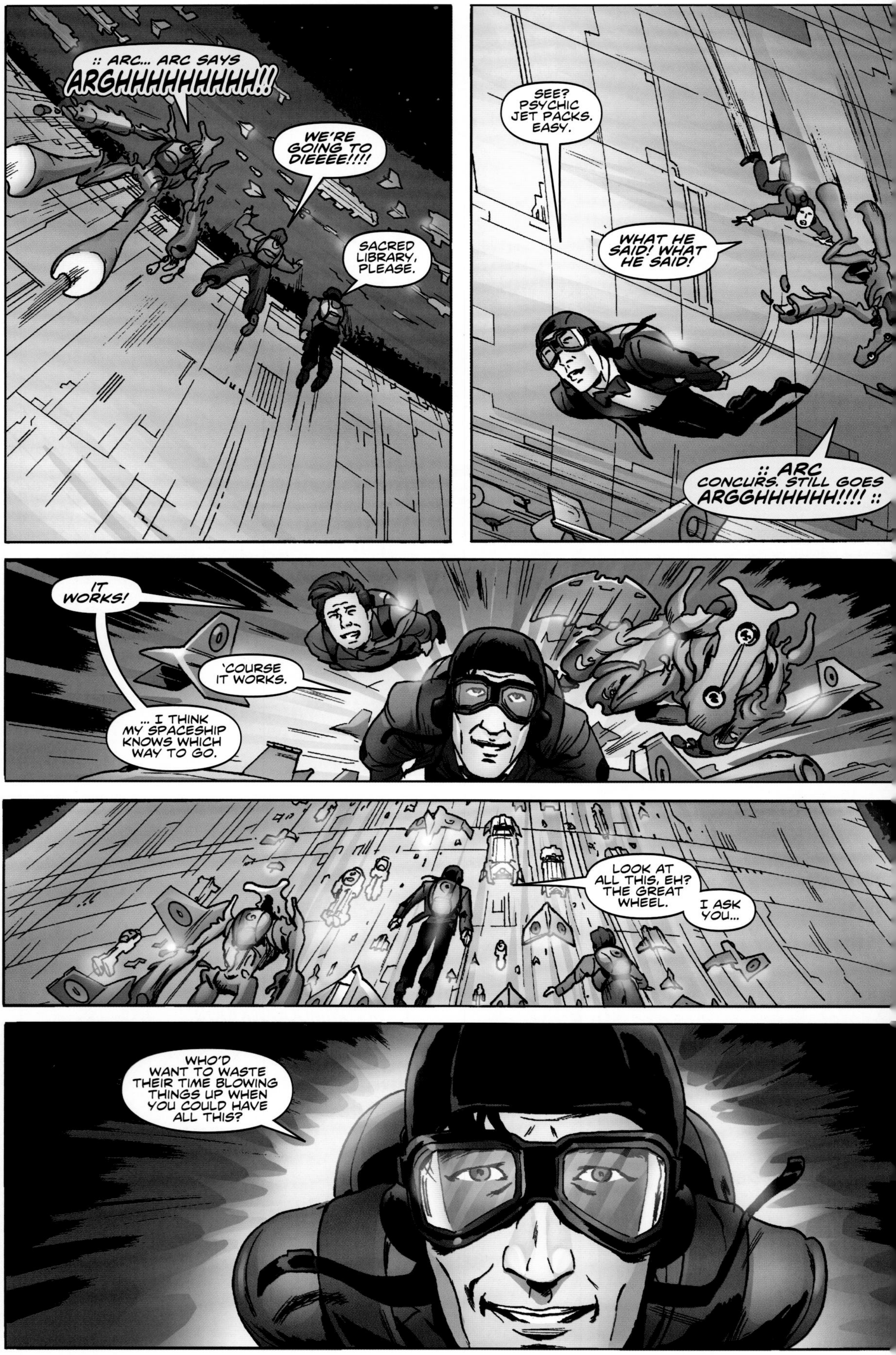
:: ARC... ARC SAYS
ARGHHHHHHHHH!!
WE'RE GOING TO DIEEEE!!!!
SACRED LIBRARY, PLEASE.
SEE? PSYCHIC JET PACKS. EASY.
WHAT HE SAID! WHAT HE SAID!
:: ARC CONCURS. STILL GOES ARGGHHHHHH!!!! ::
IT WORKS!
'COURSE IT WORKS.
... I THINK MY SPACESHIP KNOWS WHICH WAY TO GO.
LOOK AT ALL THIS, EH? THE GREAT WHEEL.
I ASK YOU...
WHO'D WANT TO WASTE THEIR TIME BLOWING THINGS UP WHEN YOU COULD HAVE ALL THIS?

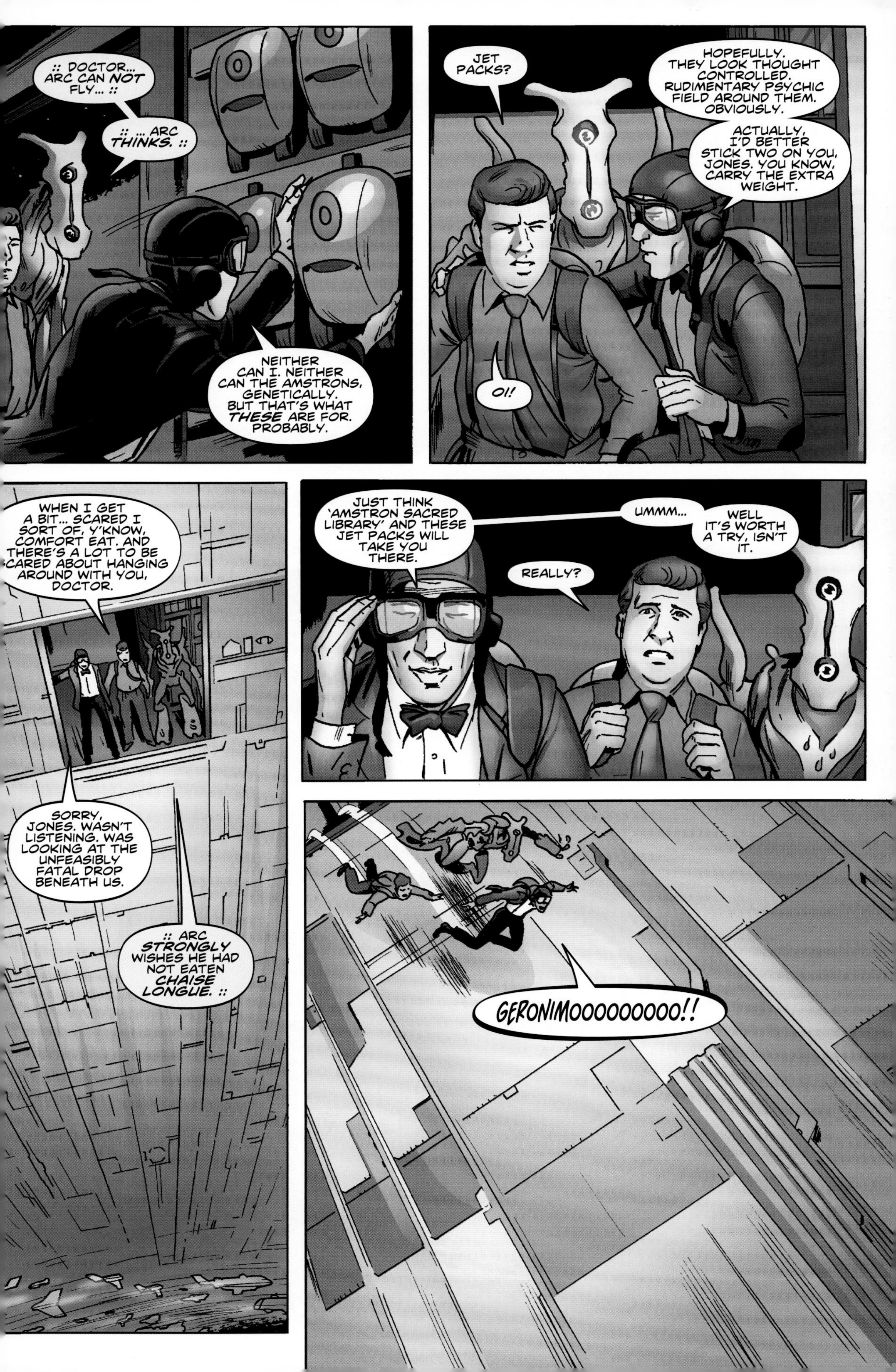
:: DOCTOR... ARC CAN NOT FLY... ::
:: ... ARC THINKS. ::
NEITHER CAN I. NEITHER CAN THE AMSTRONS, GENETICALLY. BUT THAT'S WHAT THESE ARE FOR. PROBABLY.
JET PACKS?
HOPEFULLY. THEY LOOK THOUGHT CONTROLLED. RUDIMENTARY PSYCHIC FIELD AROUND THEM. OBVIOUSLY.
ACTUALLY, I'D BETTER STICK TWO ON YOU, JONES. YOU KNOW, CARRY THE EXTRA WEIGHT.
OI!
WHEN I GET A BIT... SCARED I SORT OF, Y'KNOW, COMFORT EAT. AND THERE'S A LOT TO BE SCARED ABOUT HANGING AROUND WITH YOU, DOCTOR.
SORRY, JONES. WASN'T LISTENING. WAS LOOKING AT THE UNFEASIBLY FATAL DROP BENEATH US.
:: ARC STRONGLY WISHES HE HAD NOT EATEN CHAISE LONGUE. ::
JUST THINK 'AMSTRON SACRED LIBRARY' AND THESE JET PACKS WILL TAKE YOU THERE.
UMMM...
REALLY?
WELL IT'S WORTH A TRY, ISN'T IT.
GERONIMOOOOOOOOO!!

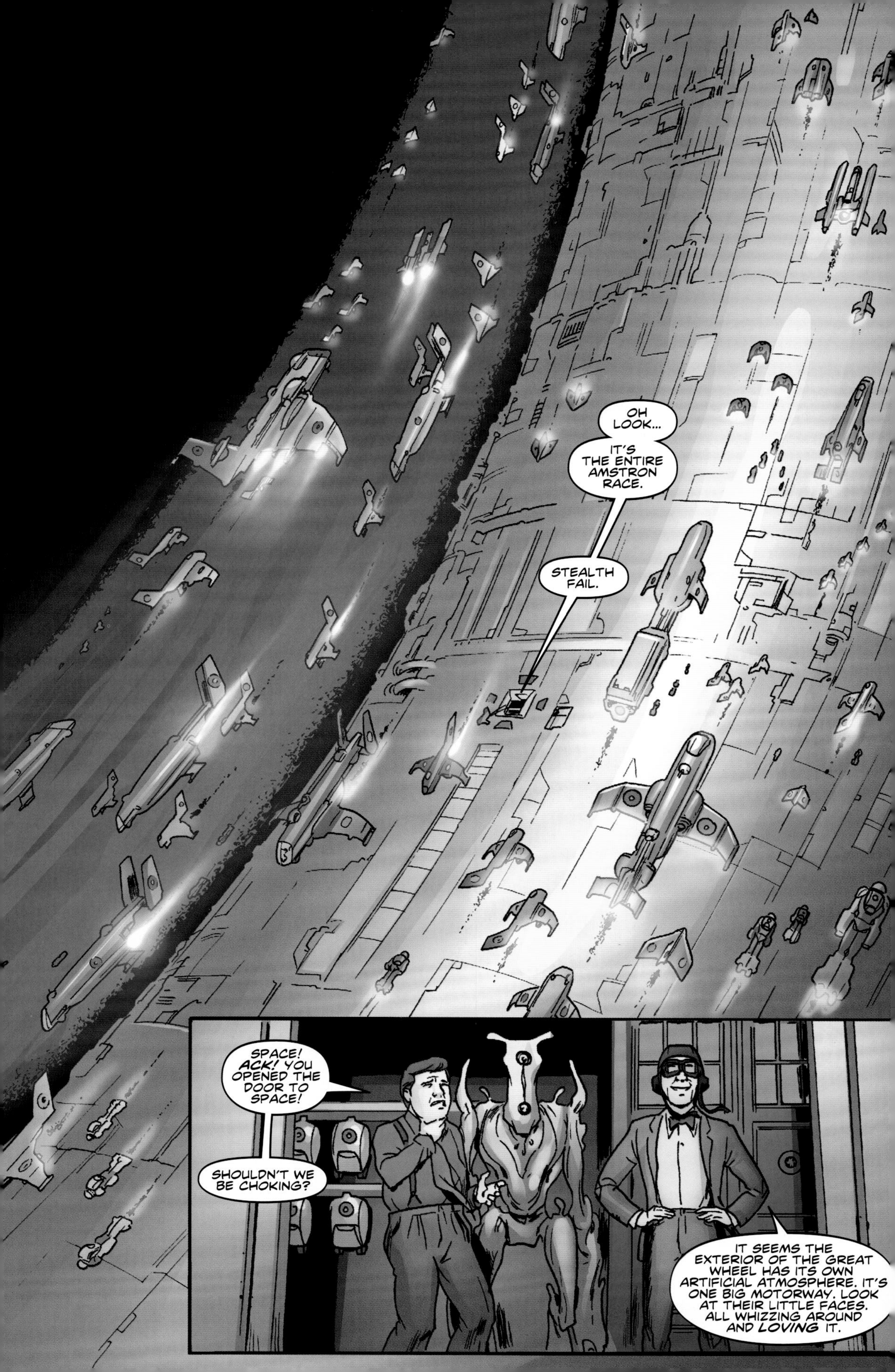
OH LOOK...
IT'S THE ENTIRE AMSTRON RACE.
STEALTH FAIL.
SPACE! ACK! YOU OPENED THE DOOR TO SPACE!
SHOULDN'T WE BE CHOKING?
IT SEEMS THE EXTERIOR OF THE GREAT WHEEL HAS ITS OWN ARTIFICIAL ATMOSPHERE. IT'S ONE BIG MOTORWAY. LOOK AT THEIR LITTLE FACES. ALL WHIZZING AROUND AND LOVING IT.

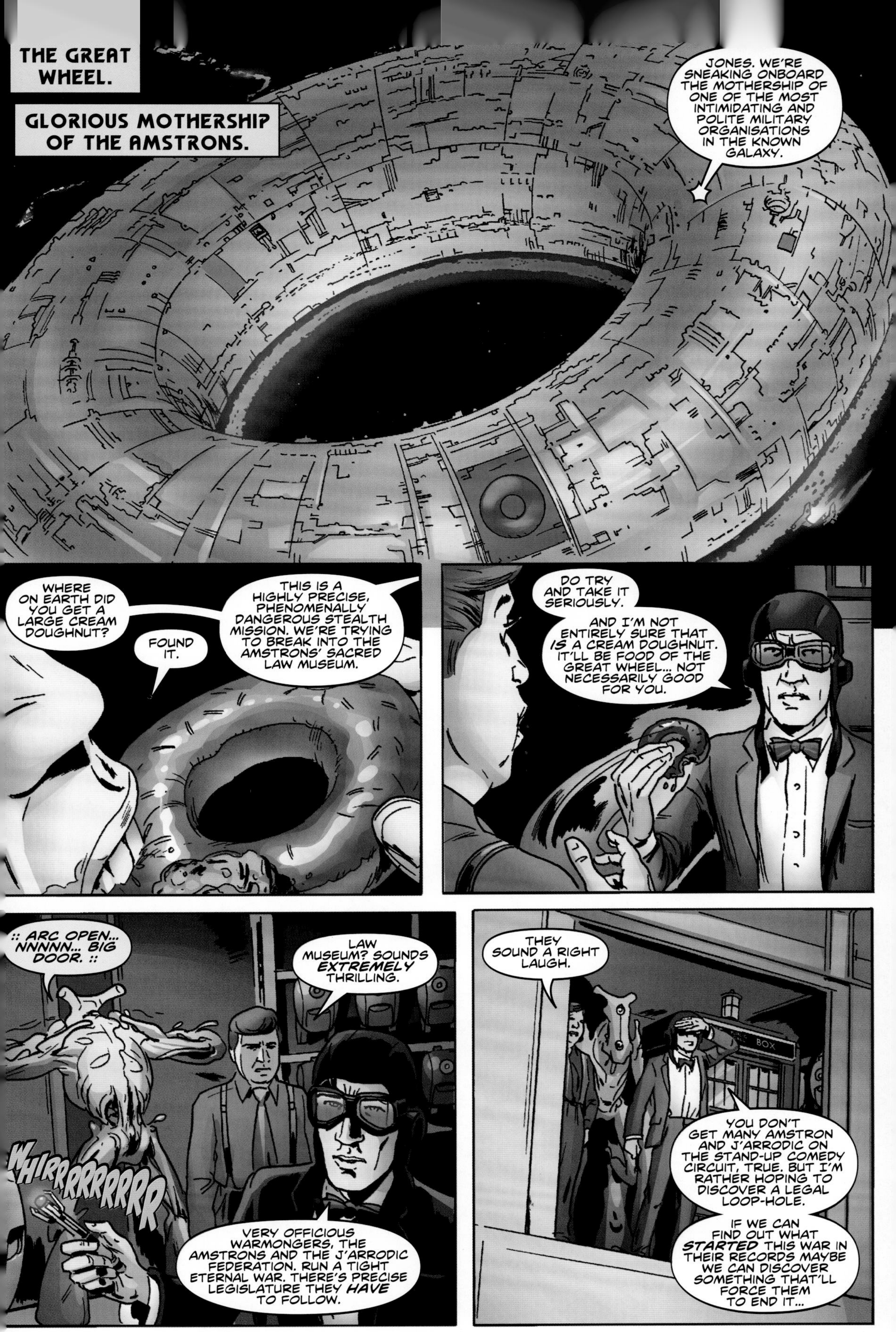
THE GREAT WHEEL.
GLORIOUS MOTHERSHIP OF THE AMSTRONS.
JONES. WE'RE SNEAKING ONBOARD THE MOTHERSHIP OF ONE OF THE MOST INTIMIDATING AND POLITE MILITARY ORGANISATIONS IN THE KNOWN GALAXY.
WHERE ON EARTH DID YOU GET A LARGE CREAM DOUGHNUT?
FOUND IT.
THIS IS A HIGHLY PRECISE, PHENOMENALLY DANGEROUS STEALTH MISSION. WE'RE TRYING TO BREAK INTO THE AMSTRONS' SACRED LAW MUSEUM.
DO TRY AND TAKE IT SERIOUSLY.
AND I'M NOT ENTIRELY SURE THAT *IS* A CREAM DOUGHNUT. IT'LL BE FOOD OF THE GREAT WHEEL... NOT NECESSARILY GOOD FOR YOU.
:: ARC OPEN... NNNNN... BIG DOOR. ::
LAW MUSEUM? SOUNDS ***EXTREMELY*** THRILLING.
WHIRRRRRRRRR
VERY OFFICIOUS WARMONGERS, THE AMSTRONS AND THE J'ARRODIC FEDERATION. RUN A TIGHT ETERNAL WAR. THERE'S PRECISE LEGISLATURE THEY ***HAVE*** TO FOLLOW.
THEY SOUND A RIGHT LAUGH.
YOU DON'T GET MANY AMSTRON AND J'ARRODIC ON THE STAND-UP COMEDY CIRCUIT, TRUE. BUT I'M RATHER HOPING TO DISCOVER A LEGAL LOOP-HOLE.
IF WE CAN FIND OUT WHAT ***STARTED*** THIS WAR IN THEIR RECORDS MAYBE WE CAN DISCOVER SOMETHING THAT'LL FORCE THEM TO END IT...

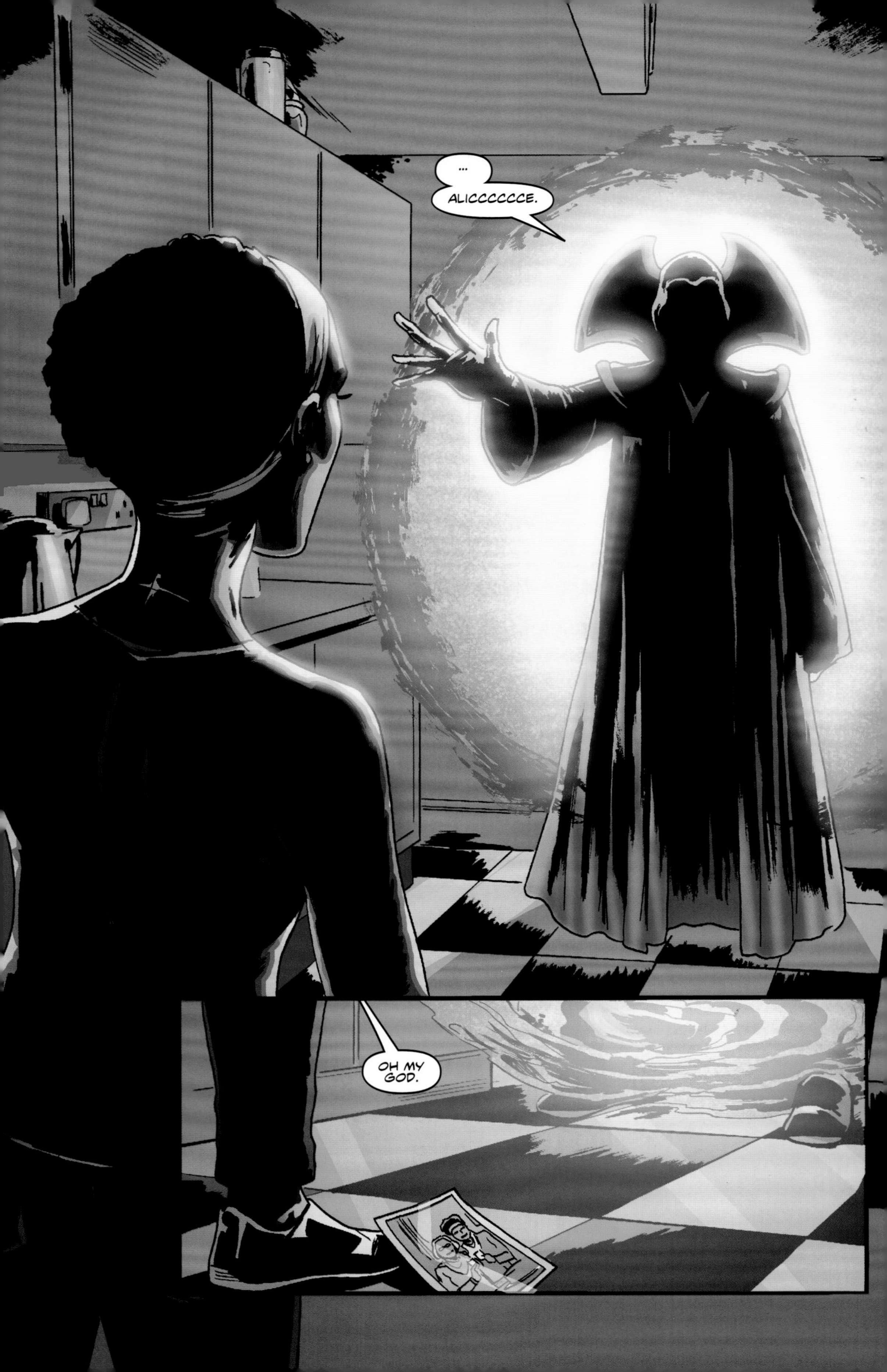
...
ALICCCCCCE.
OH MY GOD.

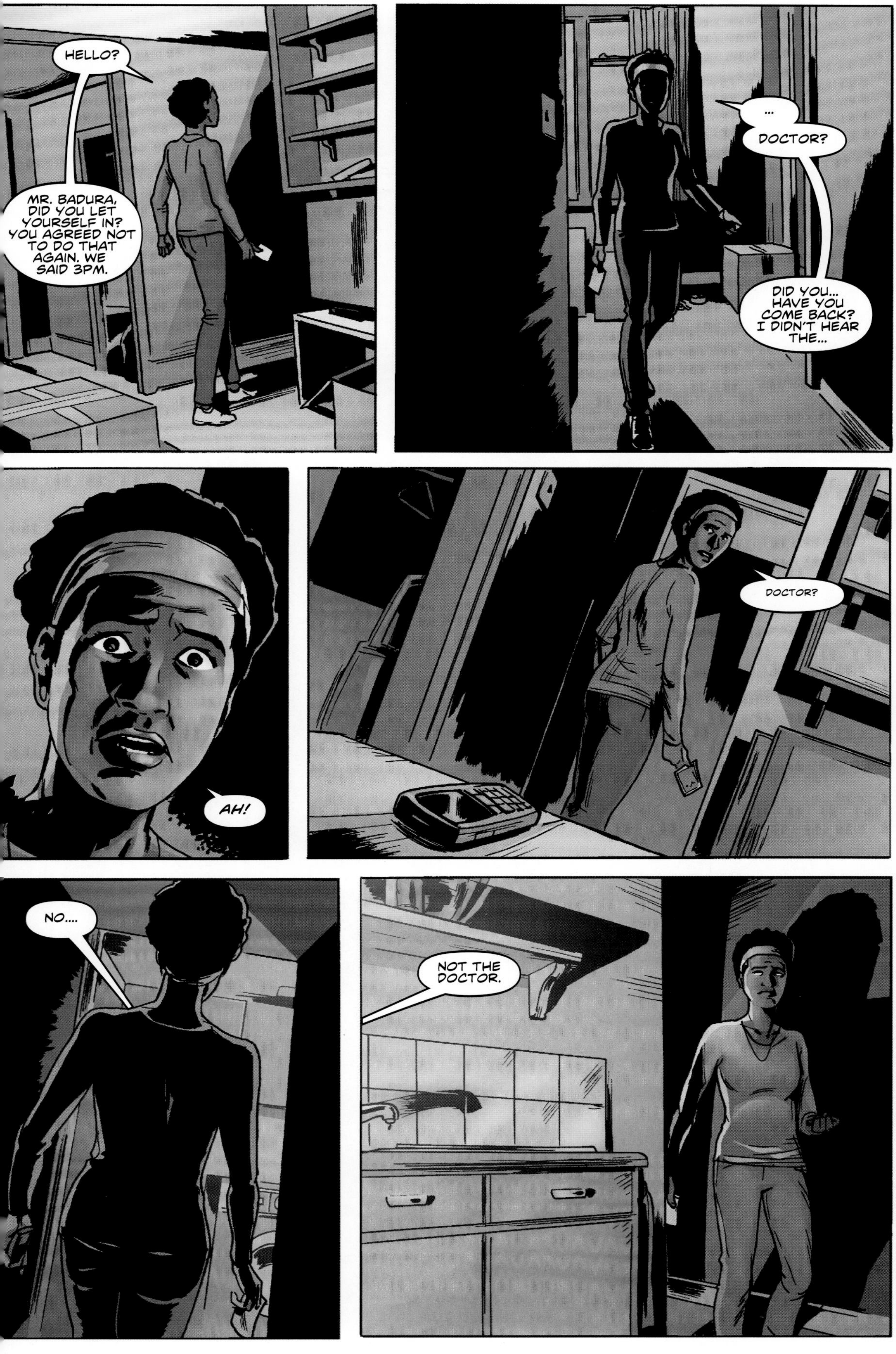
HELLO?
MR. BADURA, DID YOU LET YOURSELF IN? YOU AGREED NOT TO DO THAT AGAIN. WE SAID 3PM.
...
DOCTOR?
DID YOU... HAVE YOU COME BACK? I DIDN'T HEAR THE...
AH!
DOCTOR?
NO....
NOT THE DOCTOR.

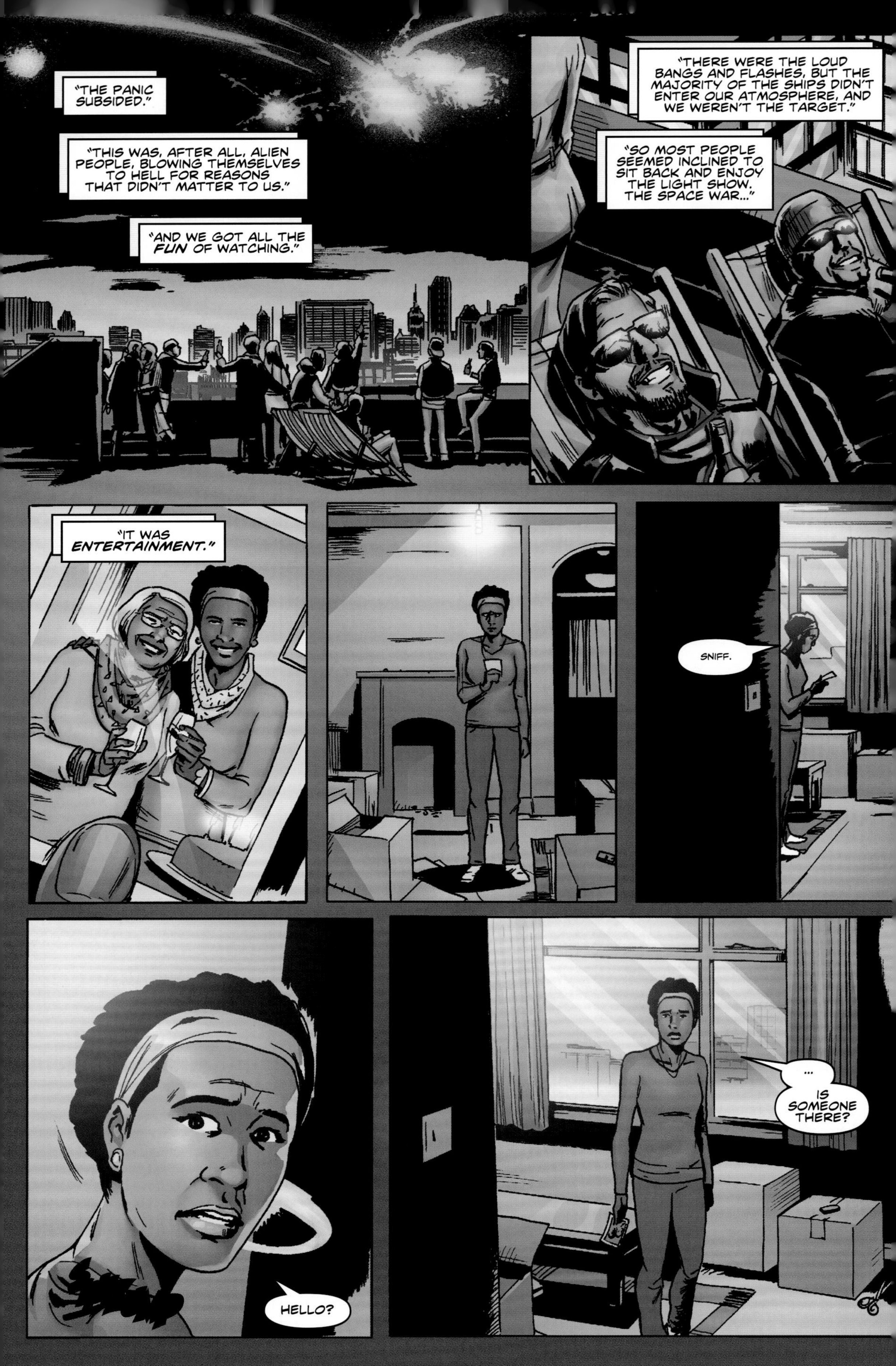
"THE PANIC SUBSIDED."
"THIS WAS, AFTER ALL, ALIEN PEOPLE, BLOWING THEMSELVES TO HELL FOR REASONS THAT DIDN'T MATTER TO US."
"AND WE GOT ALL THE *FUN* OF WATCHING."
"THERE WERE THE LOUD BANGS AND FLASHES, BUT THE MAJORITY OF THE SHIPS DIDN'T ENTER OUR ATMOSPHERE, AND WE WEREN'T THE TARGET."
"SO MOST PEOPLE SEEMED INCLINED TO SIT BACK AND ENJOY THE LIGHT SHOW. THE SPACE WAR..."
"IT WAS *ENTERTAINMENT*."
SNIFF.
HELLO?
... IS SOMEONE THERE?

"I ARGUED WITH THE DOCTOR. SAID MY THINGS COULD WAIT AND I'D COME WITH THEM BUT HE WOULDN'T HAVE IT. SAID HE'D BE BACK FOR ME SOON."

"HE SAID LIFE *SHOULDN'T* CHANGE ON EARTH BECAUSE OF THIS. THAT THE ORDINARY THINGS, THEY WERE A FREEDOM THAT GOOD PEOPLE HAD *EARNED*."

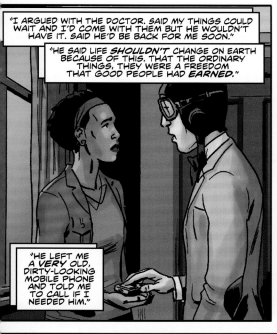

"HE LEFT ME A *VERY* OLD, DIRTY-LOOKING MOBILE PHONE AND TOLD ME TO CALL IF I NEEDED HIM."

"HE TOLD JONES OFF FOR EATING WHAT WAS LEFT IN MY FRIDGE."

"JONES HAD BEEN EATING A *LOT* LATELY, FOR SOME REASON. THE TALL PALE EARL HAD GONE A BIT... PORKY. WE WERE CONCERNED."

"OH, AND HE TOLD ARC OFF FOR EATING MUM'S OLD CHAISE LONGUE, TOO."

"AND THEN HE WAS GONE."

"I WAS WORRIED ABOUT HIM. HE ACTS THE FOOL AND PLAYS FOR LAUGHS, BUT THERE'S MOMENTS WHERE YOU GET A GLIMPSE OF SOMETHING ELSE..."

"HE CHANGES WHEN WAR IS MENTIONED."

"BUT WAR WAS WHAT EARTH SUDDENLY HAD ON ITS BORDER. THERE WAS WIDESPREAD PANIC..."

"UP UNTIL THE POINT THAT THE AMBASSADORS FOR THE AMSTRONS AND THE J'ARRODIC FEDERATION INFORMED EARTH'S LEADERS THAT THEY 'MEAN US NO HARM.'"

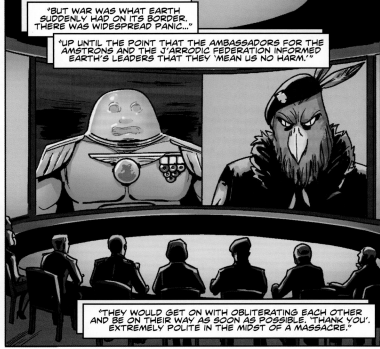

"THEY WOULD GET ON WITH OBLITERATING EACH OTHER AND BE ON THEIR WAY AS SOON AS POSSIBLE. 'THANK YOU'. EXTREMELY POLITE IN THE MIDST OF A MASSACRE."

CHAPTER 7

THE ETERNAL DOGFIGHT

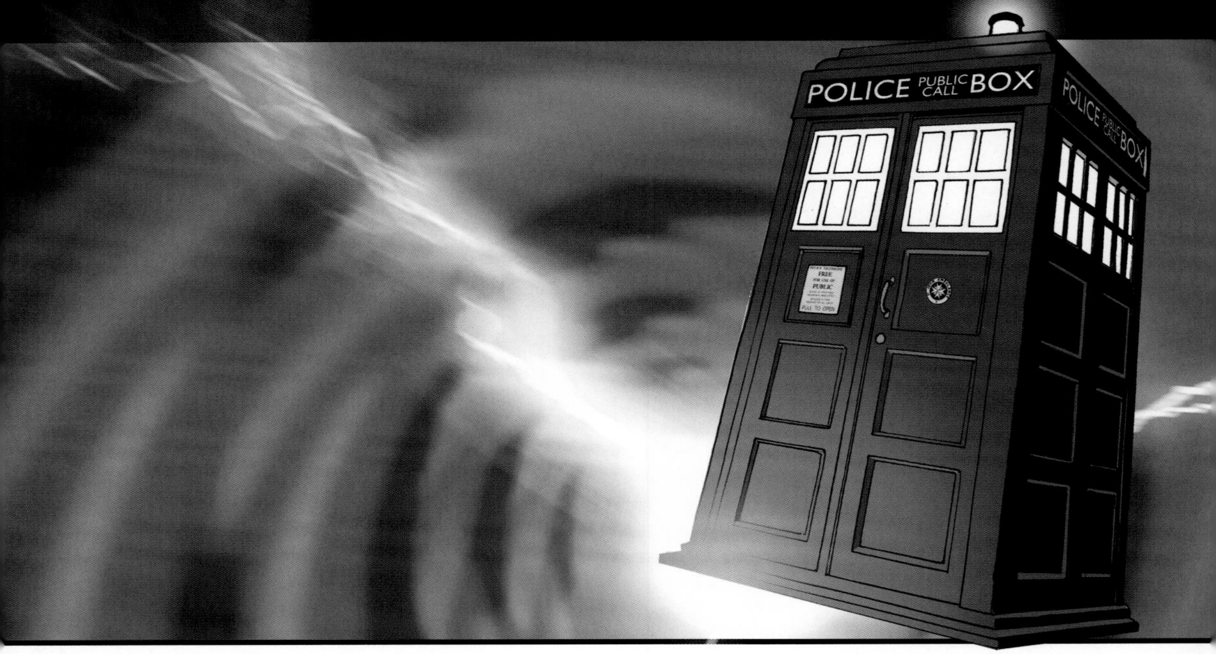
POLICE PUBLIC CALL BOX
POLICE PUBLIC CALL BOX

WRITER
ROB WILLIAMS

ARTIST
WARREN PLEECE

COLORIST
HI-FI

LETTERER
RICHARD STARKINGS AND COMICRAFT'S JIMMY BETANCOURT

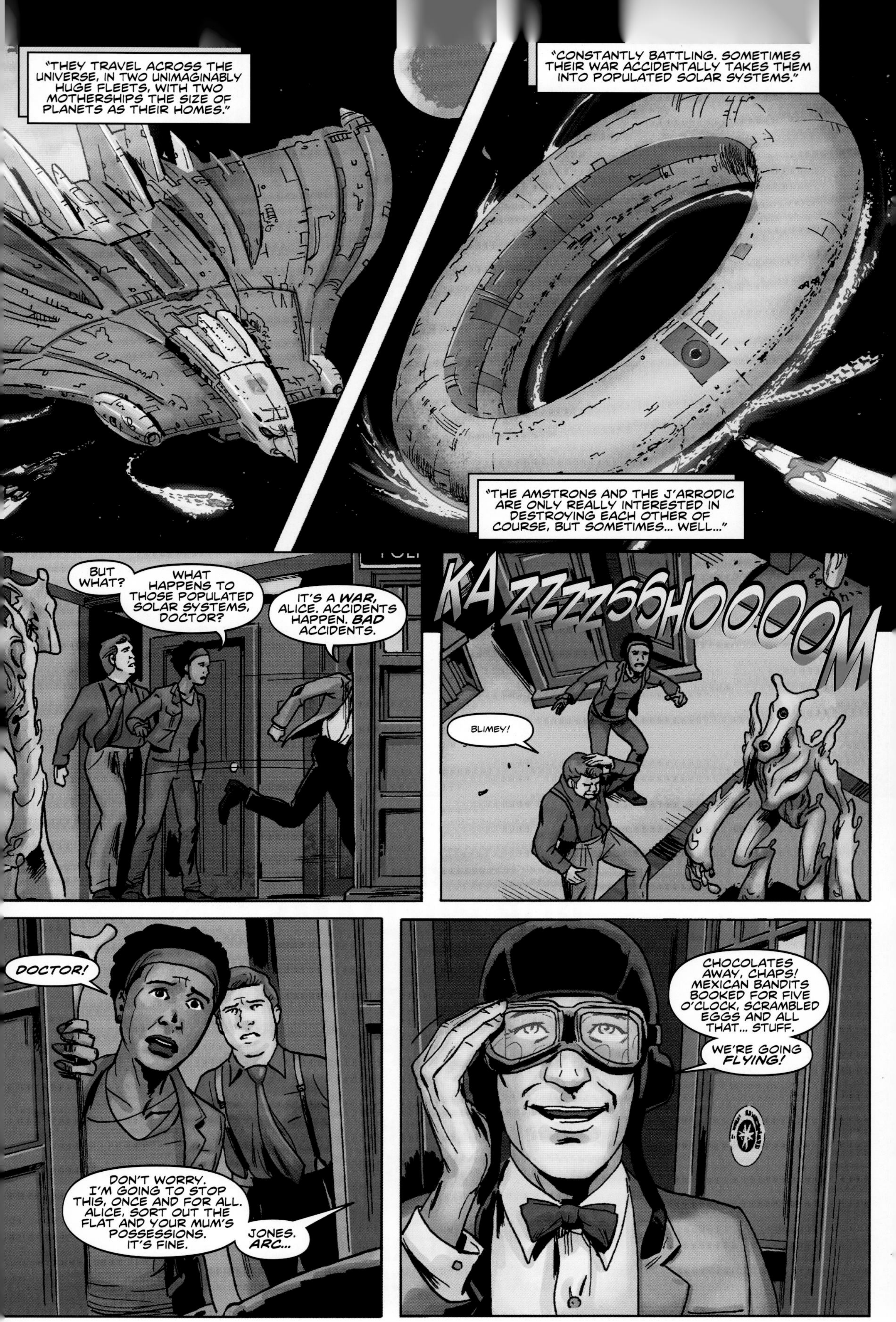
"THEY TRAVEL ACROSS THE UNIVERSE, IN TWO UNIMAGINABLY HUGE FLEETS, WITH TWO MOTHERSHIPS THE SIZE OF PLANETS AS THEIR HOMES."
"CONSTANTLY BATTLING. SOMETIMES THEIR WAR ACCIDENTALLY TAKES THEM INTO POPULATED SOLAR SYSTEMS."
"THE AMSTRONS AND THE J'ARRODIC ARE ONLY REALLY INTERESTED IN DESTROYING EACH OTHER OF COURSE, BUT SOMETIMES... WELL..."
BUT WHAT?
WHAT HAPPENS TO THOSE POPULATED SOLAR SYSTEMS, DOCTOR?
IT'S A *WAR*, ALICE. ACCIDENTS HAPPEN. ***BAD*** ACCIDENTS.
KA ZZZZSSHOOOOOM
BLIMEY!
DOCTOR!
DON'T WORRY. I'M GOING TO STOP THIS, ONCE AND FOR ALL. ALICE, SORT OUT THE FLAT AND YOUR MUM'S POSSESSIONS. IT'S FINE.
JONES. *ARC...*
CHOCOLATES AWAY, CHAPS! MEXICAN BANDITS BOOKED FOR FIVE O'CLOCK, SCRAMBLED EGGS AND ALL THAT... STUFF.
WE'RE GOING *FLYING!*

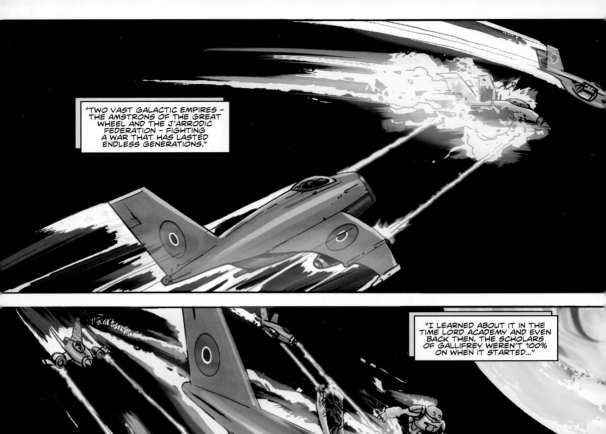

"TWO VAST GALACTIC EMPIRES – THE AMSTRONS OF THE GREAT WHEEL AND THE J'ARRODIC FEDERATION – FIGHTING A WAR THAT HAS LASTED ENDLESS GENERATIONS."

"I LEARNED ABOUT IT IN THE TIME LORD ACADEMY AND EVEN BACK THEN, THE SCHOLARS OF GALLIFREY WEREN'T 100% ON WHEN IT STARTED..."

"OR *WHY* THEY ORIGINALLY STARTED FIGHTING..."

IT'S SAID THAT BOTH THEIR HOME PLANETS WERE LOST EARLY IN THE CONFLICT.

IMAGINE THAT, EH? SEEING YOUR HOME PLANET DESTROYED...

IMAGINE WHAT THAT DOES TO YOU.

POLICE PUBLIC CALL BOX

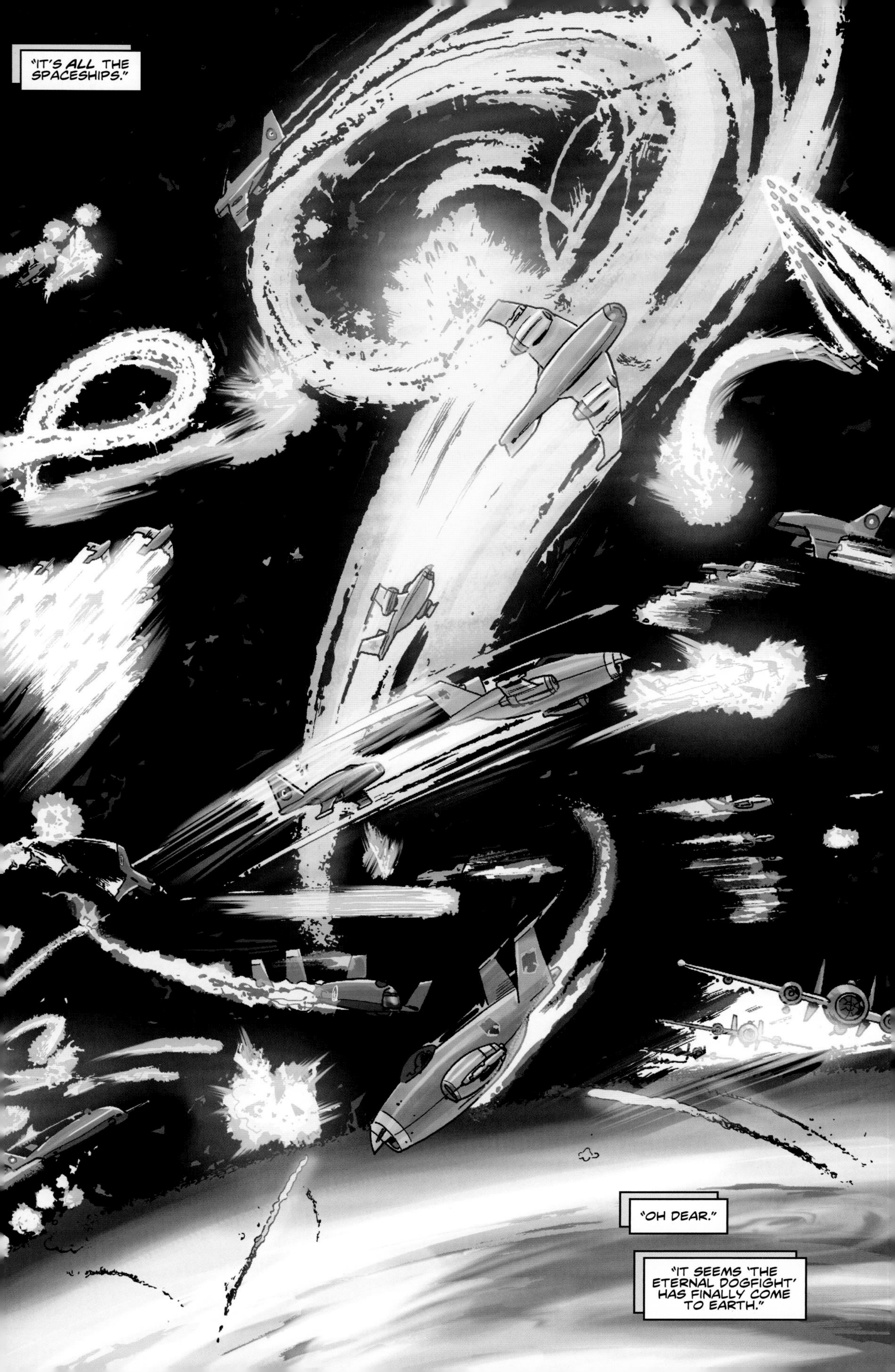
"IT'S ALL THE SPACESHIPS."
"OH DEAR."
"IT SEEMS 'THE ETERNAL DOGFIGHT' HAS FINALLY COME TO EARTH."

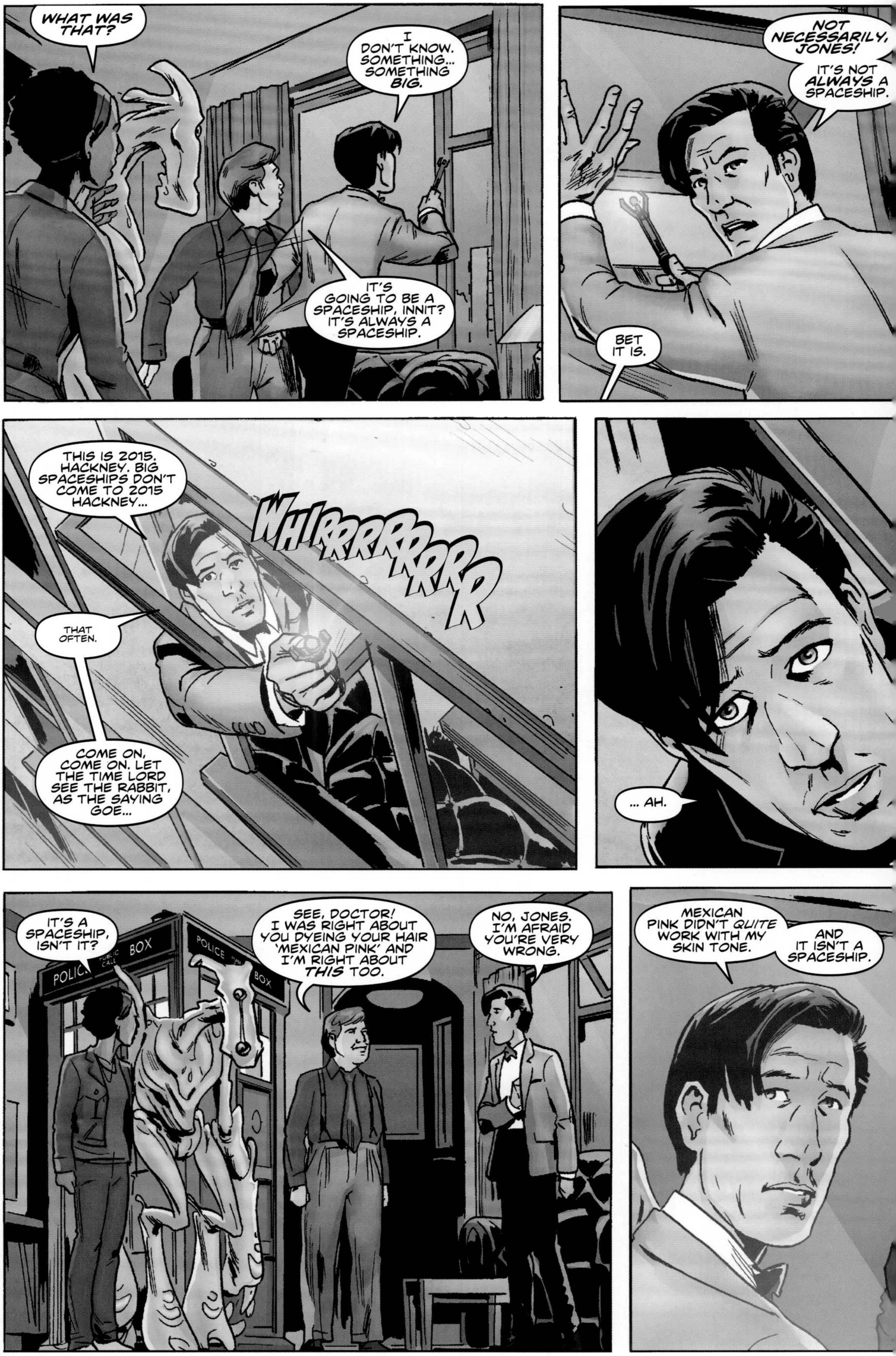
WHAT WAS THAT?
I DON'T KNOW. SOMETHING... SOMETHING BIG.
IT'S GOING TO BE A SPACESHIP, INNIT? IT'S ALWAYS A SPACESHIP.
NOT NECESSARILY, JONES!
IT'S NOT ALWAYS A SPACESHIP.
BET IT IS.
THIS IS 2015. HACKNEY. BIG SPACESHIPS DON'T COME TO 2015 HACKNEY...
WHIRRRRRRRRR
THAT OFTEN.
COME ON, COME ON. LET THE TIME LORD SEE THE RABBIT, AS THE SAYING GOE...
... AH.
IT'S A SPACESHIP, ISN'T IT?
POLICE PUBLIC CALL BOX
SEE, DOCTOR! I WAS RIGHT ABOUT YOU DYEING YOUR HAIR 'MEXICAN PINK' AND I'M RIGHT ABOUT THIS TOO.
NO, JONES. I'M AFRAID YOU'RE VERY WRONG.
MEXICAN PINK DIDN'T QUITE WORK WITH MY SKIN TONE.
AND IT ISN'T A SPACESHIP.

All of time and space to travel to...

But Alice Obiefune just wanted to go home.

VWOORRRP VWOORRRP

Grief is a funny thing. It plays tricks on you...

I DON'T NEED LONG, DOCTOR. COUPLE OF DAYS, PROBABLY.

I JUST NEVER SORTED OUT THE STORAGE FOR A LOT OF MUM'S STUFF BEFORE WE LEFT AND I NEED TO FIND SOMEWHERE NEW TO LIVE.

You forget it's there a lot of the time. And then two seconds later you hate yourself for feeling that your heart isn't broken...

YOU DON'T, ALICE.

THERE'S PLENTY OF ROOM FOR YOU ON THE TARDIS.

... and then you remember that it IS.

NOT FOREVER...

NO.

OUTTA ME WAY! I WANT TO SEE WOT'S IN A 2015 RECORD COLLECTION!

JONES. ARC. WE'RE NOT STAYING. ALICE NEEDS A LITTLE TIME TO SORT OUT SOME PERSONAL THINGS. AND JONES, DON'T EAT ANYTHI!...

KERPLLLOOOOOOOM

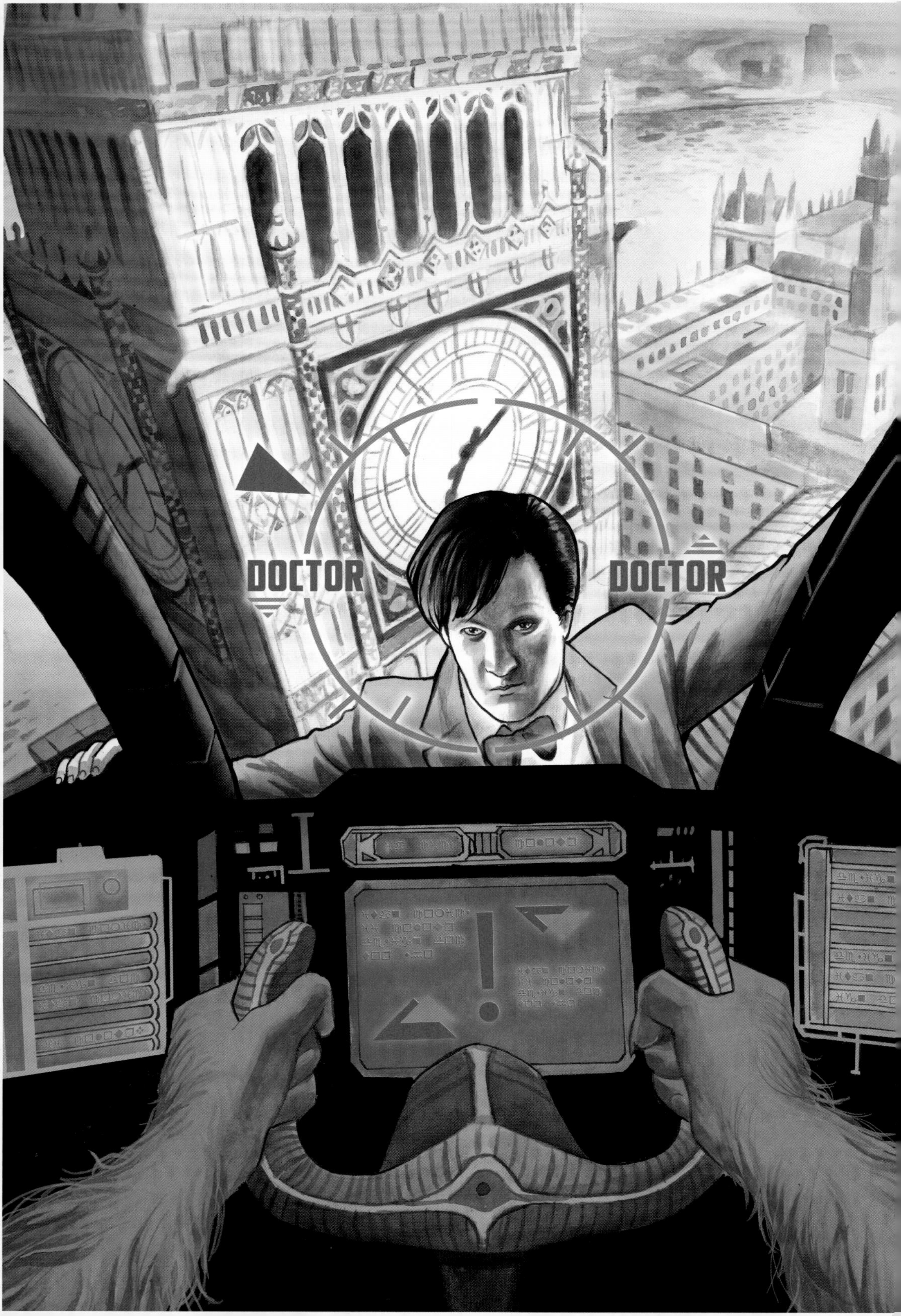
DOCTOR
DOCTOR

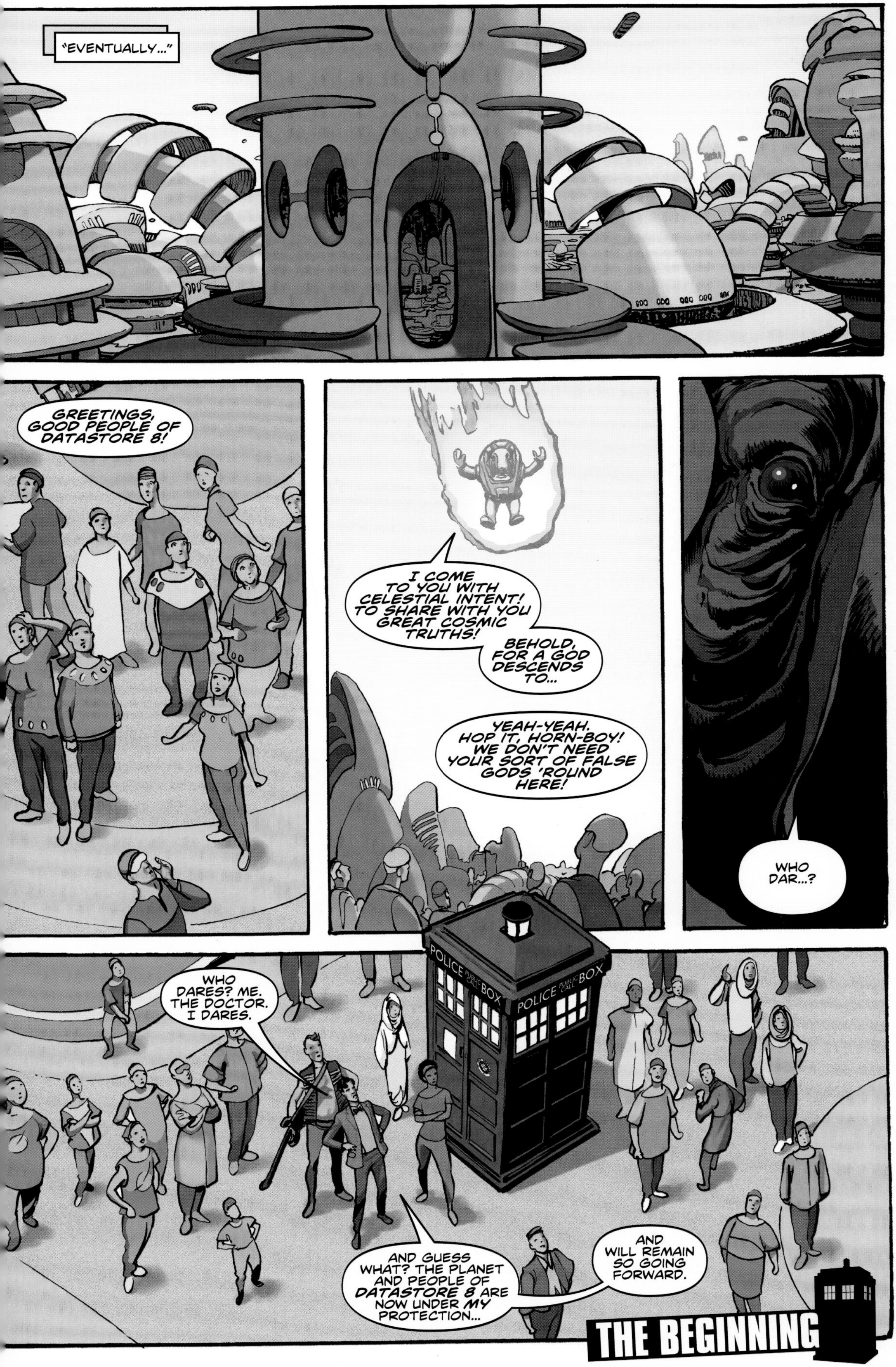
"EVENTUALLY..."
GREETINGS, GOOD PEOPLE OF DATASTORE 8!
I COME TO YOU WITH CELESTIAL INTENT! TO SHARE WITH YOU GREAT COSMIC TRUTHS!
BEHOLD, FOR A GOD DESCENDS TO...
YEAH-YEAH. HOP IT, HORN-BOY! WE DON'T NEED YOUR SORT OF FALSE GODS 'ROUND HERE!
WHO DAR...?
WHO DARES? ME. THE DOCTOR. I DARES.
POLICE PUBLIC CALL BOX
AND GUESS WHAT? THE PLANET AND PEOPLE OF DATASTORE 8 ARE NOW UNDER MY PROTECTION...
AND WILL REMAIN SO GOING FORWARD.
THE BEGINNING

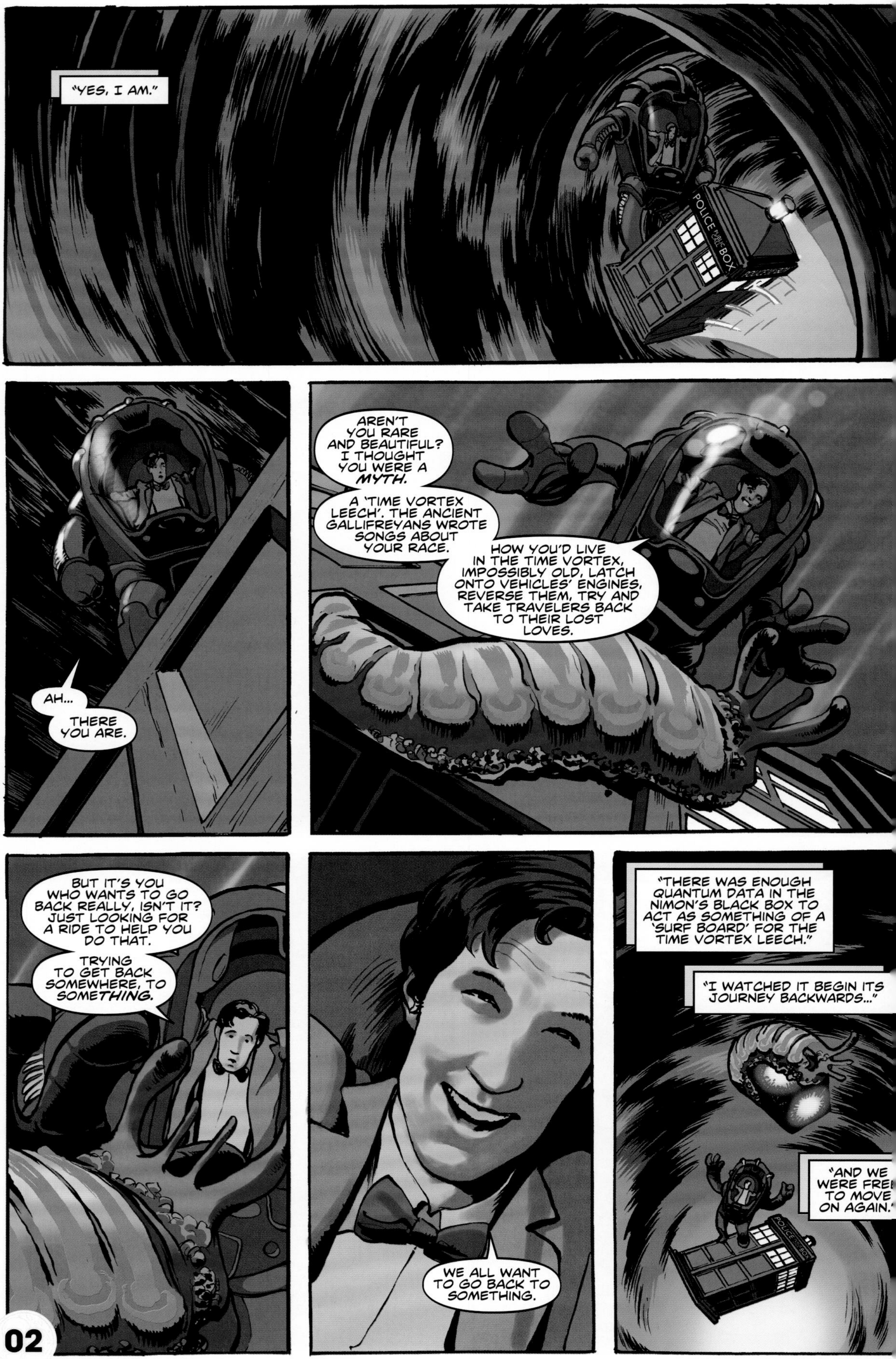
"YES, I AM."
AH... THERE YOU ARE.
AREN'T YOU RARE AND BEAUTIFUL? I THOUGHT YOU WERE A *MYTH.*
A 'TIME VORTEX LEECH'. THE ANCIENT GALLIFREYANS WROTE SONGS ABOUT YOUR RACE.
HOW YOU'D LIVE IN THE TIME VORTEX, IMPOSSIBLY OLD, LATCH ONTO VEHICLES' ENGINES, REVERSE THEM, TRY AND TAKE TRAVELERS BACK TO THEIR LOST LOVES.
BUT IT'S YOU WHO WANTS TO GO BACK REALLY, ISN'T IT? JUST LOOKING FOR A RIDE TO HELP YOU DO THAT.
TRYING TO GET BACK SOMEWHERE, TO SOME*THING.*
WE ALL WANT TO GO BACK TO SOMETHING.
"THERE WAS ENOUGH QUANTUM DATA IN THE NIMON'S BLACK BOX TO ACT AS SOMETHING OF A 'SURF BOARD' FOR THE TIME VORTEX LEECH."
"I WATCHED IT BEGIN ITS JOURNEY BACKWARDS..."
"AND WE WERE FREE TO MOVE ON AGAIN."

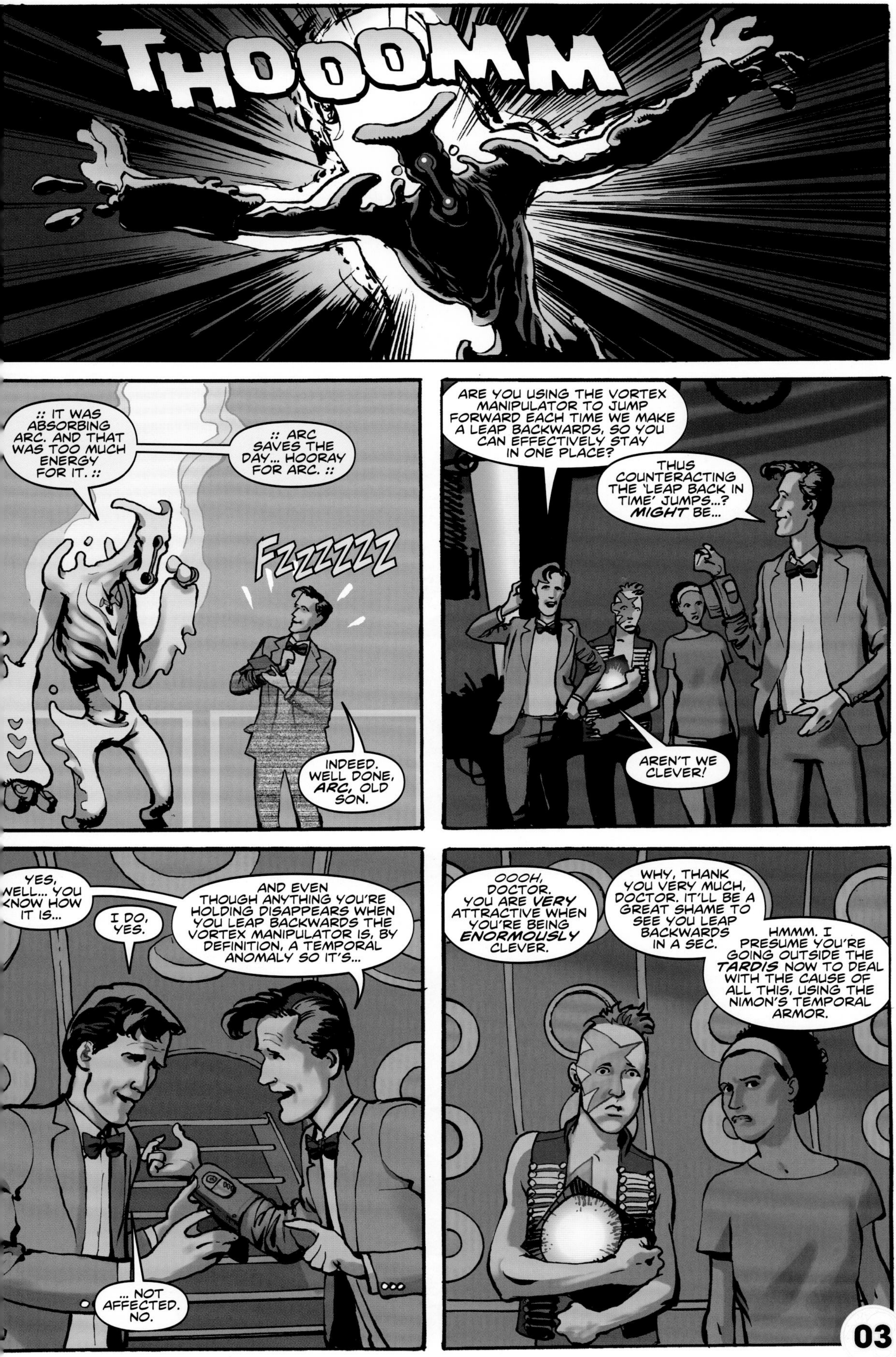
THOOOMM
:: IT WAS ABSORBING ARC. AND THAT WAS TOO MUCH ENERGY FOR IT. ::
:: ARC SAVES THE DAY... HOORAY FOR ARC. ::
FZZZZZZ
INDEED. WELL DONE, *ARC,* OLD SON.
ARE YOU USING THE VORTEX MANIPULATOR TO JUMP FORWARD EACH TIME WE MAKE A LEAP BACKWARDS, SO YOU CAN EFFECTIVELY STAY IN ONE PLACE?
THUS COUNTERACTING THE 'LEAP BACK IN TIME' JUMPS...? *MIGHT* BE...
AREN'T WE CLEVER!
YES, WELL... YOU KNOW HOW IT IS...
I DO, YES.
AND EVEN THOUGH ANYTHING YOU'RE HOLDING DISAPPEARS WHEN YOU LEAP BACKWARDS THE VORTEX MANIPULATOR IS, BY DEFINITION, A TEMPORAL ANOMALY SO IT'S...
... NOT AFFECTED. NO.
OOOH, DOCTOR. YOU ARE *VERY* ATTRACTIVE WHEN YOU'RE BEING *ENORMOUSLY* CLEVER.
WHY, THANK YOU VERY MUCH, DOCTOR. IT'LL BE A GREAT SHAME TO SEE YOU LEAP BACKWARDS IN A SEC.
HMMM. I PRESUME YOU'RE GOING OUTSIDE THE *TARDIS* NOW TO DEAL WITH THE CAUSE OF ALL THIS, USING THE NIMON'S TEMPORAL ARMOR.

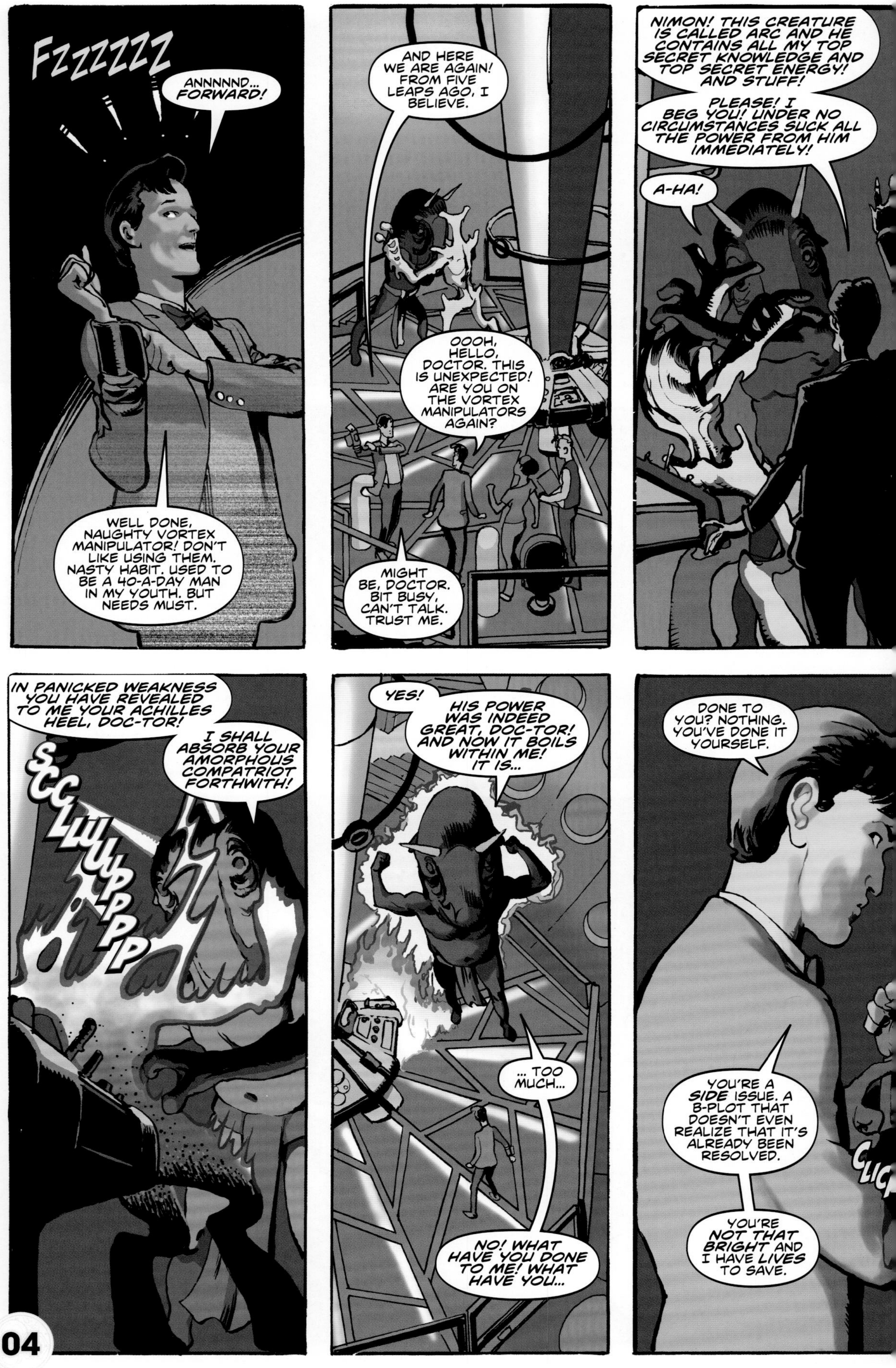
FZZZZZZ
ANNNNND... FORWARD!
WELL DONE, NAUGHTY VORTEX MANIPULATOR! DON'T LIKE USING THEM. NASTY HABIT. USED TO BE A 40-A-DAY MAN IN MY YOUTH. BUT NEEDS MUST.
AND HERE WE ARE AGAIN! FROM FIVE LEAPS AGO, I BELIEVE.
OOOH, HELLO, DOCTOR. THIS IS UNEXPECTED! ARE YOU ON THE VORTEX MANIPULATORS AGAIN?
MIGHT BE, DOCTOR. BIT BUSY, CAN'T TALK. TRUST ME.
NIMON! THIS CREATURE IS CALLED ARC AND HE CONTAINS ALL MY TOP SECRET KNOWLEDGE AND TOP SECRET ENERGY! AND STUFF!
PLEASE! I BEG YOU! UNDER NO CIRCUMSTANCES SUCK ALL THE POWER FROM HIM IMMEDIATELY!
A-HA!
IN PANICKED WEAKNESS YOU HAVE REVEALED TO ME YOUR ACHILLES HEEL, DOC-TOR!
I SHALL ABSORB YOUR AMORPHOUS COMPATRIOT FORTHWITH!
SCCLUUUPPPP
YES!
HIS POWER WAS INDEED GREAT, DOC-TOR! AND NOW IT BOILS WITHIN ME! IT IS...
... TOO MUCH...
NO! WHAT HAVE YOU DONE TO ME! WHAT HAVE YOU...
DONE TO YOU? NOTHING. YOU'VE DONE IT YOURSELF.
YOU'RE A SIDE ISSUE. A B-PLOT THAT DOESN'T EVEN REALIZE THAT IT'S ALREADY BEEN RESOLVED.
YOU'RE NOT THAT BRIGHT AND I HAVE LIVES TO SAVE.
CLIC

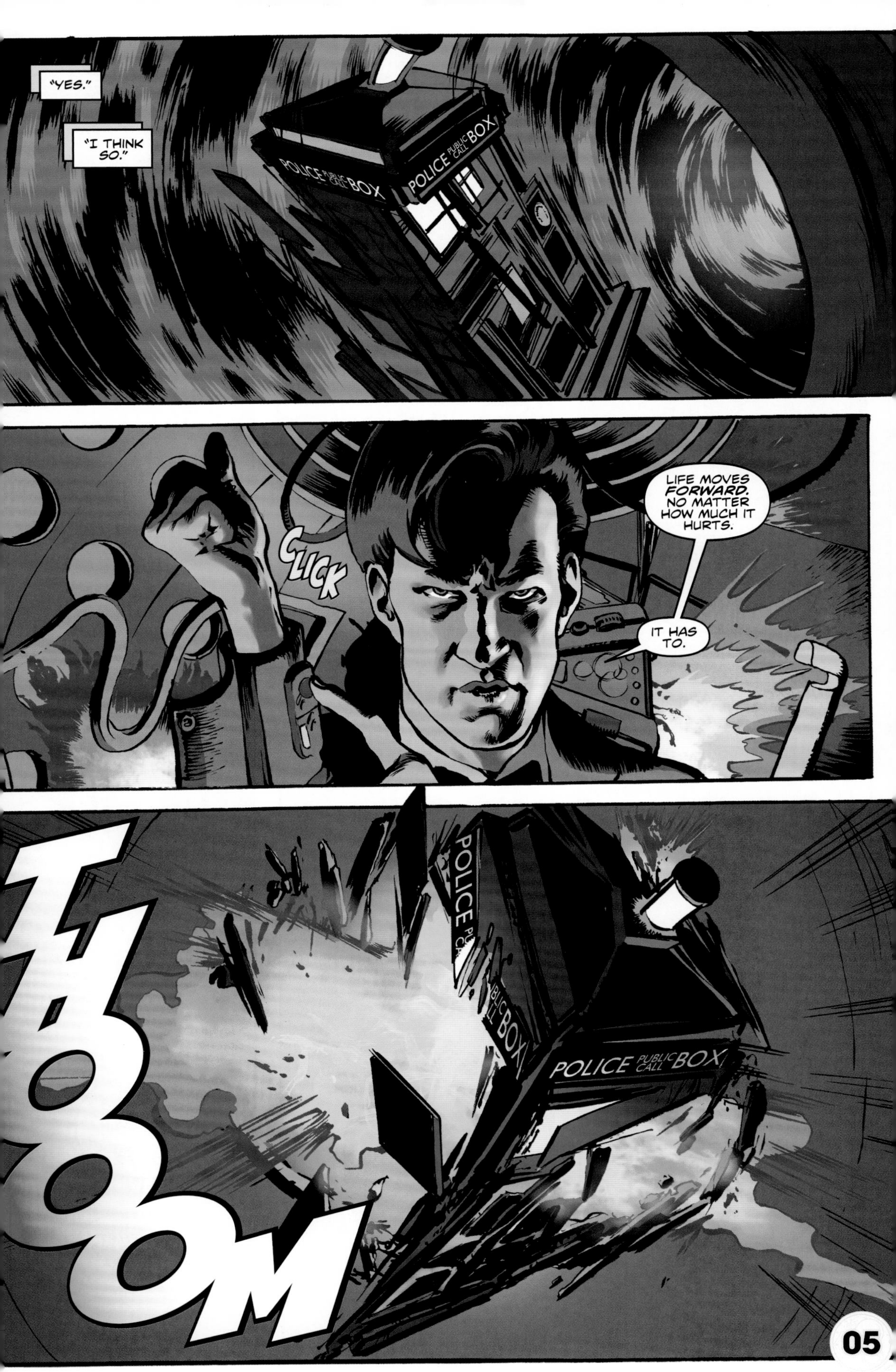
"YES."
"I THINK SO."
POLICE PUBLIC CALL BOX
LIFE MOVES FORWARD. NO MATTER HOW MUCH IT HURTS.
CLICK
IT HAS TO.
THOOOM
POLICE PUBLIC CALL BOX

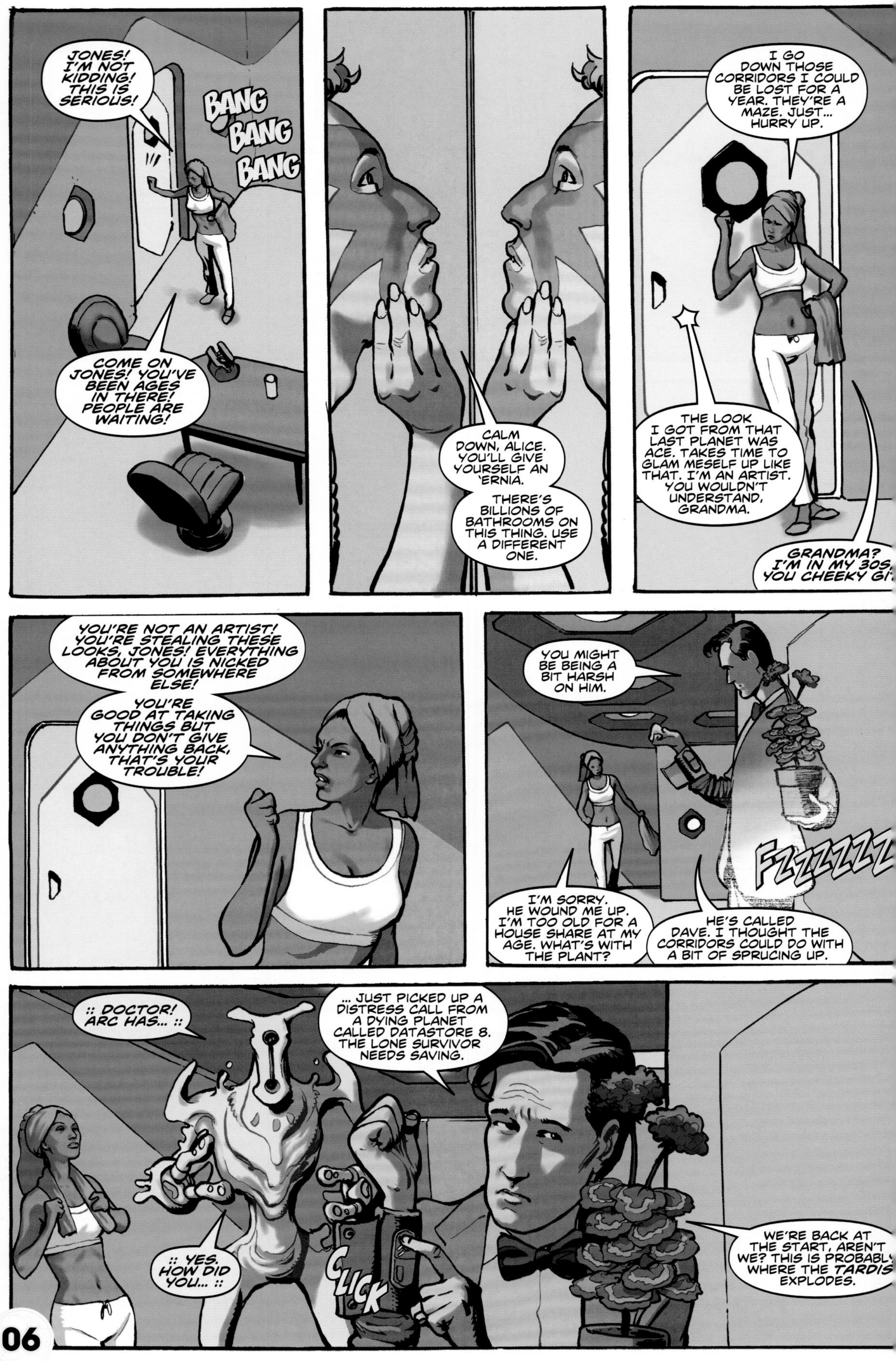
JONES! I'M NOT KIDDING! THIS IS SERIOUS!
BANG BANG BANG
COME ON JONES! YOU'VE BEEN AGES IN THERE! PEOPLE ARE WAITING!
CALM DOWN, ALICE. YOU'LL GIVE YOURSELF AN 'ERNIA.
THERE'S BILLIONS OF BATHROOMS ON THIS THING. USE A DIFFERENT ONE.
I GO DOWN THOSE CORRIDORS I COULD BE LOST FOR A YEAR. THEY'RE A MAZE. JUST... HURRY UP.
THE LOOK I GOT FROM THAT LAST PLANET WAS ACE. TAKES TIME TO GLAM MESELF UP LIKE THAT. I'M AN ARTIST. YOU WOULDN'T UNDERSTAND, GRANDMA.
GRANDMA? I'M IN MY 30S, YOU CHEEKY
YOU'RE NOT AN ARTIST! YOU'RE STEALING THESE LOOKS, JONES! EVERYTHING ABOUT YOU IS NICKED FROM SOMEWHERE ELSE!
YOU'RE GOOD AT TAKING THINGS BUT YOU DON'T GIVE ANYTHING BACK, THAT'S YOUR TROUBLE!
YOU MIGHT BE BEING A BIT HARSH ON HIM.
I'M SORRY. HE WOUND ME UP. I'M TOO OLD FOR A HOUSE SHARE AT MY AGE. WHAT'S WITH THE PLANT?
HE'S CALLED DAVE. I THOUGHT THE CORRIDORS COULD DO WITH A BIT OF SPRUCING UP.
:: DOCTOR! ARC HAS... ::
... JUST PICKED UP A DISTRESS CALL FROM A DYING PLANET CALLED DATASTORE 8. THE LONE SURVIVOR NEEDS SAVING.
:: YES. HOW DID YOU... ::
CLICK
WE'RE BACK AT THE START, AREN'T WE? THIS IS PROBABLY WHERE THE TARDIS EXPLODES.

KRRUMMMBLEE

"DATASTORE 8 WAS A *GREAT* SCIENTIFIC CIVILIZATION. A PLANET WHOSE TECTONIC PLATES WERE EVEN BONDED TOGETHER BY LINES OF PURE ELECTROMAGNETISM."

"BUILT ON *LEARNING.* RAISED ON THE STUDY OF QUANTUM MECHANICS AND TEMPORAL UNDERSTANDING."

"UNTIL *YOU* ARRIVED."

"AND DID WHAT *NIMONS* DO."

"CONVINCED THEM YOU WERE A GOD."

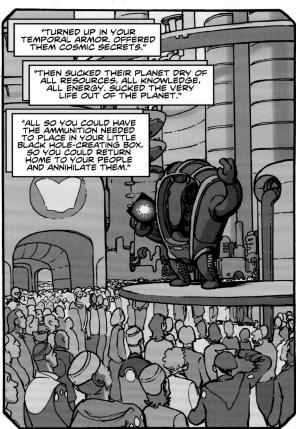

"TURNED UP IN YOUR TEMPORAL ARMOR. OFFERED THEM COSMIC SECRETS."

"THEN SUCKED THEIR PLANET DRY OF ALL RESOURCES, ALL KNOWLEDGE, ALL ENERGY. SUCKED THE VERY LIFE OUT OF THE PLANET."

"ALL SO YOU COULD HAVE THE AMMUNITION NEEDED TO PLACE IN YOUR LITTLE BLACK HOLE-CREATING BOX, SO YOU COULD RETURN HOME TO YOUR PEOPLE AND ANNIHILATE THEM."

DOCTOR!

"AND THEN YOU CALL MY TARDIS HERE BECAUSE ITS ENGINES WOULD BE THE OVEN NEEDED TO BAKE UP YOUR PATHETIC LITTLE BLACK HOLE BOMB!"

DOCTOR! WE'RE BURNING UP! DEMATERIALIZE US! DOCTOR!!! DOCTO...

07

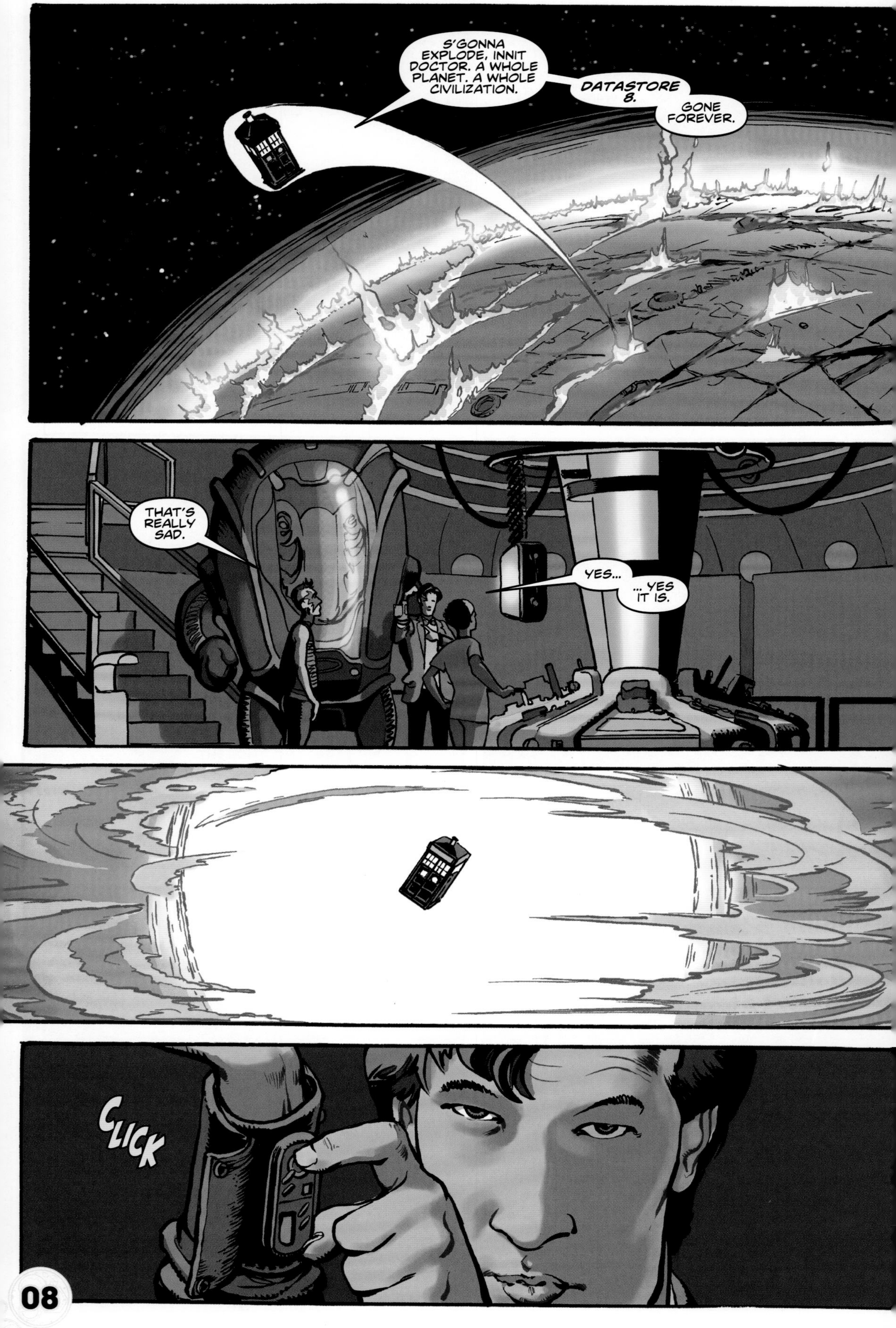
S'GONNA EXPLODE, INNIT DOCTOR. A WHOLE PLANET. A WHOLE CIVILIZATION.
DATASTORE 8.
GONE FOREVER.
THAT'S REALLY SAD.
YES...
... YES IT IS.
CLICK

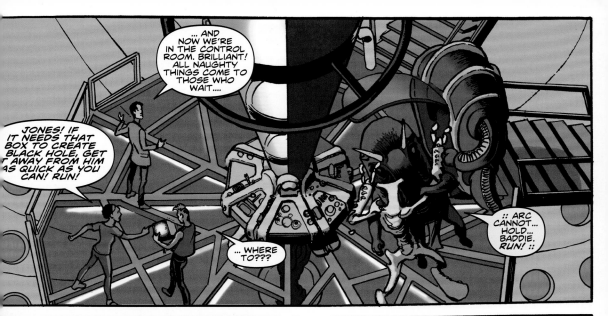

... AND NOW WE'RE IN THE CONTROL ROOM. BRILLIANT! ALL NAUGHTY THINGS COME TO THOSE WHO WAIT....

JONES! IF IT NEEDS THAT BOX TO CREATE BLACK HOLE, GET IT AWAY FROM HIM AS QUICK AS YOU CAN! RUN!

... WHERE TO???

:: ARC CANNOT... HOLD... BADDIE. RUN! ::

I DON'T KNOW. THE *TARDIS* CORRIDORS ARE A BLOODY MAZE! GO GET LOST IN THEM!

YOU'D LIKE ME TO GET LOST, WOULDN'T YOU?

HANG ON, JONES. BEFORE YOU RUN OFF, FAIL AND THEN, RATHER ADMIRABLY, GAIN REDEMPTION... JUST WANT TO CHECK SOMETHING.

DOCTOR! WHAT ARE YOU *DOING?* ARC CAN'T HOLD HIM FOREVER.

WHIRRRRRR

NO, THOUGHT NOT. IT'S NOT THE BLACK BOX. DAVE WAS RIGHT.

COME ON... QUICK... BEFORE WE LEAP AGAIN...

YOU WOULD DO WELL TO RUN, DOC-TOR!

WHEN MY BLACK HOLE IS CREATED I SHALL HAVE MY REVENGE UPON THE NIMON RACE WHO EXILED ME! JUST AS I MURDERED THE ENTIRE POPULATION OF DATASTORE 8!!

COME ON, NAUGHTY... WHERE ARE YOU? COME TO PAPPA, NAUGHTY!

DATASTORE 8! YES!

DATASTORE... 8!

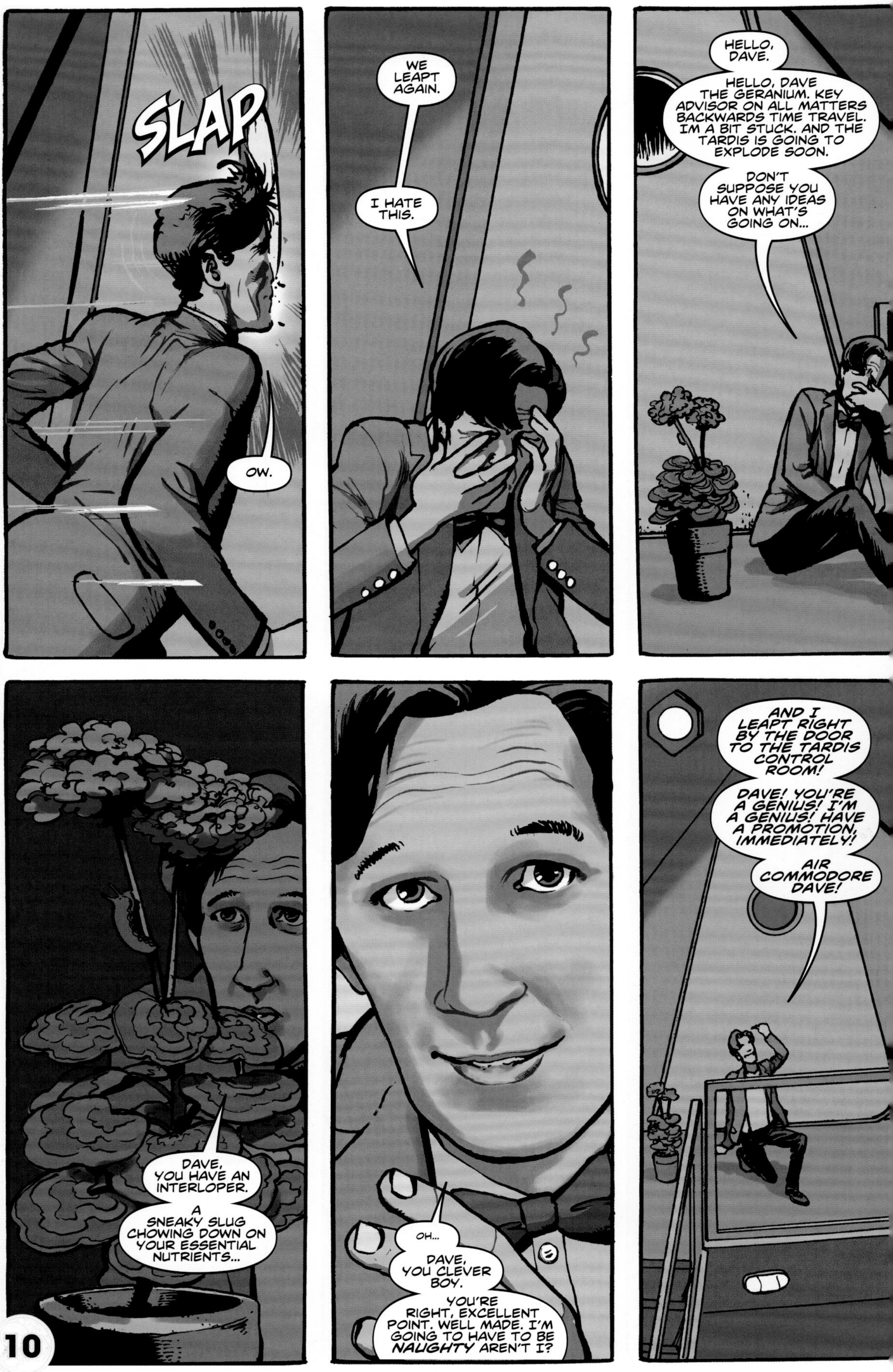
SLAP
OW.
WE LEAPT AGAIN.
I HATE THIS.
HELLO, DAVE.
HELLO, DAVE THE GERANIUM. KEY ADVISOR ON ALL MATTERS BACKWARDS TIME TRAVEL. I'M A BIT STUCK. AND THE TARDIS IS GOING TO EXPLODE SOON.
DON'T SUPPOSE YOU HAVE ANY IDEAS ON WHAT'S GOING ON...
DAVE, YOU HAVE AN INTERLOPER.
A SNEAKY SLUG CHOWING DOWN ON YOUR ESSENTIAL NUTRIENTS...
OH...
DAVE, YOU CLEVER BOY.
YOU'RE RIGHT, EXCELLENT POINT. WELL MADE. I'M GOING TO HAVE TO BE *NAUGHTY* AREN'T I?
AND I LEAPT RIGHT BY THE DOOR TO THE TARDIS CONTROL ROOM!
DAVE! YOU'RE A GENIUS! I'M A GENIUS! HAVE A PROMOTION, IMMEDIATELY!
AIR COMMODORE DAVE!

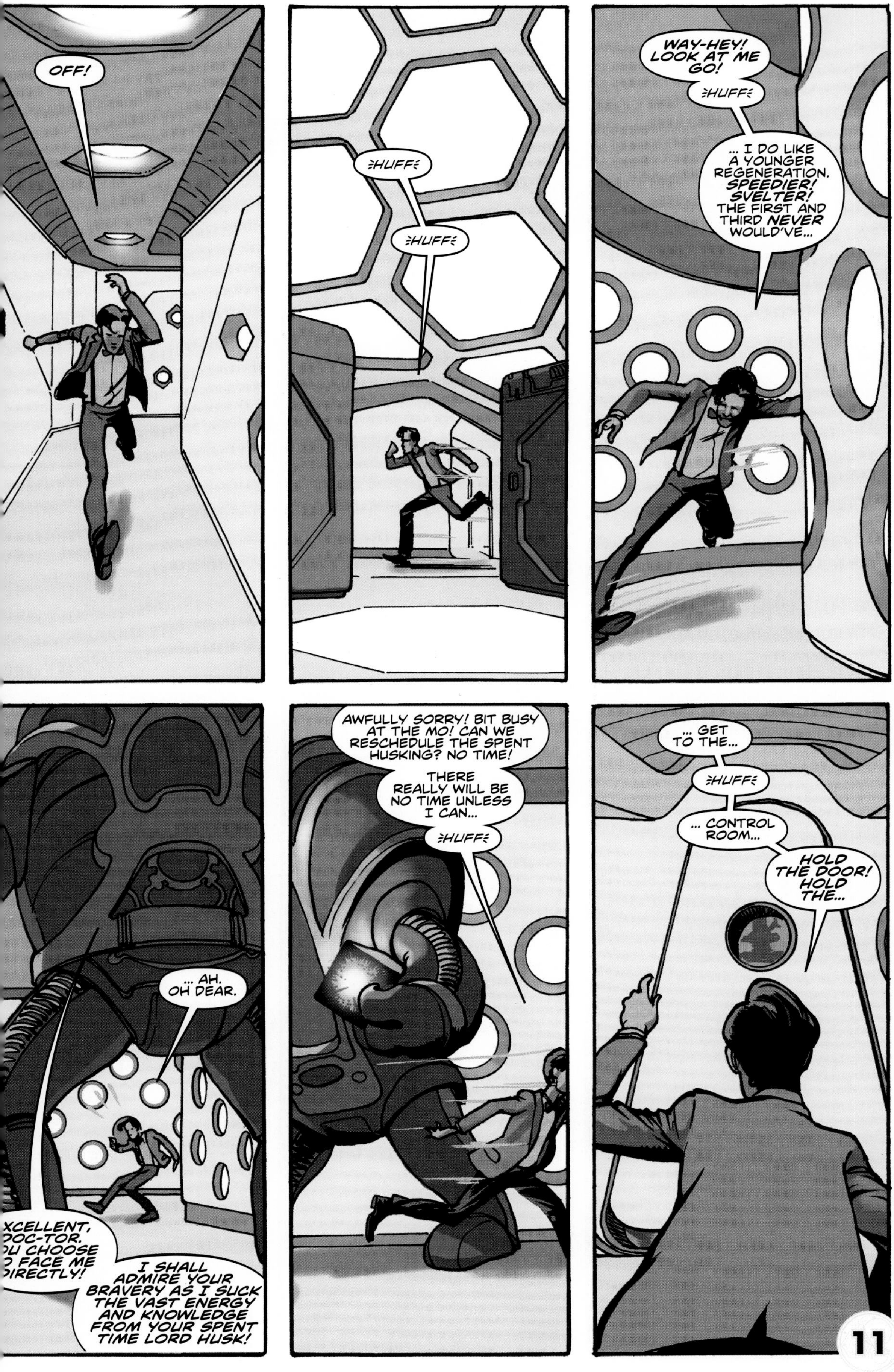
OFF!
⩩HUFF⩨
⩩HUFF⩨
WAY-HEY! LOOK AT ME GO!
⩩HUFF⩨
... I DO LIKE A YOUNGER REGENERATION. SPEEDIER! SVELTER! THE FIRST AND THIRD NEVER WOULD'VE...
... AH. OH DEAR.
XCELLENT, OC-TOR. OU CHOOSE O FACE ME IRECTLY!
I SHALL ADMIRE YOUR BRAVERY AS I SUCK THE VAST ENERGY AND KNOWLEDGE FROM YOUR SPENT TIME LORD HUSK!
AWFULLY SORRY! BIT BUSY AT THE MO! CAN WE RESCHEDULE THE SPENT HUSKING? NO TIME!
THERE REALLY WILL BE NO TIME UNLESS I CAN...
⩩HUFF⩨
... GET TO THE...
⩩HUFF⩨
... CONTROL ROOM...
HOLD THE DOOR! HOLD THE...

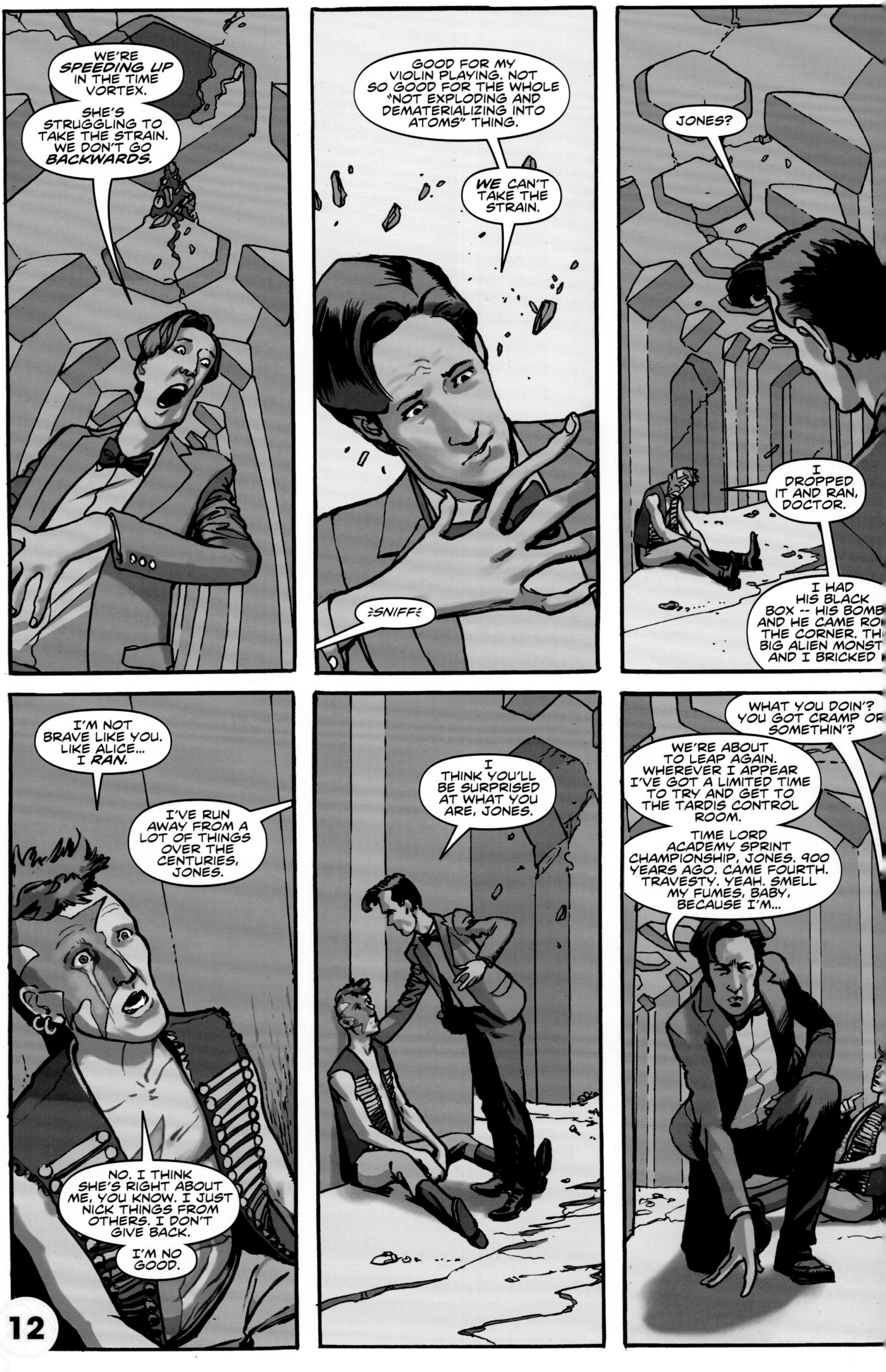
WE'RE SPEEDING UP IN THE TIME VORTEX.
SHE'S STRUGGLING TO TAKE THE STRAIN. WE DON'T GO BACKWARDS.
GOOD FOR MY VIOLIN PLAYING. NOT SO GOOD FOR THE WHOLE "NOT EXPLODING AND DEMATERIALIZING INTO ATOMS" THING.
WE CAN'T TAKE THE STRAIN.
SNIFF
JONES?
I DROPPED IT AND RAN, DOCTOR.
I HAD HIS BLACK BOX -- HIS BOMB AND HE CAME RO THE CORNER. TH BIG ALIEN MONST AND I BRICKED
I'M NOT BRAVE LIKE YOU. LIKE ALICE... I RAN.
I'VE RUN AWAY FROM A LOT OF THINGS OVER THE CENTURIES, JONES.
NO. I THINK SHE'S RIGHT ABOUT ME, YOU KNOW. I JUST NICK THINGS FROM OTHERS. I DON'T GIVE BACK.
I'M NO GOOD.
I THINK YOU'LL BE SURPRISED AT WHAT YOU ARE, JONES.
WHAT YOU DOIN'? YOU GOT CRAMP OR SOMETHIN'?
WE'RE ABOUT TO LEAP AGAIN. WHEREVER I APPEAR I'VE GOT A LIMITED TIME TO TRY AND GET TO THE TARDIS CONTROL ROOM.
TIME LORD ACADEMY SPRINT CHAMPIONSHIP, JONES. 900 YEARS AGO. CAME FOURTH. TRAVESTY. YEAH. SMELL MY FUMES, BABY, BECAUSE I'M...

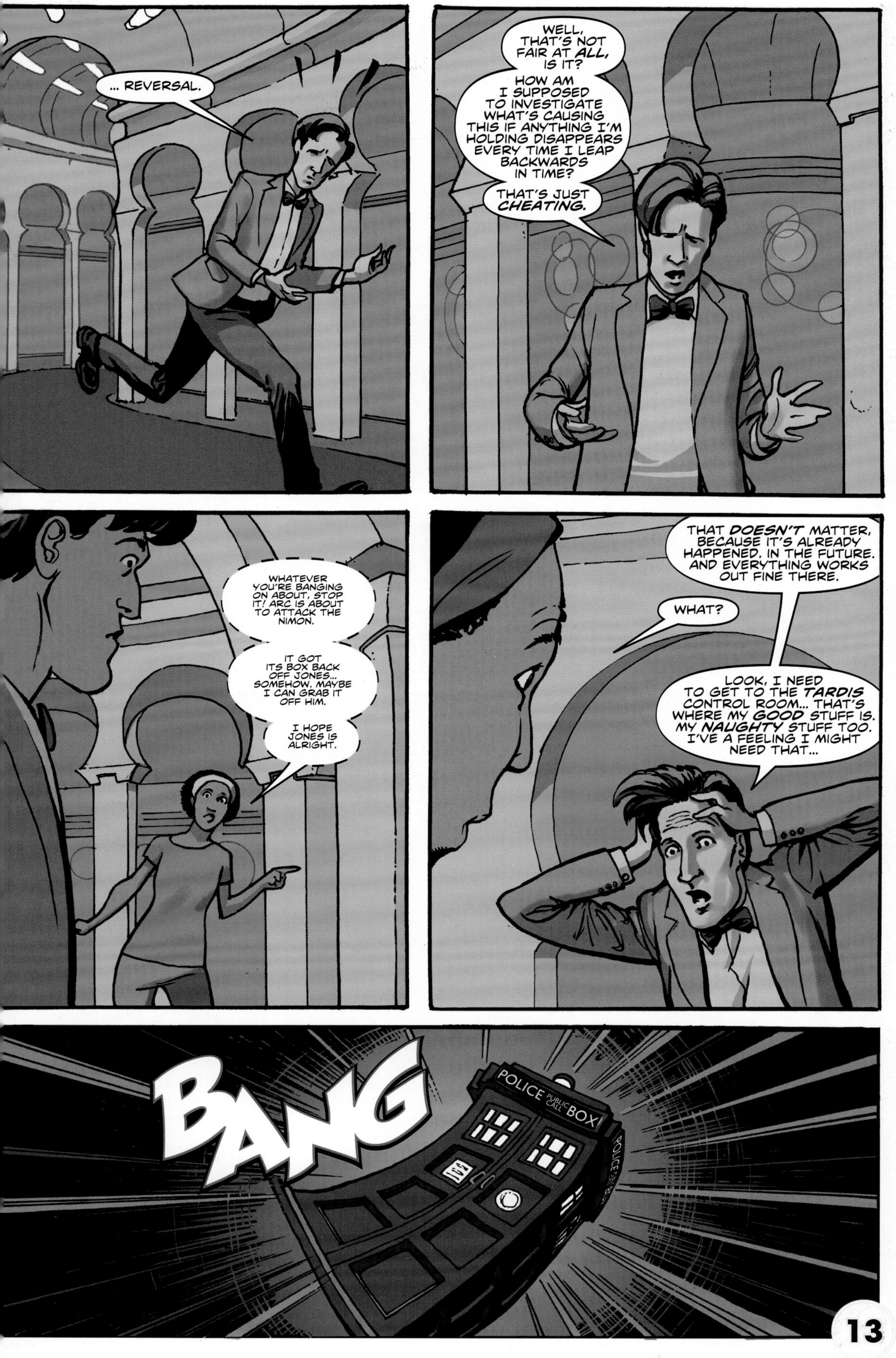
... REVERSAL.
WELL, THAT'S NOT FAIR AT ALL, IS IT?
HOW AM I SUPPOSED TO INVESTIGATE WHAT'S CAUSING THIS IF ANYTHING I'M HOLDING DISAPPEARS EVERY TIME I LEAP BACKWARDS IN TIME?
THAT'S JUST CHEATING.
WHATEVER YOU'RE BANGING ON ABOUT, STOP IT! ARC IS ABOUT TO ATTACK THE NIMON.
IT GOT ITS BOX BACK OFF JONES... SOMEHOW. MAYBE I CAN GRAB IT OFF HIM.
I HOPE JONES IS ALRIGHT.
THAT DOESN'T MATTER, BECAUSE IT'S ALREADY HAPPENED. IN THE FUTURE. AND EVERYTHING WORKS OUT FINE THERE.
WHAT?
LOOK, I NEED TO GET TO THE TARDIS CONTROL ROOM... THAT'S WHERE MY GOOD STUFF IS. MY NAUGHTY STUFF TOO. I'VE A FEELING I MIGHT NEED THAT...
BANG
POLICE PUBLIC CALL BOX

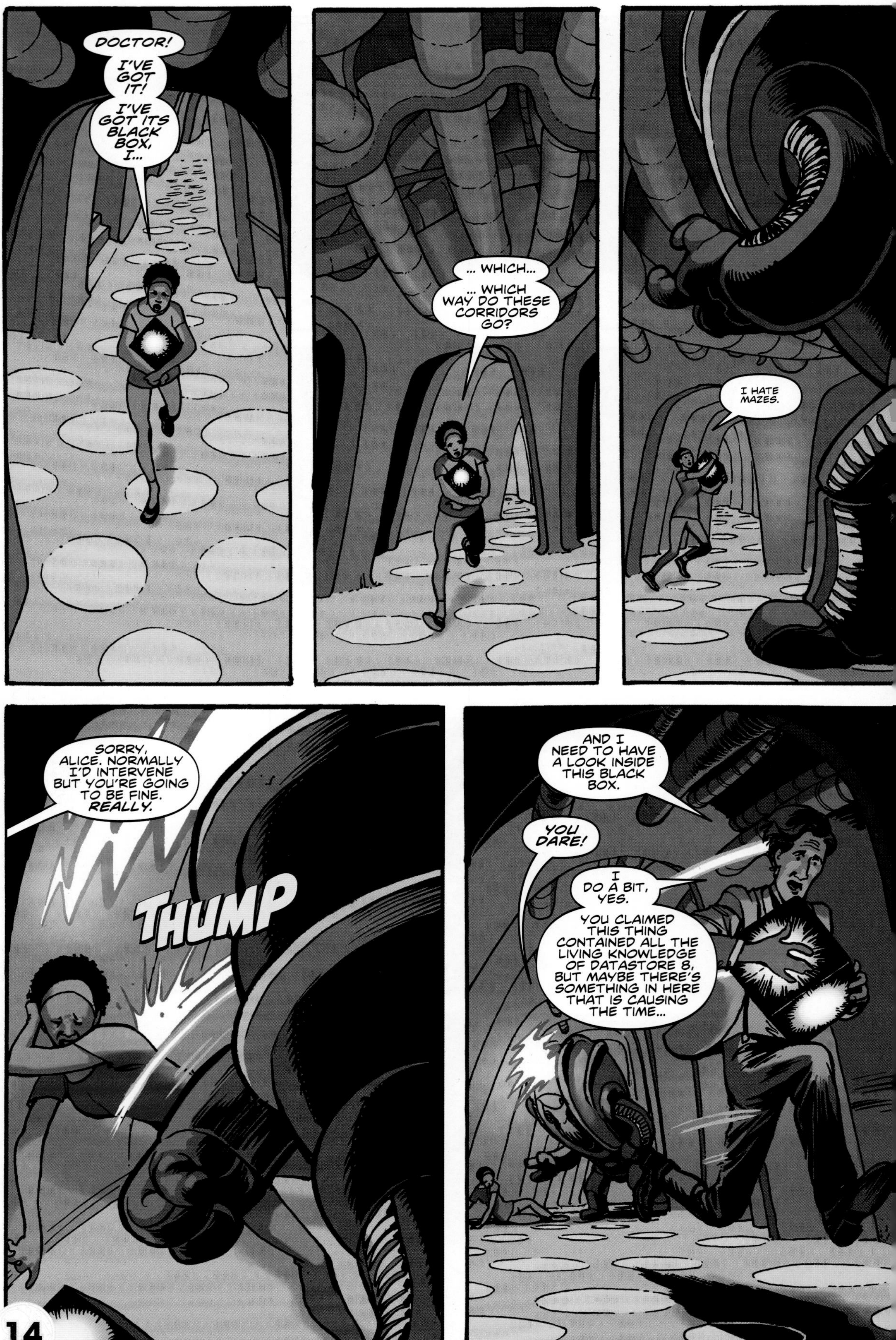
DOCTOR!
I'VE GOT IT!
I'VE GOT ITS BLACK BOX, I...
... WHICH...
... WHICH WAY DO THESE CORRIDORS GO?
I HATE MAZES.
SORRY, ALICE. NORMALLY I'D INTERVENE BUT YOU'RE GOING TO BE FINE. REALLY.
THUMP
AND I NEED TO HAVE A LOOK INSIDE THIS BLACK BOX.
YOU DARE!
I DO A BIT, YES.
YOU CLAIMED THIS THING CONTAINED ALL THE LIVING KNOWLEDGE OF DATASTORE 8, BUT MAYBE THERE'S SOMETHING IN HERE THAT IS CAUSING THE TIME...

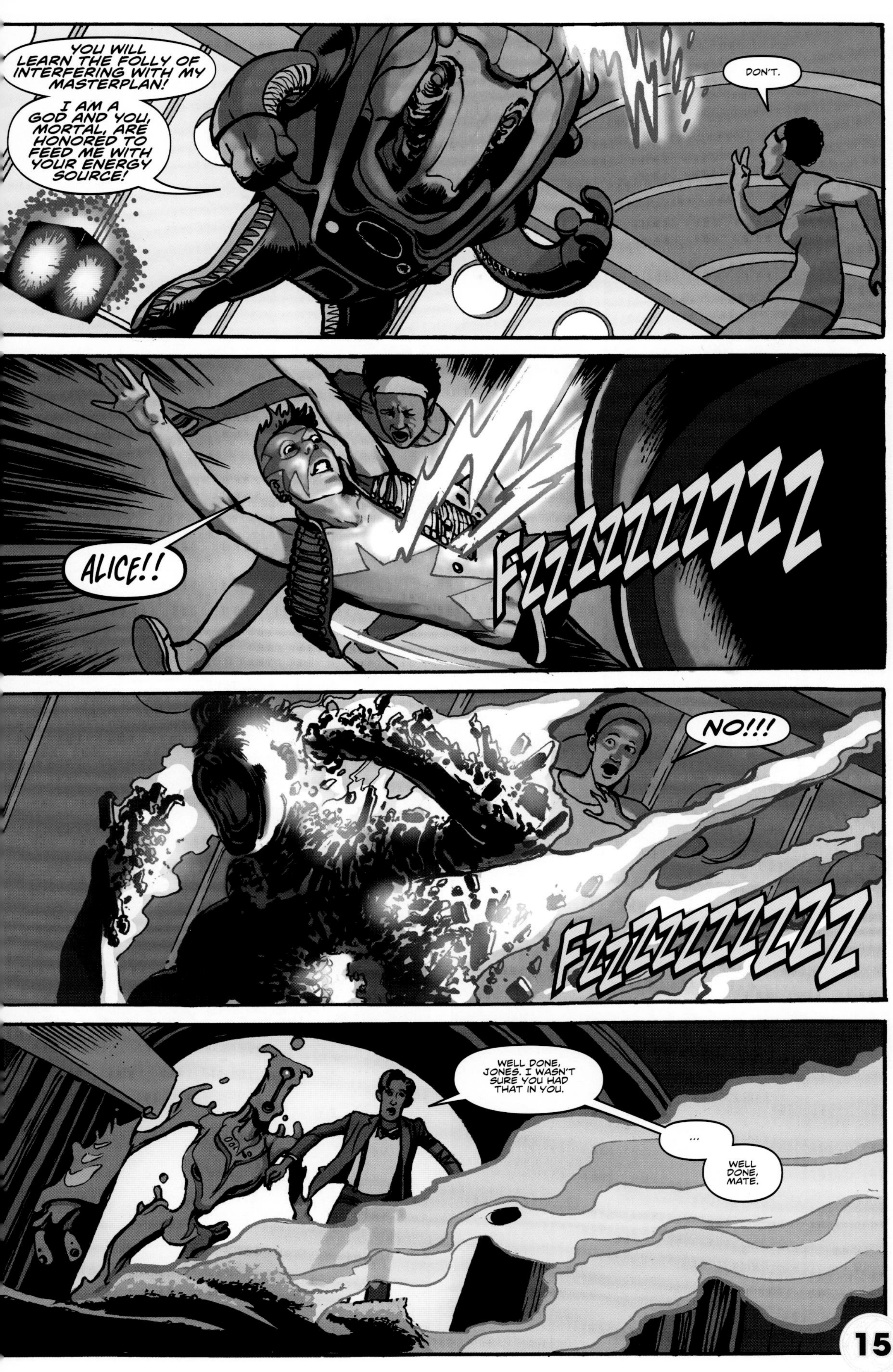
YOU WILL LEARN THE FOLLY OF INTERFERING WITH MY MASTERPLAN!
I AM A GOD AND YOU, MORTAL, ARE HONORED TO FEED ME WITH YOUR ENERGY SOURCE!
DON'T.
ALICE!!
FZZZZZZZZZZ
NO!!!
FZZZZZZZZZZ
WELL DONE, JONES. I WASN'T SURE YOU HAD THAT IN YOU.
...
WELL DONE, MATE.

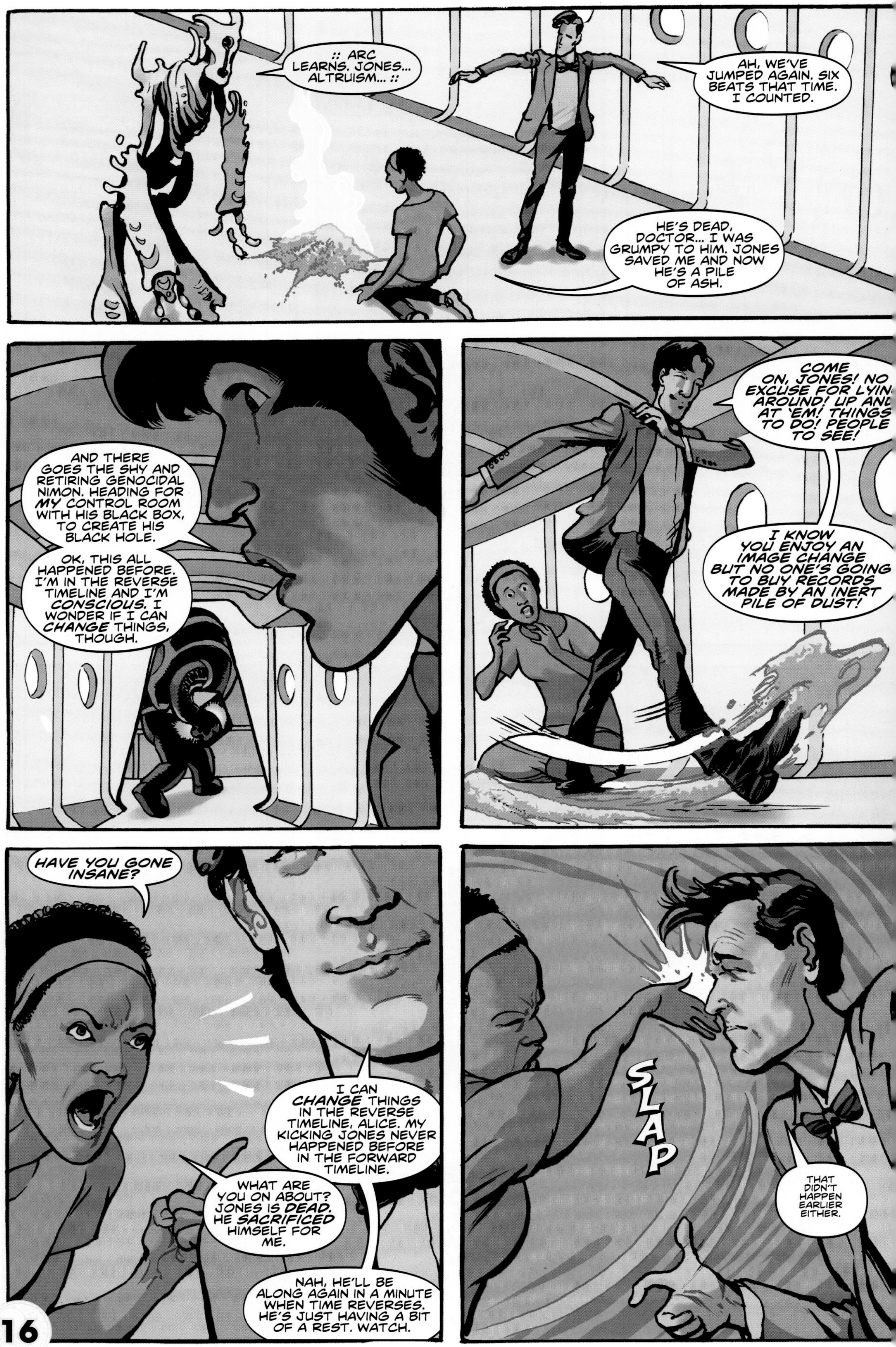
:: ARC LEARNS. JONES... ALTRUISM... ::
AH, WE'VE JUMPED AGAIN. SIX BEATS THAT TIME. I COUNTED.
HE'S DEAD, DOCTOR... I WAS GRUMPY TO HIM. JONES SAVED ME AND NOW HE'S A PILE OF ASH.
AND THERE GOES THE SHY AND RETIRING GENOCIDAL NIMON. HEADING FOR *MY* CONTROL ROOM WITH HIS BLACK BOX, TO CREATE HIS BLACK HOLE.
OK, THIS ALL HAPPENED BEFORE. I'M IN THE REVERSE TIMELINE AND I'M *CONSCIOUS*. I WONDER IF I CAN *CHANGE* THINGS, THOUGH.
COME ON, JONES! NO EXCUSE FOR LYIN AROUND! UP AND AT 'EM! THINGS TO DO! PEOPLE TO SEE!
I KNOW YOU ENJOY AN IMAGE CHANGE BUT NO ONE'S GOING TO BUY RECORDS MADE BY AN INERT PILE OF DUST!
HAVE YOU GONE INSANE?
I CAN *CHANGE* THINGS IN THE REVERSE TIMELINE, ALICE. MY KICKING JONES NEVER HAPPENED BEFORE IN THE FORWARD TIMELINE.
WHAT ARE YOU ON ABOUT? JONES IS *DEAD*. HE *SACRIFICED* HIMSELF FOR ME.
NAH, HE'LL BE ALONG AGAIN IN A MINUTE WHEN TIME REVERSES. HE'S JUST HAVING A BIT OF A REST. WATCH.
SLAP
THAT DIDN'T HAPPEN EARLIER EITHER.

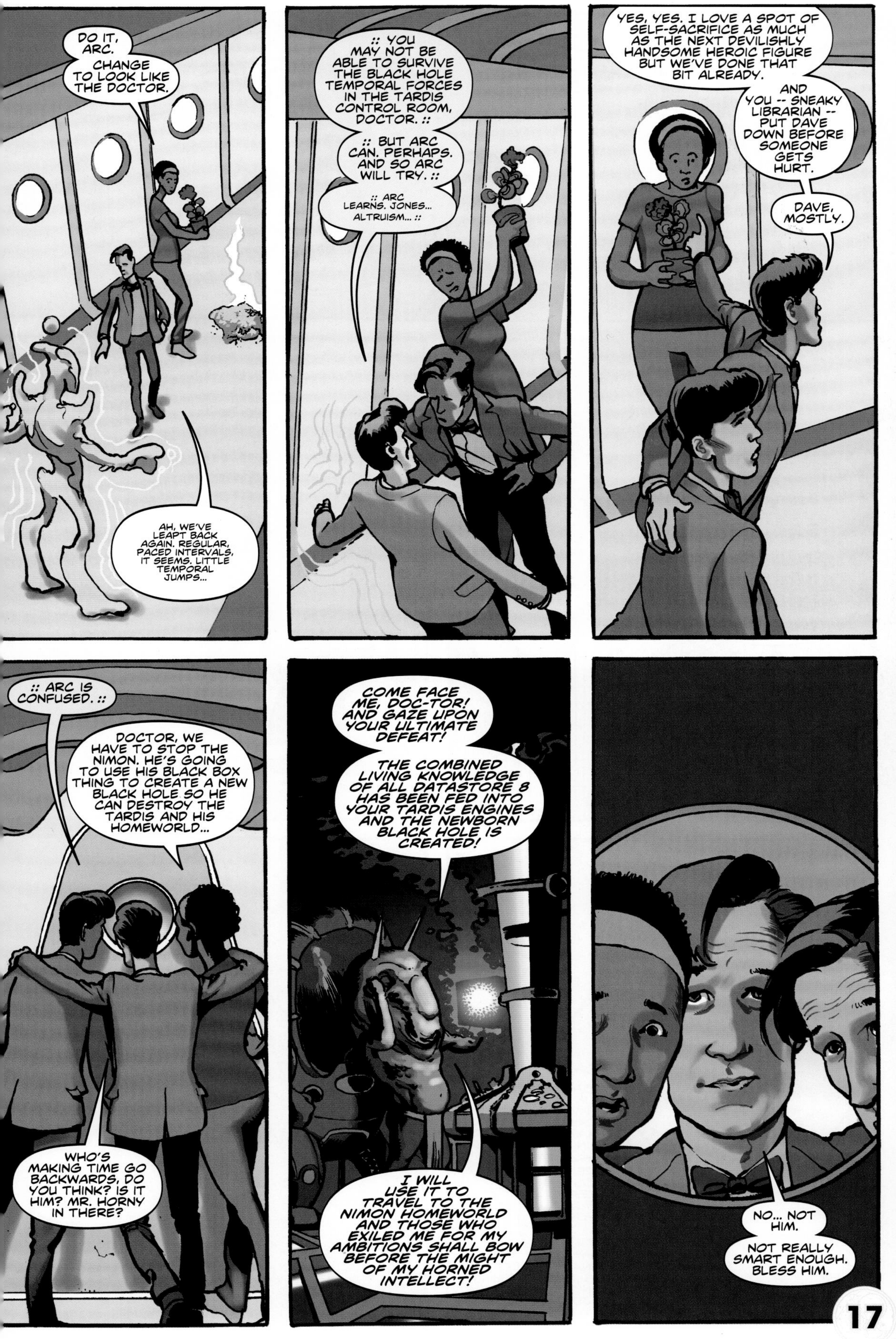
DO IT, ARC. CHANGE TO LOOK LIKE THE DOCTOR.
AH, WE'VE LEAPT BACK AGAIN. REGULAR, PACED INTERVALS, IT SEEMS. LITTLE TEMPORAL JUMPS...
:: YOU MAY NOT BE ABLE TO SURVIVE THE BLACK HOLE TEMPORAL FORCES IN THE TARDIS CONTROL ROOM, DOCTOR. ::
:: BUT ARC CAN. PERHAPS. AND SO ARC WILL TRY. ::
:: ARC LEARNS. JONES... ALTRUISM... ::
YES, YES. I LOVE A SPOT OF SELF-SACRIFICE AS MUCH AS THE NEXT DEVILISHLY HANDSOME HEROIC FIGURE BUT WE'VE DONE THAT BIT ALREADY.
AND YOU -- SNEAKY LIBRARIAN -- PUT DAVE DOWN BEFORE SOMEONE GETS HURT.
DAVE, MOSTLY.
:: ARC IS CONFUSED. ::
DOCTOR, WE HAVE TO STOP THE NIMON. HE'S GOING TO USE HIS BLACK BOX THING TO CREATE A NEW BLACK HOLE SO HE CAN DESTROY THE TARDIS AND HIS HOMEWORLD...
WHO'S MAKING TIME GO BACKWARDS, DO YOU THINK? IS IT HIM? MR. HORNY IN THERE?
COME FACE ME, DOC-TOR! AND GAZE UPON YOUR ULTIMATE DEFEAT!
THE COMBINED LIVING KNOWLEDGE OF ALL DATASTORE 8 HAS BEEN FED INTO YOUR TARDIS ENGINES AND THE NEWBORN BLACK HOLE IS CREATED!
I WILL USE IT TO TRAVEL TO THE NIMON HOMEWORLD AND THOSE WHO EXILED ME FOR MY AMBITIONS SHALL BOW BEFORE THE MIGHT OF MY HORNED INTELLECT!
NO... NOT HIM.
NOT REALLY SMART ENOUGH. BLESS HIM.

CHAPTER 6

SPACE IN DIMENSION RELATIVE AND TIME

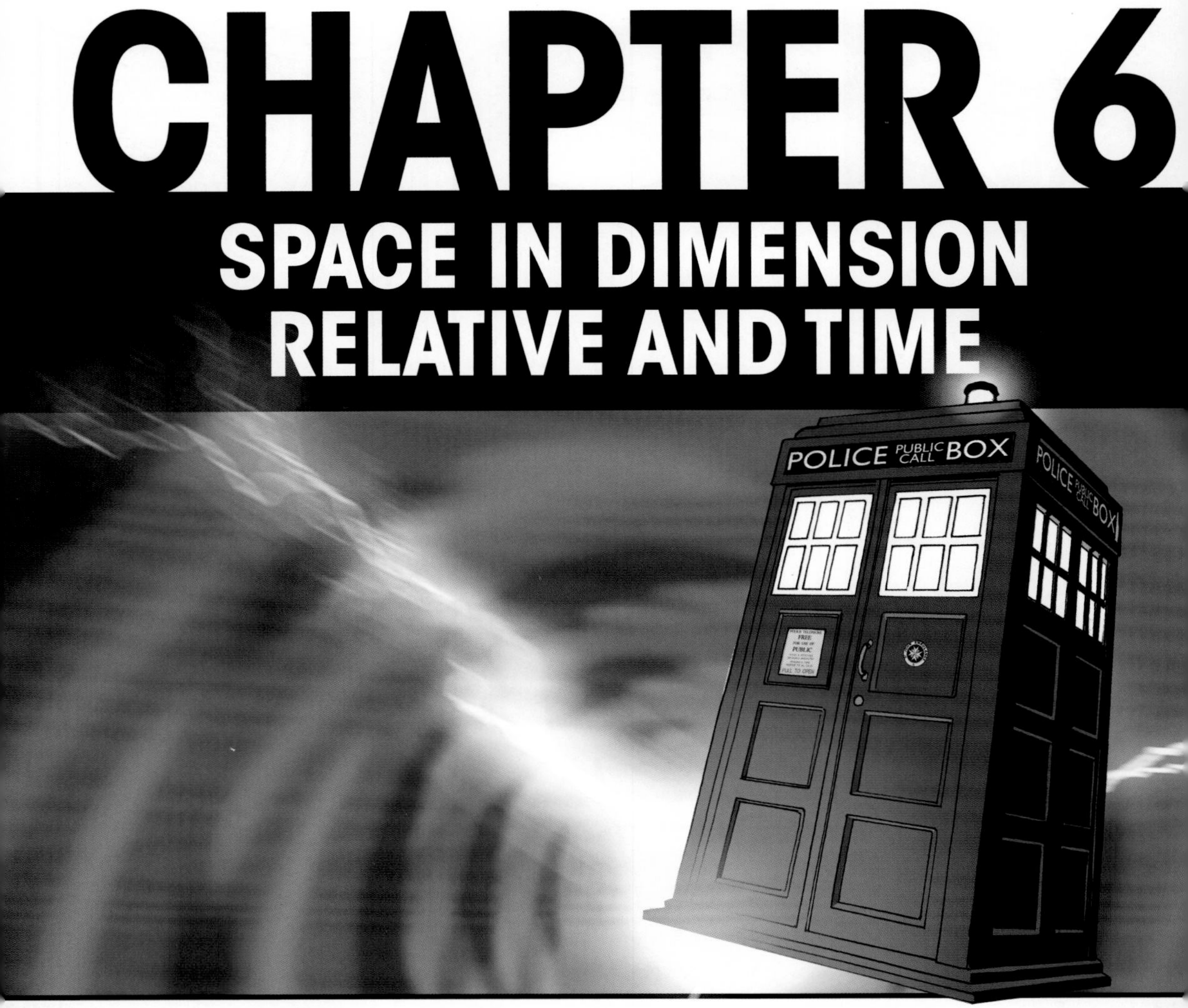
POLICE PUBLIC CALL BOX
POLICE PUBLIC CALL BOX

WRITER
ROB WILLIAMS

ARTIST
SIMON FRASER

COLORIST
GARY CALDWELL

LETTERER
RICHARD STARKINGS AND COMICRAFT'S JIMMY BETANCOURT

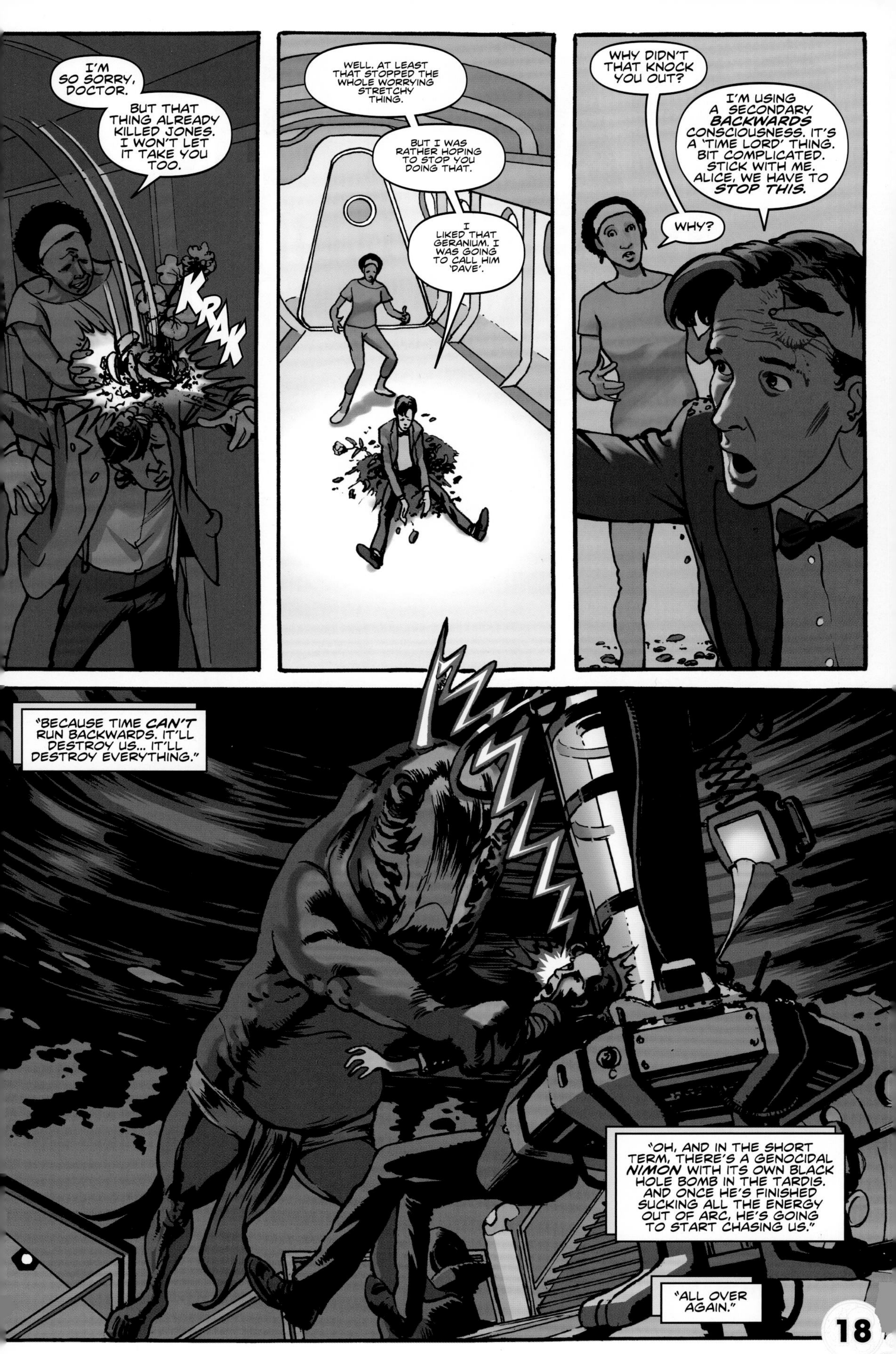
I'M SO SORRY, DOCTOR.
BUT THAT THING ALREADY KILLED JONES. I WON'T LET IT TAKE YOU TOO.
KRAK
WELL. AT LEAST THAT STOPPED THE WHOLE WORRYING STRETCHY THING.
BUT I WAS RATHER HOPING TO STOP YOU DOING THAT.
I LIKED THAT GERANIUM. I WAS GOING TO CALL HIM 'DAVE'.
WHY DIDN'T THAT KNOCK YOU OUT?
I'M USING A SECONDARY BACKWARDS CONSCIOUSNESS. IT'S A 'TIME LORD' THING. BIT COMPLICATED. STICK WITH ME. ALICE, WE HAVE TO STOP THIS.
WHY?
"BECAUSE TIME CAN'T RUN BACKWARDS. IT'LL DESTROY US... IT'LL DESTROY EVERYTHING."
"OH, AND IN THE SHORT TERM, THERE'S A GENOCIDAL NIMON WITH ITS OWN BLACK HOLE BOMB IN THE TARDIS. AND ONCE HE'S FINISHED SUCKING ALL THE ENERGY OUT OF ARC, HE'S GOING TO START CHASING US."
"ALL OVER AGAIN."

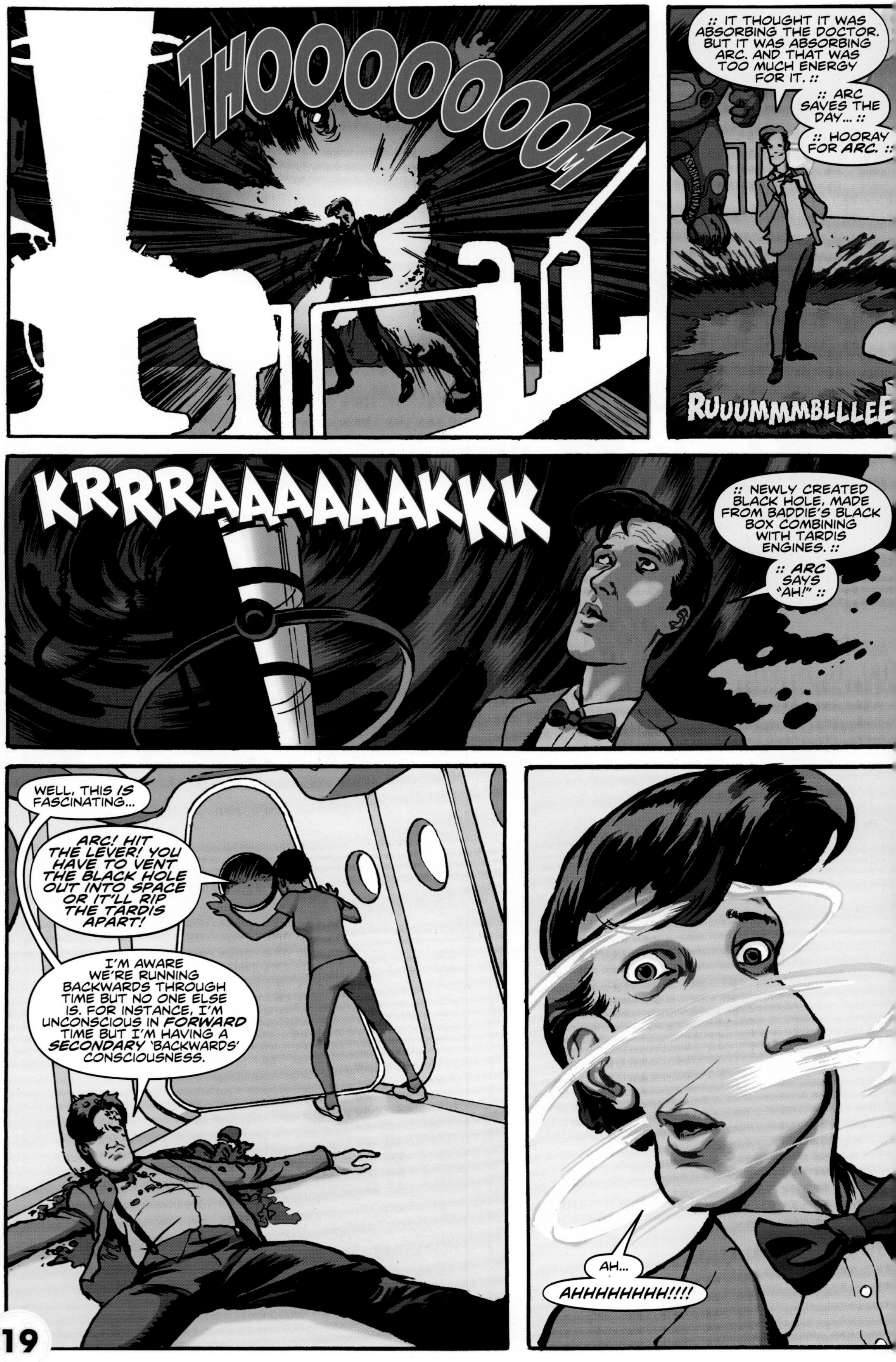

THOOOOOOOM
:: IT THOUGHT IT WAS ABSORBING THE DOCTOR. BUT IT WAS ABSORBING ARC. AND THAT WAS TOO MUCH ENERGY FOR IT. ::
:: ARC SAVES THE DAY... ::
:: HOORAY FOR *ARC*. ::
RUUUMMMBLLLEE
KRRRAAAAAAKKK
:: NEWLY CREATED BLACK HOLE, MADE FROM BADDIE'S BLACK BOX COMBINING WITH TARDIS ENGINES. ::
:: *ARC* SAYS "AH!" ::
WELL, THIS *IS* FASCINATING...
ARC! HIT THE LEVER! YOU HAVE TO VENT THE BLACK HOLE OUT INTO SPACE OR IT'LL RIP THE TARDIS APART!
I'M AWARE WE'RE RUNNING BACKWARDS THROUGH TIME BUT NO ONE ELSE IS. FOR INSTANCE, I'M UNCONSCIOUS IN *FORWARD* TIME BUT I'M HAVING A *SECONDARY* 'BACKWARDS' CONSCIOUSNESS.
AH...
AHHHHHHHH!!!!

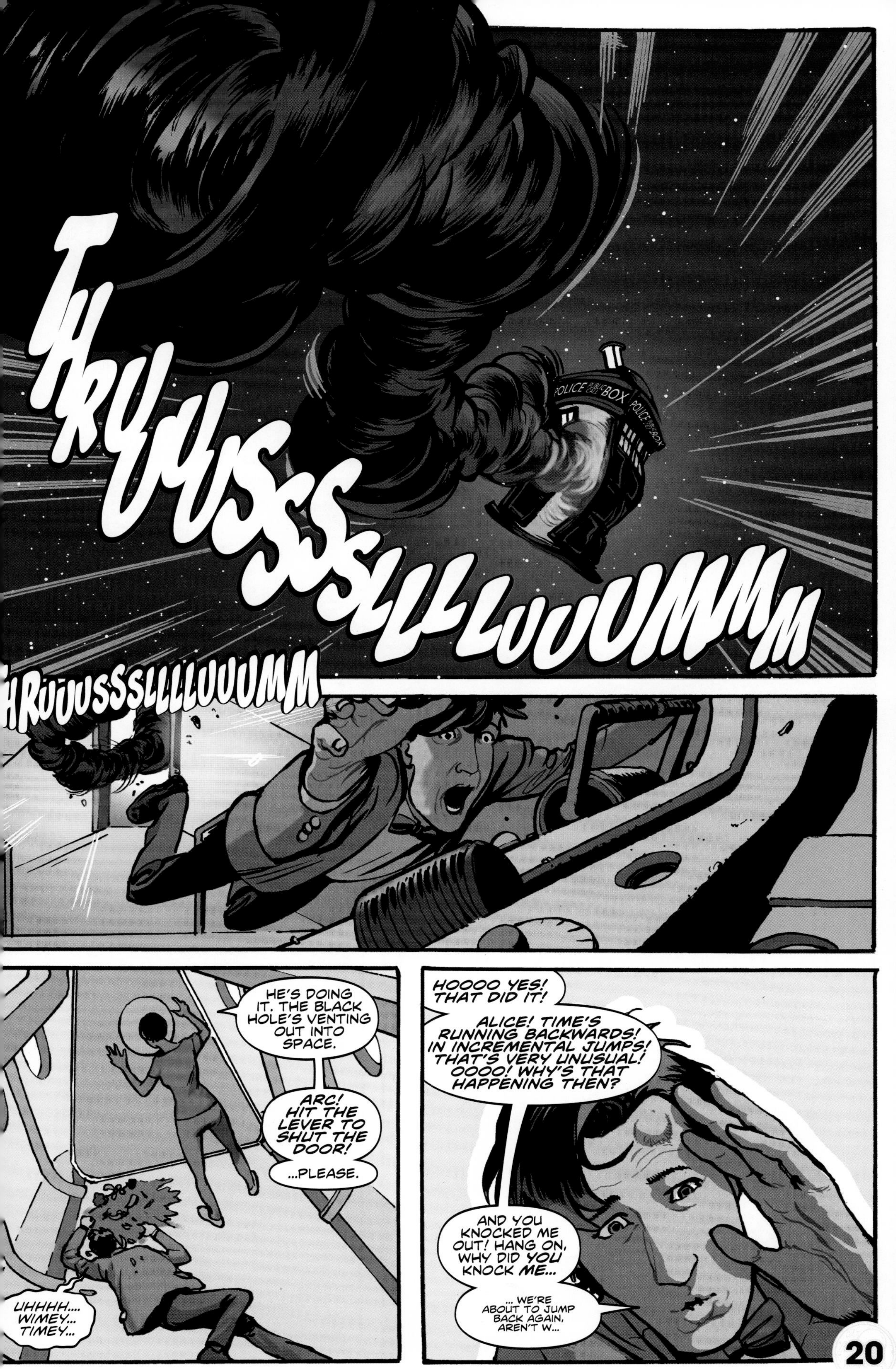
THRUUUSSSSLLLLUUUUMMMM
POLICE PUBLIC CALL BOX
HRUUUSSSSLLLLUUUMM
HE'S DOING IT. THE BLACK HOLE'S VENTING OUT INTO SPACE.
ARC! HIT THE LEVER TO SHUT THE DOOR!
...PLEASE.
UHHHH.... WIMEY... TIMEY...
HOOOO YES! THAT DID IT!
ALICE! TIME'S RUNNING BACKWARDS! IN INCREMENTAL JUMPS! THAT'S VERY UNUSUAL! OOOO! WHY'S THAT HAPPENING THEN?
AND YOU KNOCKED ME OUT! HANG ON, WHY DID YOU KNOCK ME...
... WE'RE ABOUT TO JUMP BACK AGAIN, AREN'T W...

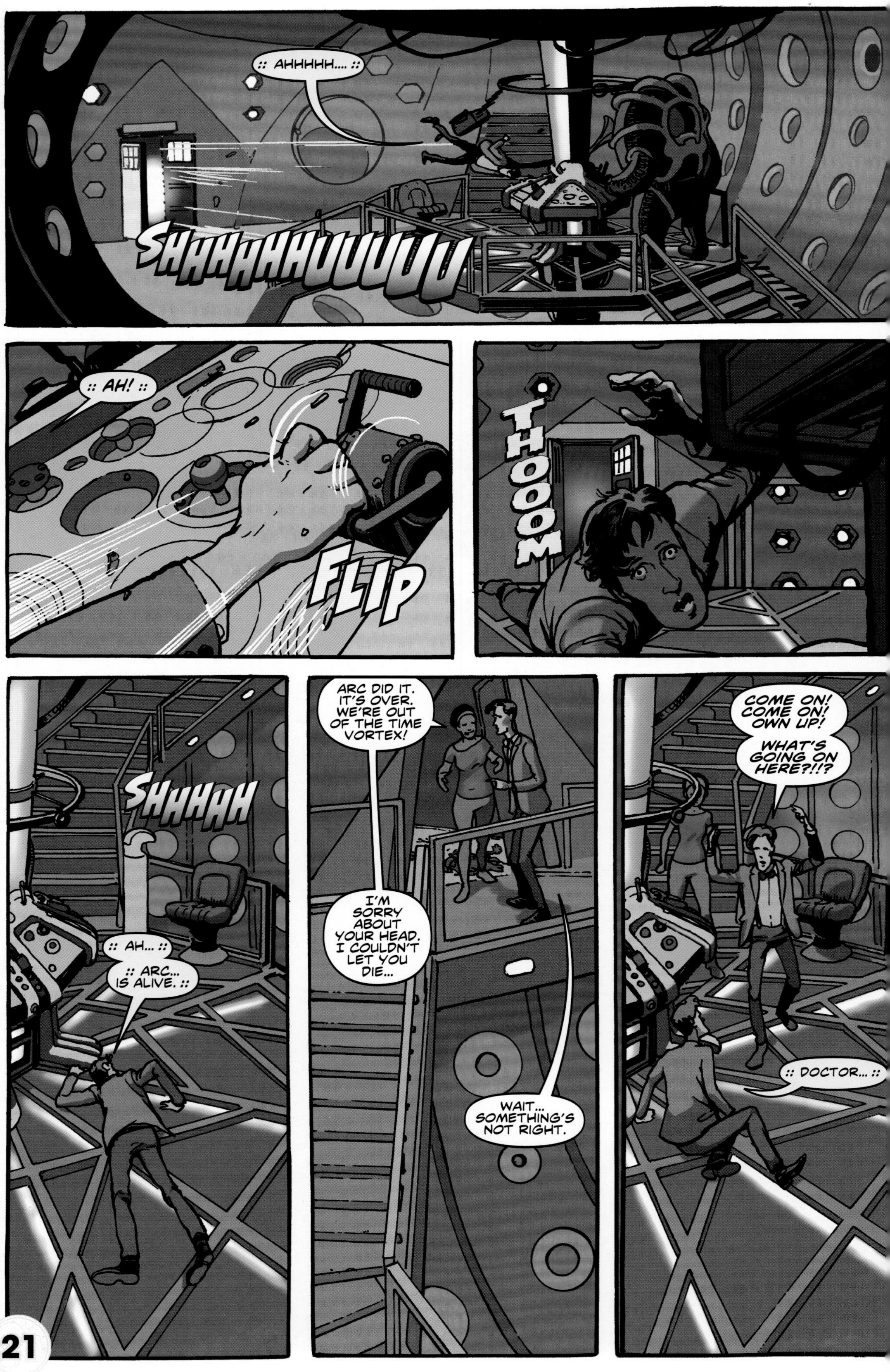
:: AHHHHH.... ::
SHHHHHHUUUUU
:: AH! ::
FLIP
THOOOM
SHHHHH
:: AH... ::
:: ARC... IS ALIVE. ::
ARC DID IT. IT'S OVER. WE'RE OUT OF THE TIME VORTEX!
I'M SORRY ABOUT YOUR HEAD. I COULDN'T LET YOU DIE...
WAIT... SOMETHING'S NOT RIGHT.
COME ON! COME ON! OWN UP!
WHAT'S GOING ON HERE?!!?
:: DOCTOR... ::

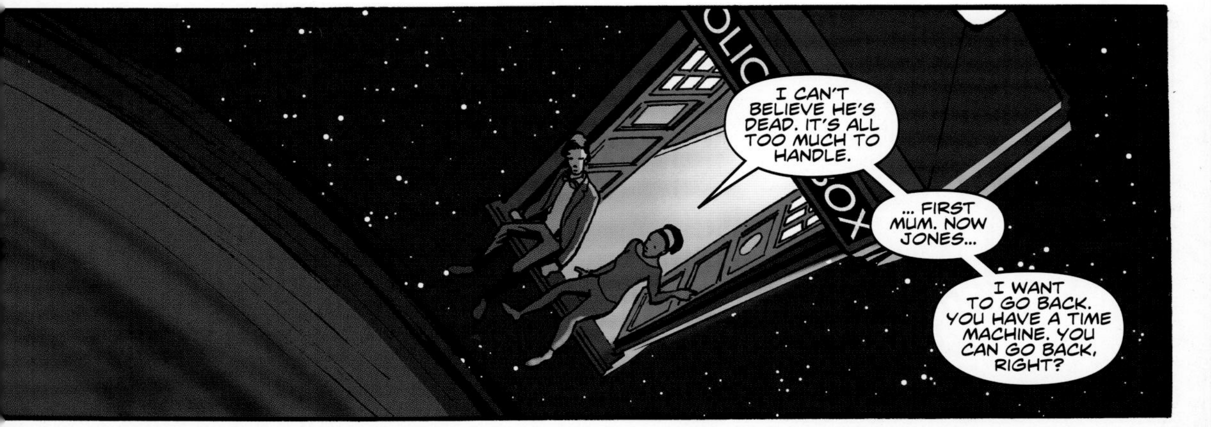
I CAN'T BELIEVE HE'S DEAD. IT'S ALL TOO MUCH TO HANDLE.
... FIRST MUM. NOW JONES...
I WANT TO GO BACK. YOU HAVE A TIME MACHINE. YOU CAN GO BACK, RIGHT?
POLICE BOX

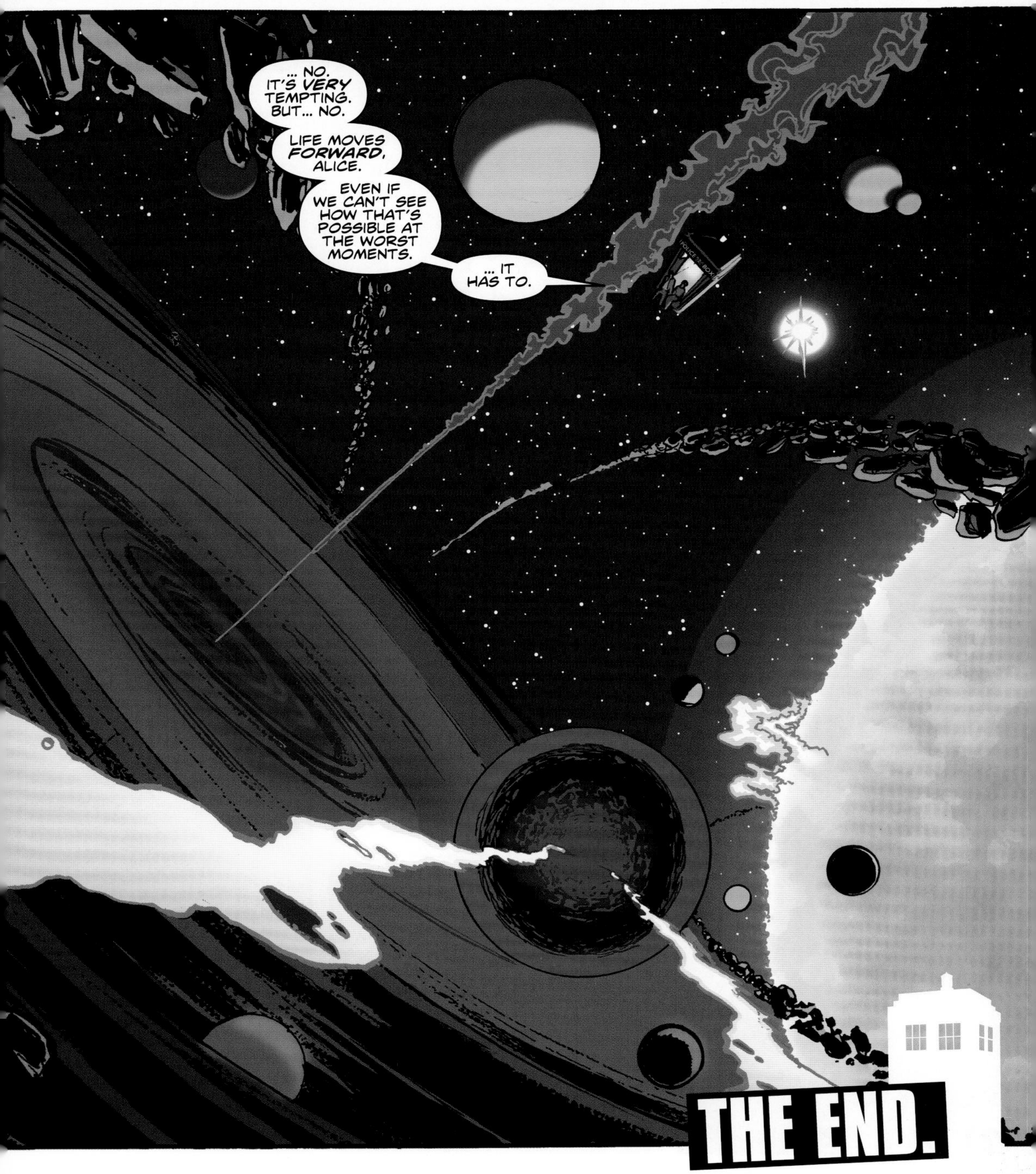
... NO. IT'S VERY TEMPTING. BUT... NO.
LIFE MOVES FORWARD, ALICE.
EVEN IF WE CAN'T SEE HOW THAT'S POSSIBLE AT THE WORST MOMENTS.
... IT HAS TO.
THE END.

BBC

DOCTOR WHO

THE ELEVENTH DOCTOR

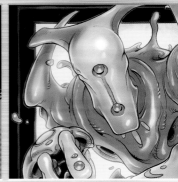

ALICE

Having lost her mother to illness and facing eviction from her landlord, former Library Assistant Alice Obiefune felt like her life was falling apart. Then she met the Doctor! Now she's determined to see all the beauty and strangeness of the universe as she travels with him in the TARDIS!

JONES

Initially a forgettable skiffle musician, Jones is destined to become a rock god! He was also Alice's mother's favorite musician. He changes his look as often as his underwear (*regularly*, thank you very much)! He's traveling with the Doctor in the hope it ignites his creative spark.

ARC

A shapeshifter, dubbed 'Autonomous Reasoning Center' by the rogue corporate scientists of SERVEYOUinc, ARC can shift form into anything it chooses. Having found its own voice, ARC now travels with the Doctor, enjoying the life of adventure while searching for the truth behind its mysterious origin...

PREVIOUSLY...

Alice, Jones, ARC and the Doctor: together, they're exploring all of time and space!

Alice first met the Doctor when she helped save London from a rainbow-colored alien dog.
The chameleonic Jones joined the crew when he snuck on board the TARDIS after a disastrous debut gig.
ARC boarded from a grim research base, where its probing attempts to communicate were terribly misunderstood.

Through all their adventures, the mysterious and malign SERVEYOUinc corporation has lurked...
personified by the tempting Talent Scout, who only wants to offer you... everything!

When you've finished reading the collection, please email your thoughts to doctorwhocomic@titanemail.com

DOCTOR WHO

THE ELEVENTH DOCTOR

VOL 2: SERVE YOU

WRITERS:
AL EWING & ROB WILLIAMS

ARTISTS:
SIMON FRASER
BOO COOK
WARREN PLEECE

COLORISTS:
GARY CALDWELL
HI-FI

LETTERS: RICHARD STARKINGS
AND COMICRAFT'S
JIMMY BETANCOURT

EDITOR:
ANDREW JAMES

ASSISTANT EDITOR:
KIRSTEN MURRAY

DESIGNER:
ROB FARMER

www.titan-comics.com

TITAN COMICS

SENIOR EDITOR
Steve White

TITAN COMICS EDITORIAL
Lizzie Kaye, Tom Williams

PRODUCTION SUPERVISORS
Maria Pearson,
Jackie Flook

PRODUCTION MANAGER
Obi Onuora

STUDIO MANAGER
Emma Smith

CIRCULATION MANAGER
Steve Tothill

SENIOR MARKETING & PRESS OFFICER
Owen Johnson

MARKETING MANAGER
Ricky Claydon

ADVERTISING MANAGER
Michelle Fairlamb

PUBLISHING MANAGER
Darryl Tothill

PUBLISHING DIRECTOR
Chris Teather

OPERATIONS DIRECTOR
Leigh Baulch

EXECUTIVE DIRECTOR
Vivian Cheung

PUBLISHER
Nick Landau

DOCTOR WHO: THE ELEVENTH DOCTOR
VOL 2: SERVE YOU
HB ISBN: 9781782761761   SB ISBN: 9781782765035

Published by Titan Comics, a division of
Titan Publishing Group, Ltd. 144 Southwark Street,
London, SE1 0UP.

A CIP catalogue record for this title is available from the British Library.
First edition: July 2015.

10 9 8 7 6 5 4 3 2 1

Printed in China. TC0294.

Titan Comics does not read or accept unsolicited DOCTOR WHO
submissions of ideas, stories or artwork.

Special thanks to
Steven Moffat, Brian Minchin, Matt Nicholls,
James Dudley, Georgie Britton, Edward
Russell, Derek Ritchie, Scott Handcock, Kirsty
Mullan, Kate Bush, Julia Nocciolino, Ed Casey,
Marcus Wilson and
Richard Cookson
for their invaluable
assistance.

BBC

DOCTOR WHO

THE ELEVENTH DOCTOR

VOL 2: SERVE YOU

"Amazing! It hit all the right notes, and got the Doctor perfect! 9/10"
COMIC BOOK CAST

"Mind-bending and impressive."
BENJAMIN HERMAN

"Balances out the serious with well-placed humor, slapstick included."
WHATCHA READING

"A fun read with some great characterization and a sense of adventure. 9 out of 10!"
COMICS VERSE

"An enjoyable romp."
FLICKERING MYTH

"9.5 out of 10!"
NERDS UNCHAINED

"Does a splendid job of capturing Matt Smith's expressions."
GEEK WITH CURVES

"The tone of the Eleventh Doctor is strong in this one."
WARPED FACTOR

"A fantastic Eleventh Doctor adventure! 9 out of 10!"
NEWSARAMA

"A great job creating a companion who can keep up with the Doctor. 10 out of 10!"
PROJECT FANDOM

"Nails the tone and spirit right out of the gate. 4 out of 5!"
COMIC BOOK RESOURCES

"A great continuation of a fabulous series. The character depth, dramatic arc and suspenseful flow make it a gripping read."
UNLEASH THE FANBOY

"Excellent script with great artwork. I've become a fan of Alice Obiefune – what a character she has become!"
TM STASH

"Compelling art."
BLEEDING COOL

"Well-written with great art!"
COMIC BASTARDS